Theological Hermeneutics

The SCM Core Texts

SCM CORE TEXT

Theological Hermeneutics

Alexander S. Jensen

scm press

British Library Cataloguing in Publication data

A catalogue record for this book is available
from the British Library

Scripture quotations are from the New Revised Standard Version of
the Bible, copyright 1989 by the Division of Christian Education of
the National Council of the Churches of Christ in the USA. Used by
permission. All rights reserved.

978 0 334 02901 4

First published in 2007 by SCM Press
9–17 St Alban's Place
London N1 0NX

www.scm-canterburypress.co.uk

SCM Press is a division of
SCM-Canterbury Press Ltd

Typeset by Regent Typesetting, London
Printed and bound in Great Britain by
William Clowes Ltd, Beccles, Suffolk

Contents

v

Feb m

For Helen

Acknowledgements

Hermeneutics has been a passion of mine since my undergraduate days. Initially, this was born out of curiosity – the word sounded attractive, my lecturers used it in interesting ways, and so I was eager to find out what was hidden behind this mysterious title. As I came to discover, the content of this field of study is even more fascinating than the title.

My first introduction to hermeneutics was by reading Jean Grondin's *Introduction to Philosophical Hermeneutics*, the German edition of which appeared some years before the English.[1] Some readers may notice how my understanding of hermeneutics is still influenced by Grondin's interpretation of Gadamer.

I am grateful to my own lecturers, and later to colleagues and students for their ongoing encouragement. Especially my students in the 'Hermeneutics and Theology' course at Trinity College, Dublin, in 2003/04 challenged me to find a way to explain complex ideas and sometimes inapproachable terminology in accessible ways. The idea for this book stems from that course, and it is based on what I learned about teaching hermeneutics in this course. I hope it will be a useful resource in the lecture theatre, an aid for the interested enquirer and a partner in discussion for the scholar.

There are many more people who have supported me in writing this book in various ways. I cannot name all the people with whom I discussed my ideas on hermeneutics. My colleagues in the theology and philosophy programmes at Murdoch University were a great support in this and many other ways. In particular, I would like to thank Dr Paul MacDonald, Prof. Trish Harris, Prof. Bill Loader and Dr Andrew Webster, all of Murdoch University, as well as Prof. John Tonkin of the University of Western Australia, for their friendship and support.

The greatest thanks, however, are due to my wife Helen for her love, patience and support. This book is dedicated to her in gratitude.

Notes

1   Jean Grondin, 1991, *Einführung in die philosophische Hermeneutik*, Darmstadt: Wissenschaftliche Buchgesellschaft; Jean Grondin, 1994, *Introduction to Philosophical Hermeneutics*, *Yale Studies in Hermeneutics*, New Haven; London: Yale University Press.

Introduction

Although this may not be immediately obvious to every reader, understanding of language is a deeply problematic activity. People often do not see this, because in most instances understanding seems to work. So what is the use of theoretical reflection on an activity that, in practice, seems to work well enough?

The great economist John Maynard Keynes once wrote that 'practical men, who believe themselves to be quite exempt from any intellectual influences, are usually the slaves of some defunct economist. Madmen in authority, who hear voices in the air, are distilling their frenzy from some academic scribbler of a few years back.'[1] In other words, if we do not reflect on our presuppositions, then we take for granted theories that were discredited long before we were born. This is not only true in the field of economics, but especially in the area of understanding, of reading and listening.

Most people read in order to learn the facts behind the text. The typical instance for this style of reading is the way we approach newspapers. When reading the newspaper, most readers would understand that they learn the facts reported in the article. They read the words of the report in the belief that through them one can reach to the objective facts behind the words. Certainly, one has to allow for some distortion due to the journalist's bias, but being aware of this, one can avoid being influenced by the writer's subjectivity. In other words, for most readers the aim of reading is to reach objectivity, to learn facts. This is not only the case with newspapers, but most people would approach most kinds of literature in this way. This naïve realism, however, is by no means the God-given or natural way of reading, but it is the result of a set of philosophical assumptions that date back to the late eighteenth century and are connected with the work of the Scottish philosopher Thomas Reid (1710–96), the founder of so-called Scottish common-sense philosophy (see pp. 82–4). In the philosophical discourse, his ideas have long been discredited, but 'practical people' still adhere to it.

The main point of Keynes' book was that ideas count. Even in a field such as economics, where it is easy to disregard theory and go for practical or common-sense solutions, theory lies behind all decisions. If one is not familiar with the theory and the ideas, then one becomes too easily the slave of some defunct theorist. It is therefore crucial to become familiar with the history of thought and the current debates in all areas where one works. This is particularly true with regard to one's approach to understanding in theology. Understanding texts, one's self, God and the world are at the heart of the theological enterprise. Consequently, if one does not make explicit one's assumptions and reflect on them critically, one is prone to be guided by unacknowledged presuppositions. In order to avoid this, it is essential to be familiar with the field of study commonly called hermeneutics.

What is hermeneutics?

Hermeneutics is the reflection on the problem of understanding. This can be taken in two ways. First, the simple meaning is that hermeneutics is the 'art of *hermeneuein*, i.e. of proclaiming, translating, explaining and interpreting',[2] or, in short, the 'art of understanding' (see p. 90). Thus hermeneutics can be seen as reflection on how we understand, usually with regard to text or speech, and what we need to do in order to avoid misunderstanding.

In this respect, hermeneutics is understood as the identification, analysis and removal of obstacles to understanding. One identifies obstacles to understanding, such as the lack of knowledge of classical Greek, medieval philosophy, or the biography of the author, and develops strategies for dealing with this. This is quite straightforward, and hardly warrants its own field of study. However, there are more complex and fundamental obstacles to understanding which need to be identified and considered.

What happens, for example, if ancient authoritative texts do not make sense any more? The ancient Greeks were faced with this issue with the *Iliad* and the *Odyssey*, which told the stories of the Trojan War and Odysseus' homecoming. These were the foundational texts of Hellenic culture, but in the sixth century BC they clashed with the maturing cultural, ethical and religious norms of Hellenic society. Consequently, the Greeks had to develop strategies which would allow them to reinterpret these texts radically while continuing to take them seriously. We will see in the next chapter how this led to the development of allegorical interpretation.

A similar difficulty arises with theological texts, both from the Bible and from the Christian tradition. Some biblical texts seem to presuppose a world-view that we do not share any more. We know that the world is not a flat disc under a dome, beyond which the chaos-waters are stored. We also know that certain medical symptoms are not caused by demon possession, but by disease. And we do not take slavery for granted in our society.

Most readers will have developed strategies to deal with these obstacles to understanding, consciously or unconsciously. However, if readers do not reflect critically on their strategies, then they are in great danger of being beholden to some defunct 'academic scribbler of a few years back'. They are likely to be unwitting adherents of some discredited hermeneutical theory. Thus critical reflection on one's own hermeneutical presuppositions is not only necessary, but essential for the intellectual integrity of the theologian, be it the academic theologian, the preacher or the interested layperson.

Finally, understanding becomes problematic in principle if we acknowledge that we cannot even completely understand ourselves. Both sensory perception as well as memories are non-conceptual and non-verbal. The fifth-century theologian Augustine of Hippo called this the *verbum interius*, the inner word. When we conceptualize our perceptions and memories, when we begin to think consciously, then the inner word enters the external word, the *verbum externum* – the pre-verbal thought becomes explicit thought. Augustine identified a fundamental obstacle in the entering of the inner word into the external word: there is always a loss (see p. 45). We cannot adequately translate our pre-verbal perceptions and memories into language. Consequently, even understanding our own selves becomes problematic. This insight, based on the work of Augustine of Hippo, lies at the heart of hermeneutical reflection since the early twentieth century (see p. 138).

So if we speak of hermeneutics as the identification, analysis and removal of obstacles to understanding, then we need to do so in the broadest possible way. Our understanding is always impeded, even our self-understanding.

For these reasons, hermeneutics is an essential part of theology. First of all, theology is about the interpretation of Christian texts, biblical and other, and the proclamation of the Christian faith on the basis of the understanding gained from these texts. Thus all issues involved in textual interpretation are of utmost importance for theology. In addition, theology attempts to express the Christian experience of God in intellectually accountable language. As I have already indicated, if there is a problem with the translation of human experience into language, then this poses a fundamental problem for Christian theology. We will see in the course of this book that, if we take these issues seriously, all theology must first and foremost be hermeneutical theology (see section 'Hermeneutical Theology', pp. 151–4).

The hermeneutic circle

One of the most basic insights in the field of hermeneutics is that understanding is always circular. From the romantic period of the early nineteenth century onwards, this phenomenon has been a major concern in hermeneutical thinking. In short, it refers to the conundrum that one can understand the whole of a text only when one has understood its parts. The parts, however, can only be properly understood in the light of the whole. In order to understand a text, one needs to enter this circle. The German theologian and philosopher Friedrich Schleiermacher (1768–1834) suggested that one enters the circle by making an informed guess (see pp. 98–9).

When I start reading a book, I make a guess as to what it may be about. While proceeding through the book, my initial guess is constantly revised in the light of the parts of the book as I go along. Assuming that the book is a good one, I may read the book again and, in the light of the understanding of the whole that I gained in the first reading, understand the parts better, which, in turn, will give me a better understanding of the whole. I may even study certain sections of the book in great detail in order to gain a more profound understanding of the whole book.

Moreover, the hermeneutic circle can be drawn wider than this. Schleiermacher also suggested that, if one endeavours to understand a particular book, it can be understood only within the context of the complete works of the author, which, in turn, requires knowledge of his or her individual works. The oeuvre of a given author, however, can only be understood within the context of the literature of his or her language. Thus there is no end to the widening of the circle.

In a later version of the circle, which is connected to the existentialist hermeneutics of Martin Heidegger and Rudolf Bultmann, the hermeneutic circle expands again, and includes the interpreter's preconceptions of the subject matter. In other words, if I read a book on theological hermeneutics, it requires that I have at least some notion of its subject matter, of the practice of reading, of theology and religion, etc. Otherwise I will not be able to make much sense of the book. Thus a preconception of the subject matter is not a hindrance to 'objective' understanding, but an essential prerequisite.

If one follows this train of thought, this has important implications for our understanding of the nature of theological language and of Christian proclamation. We will discuss these in detail in the chapter on existentialist hermeneutics (see pp. 122–4). For now, it will suffice to note that hermeneutics is essentially circular. This may be unsatisfactory for those who prefer understanding to be objective, and who do not think that prejudice, presupposition and guesswork have a place in interpretation. However, the admission that this cannot be avoided is an acknowledgement of the problematic nature of all human understanding, and the limitations of language as the medium of understanding. In this case, we can even welcome the circularity of understanding with Martin Heidegger who suggested that 'what is decisive is not to get out of the circle but to come into it in the right way'.[3] (See p. 123.)

The place of hermeneutics

After these initial definitions and distinctions, we can now locate hermeneutics. It occupies the place between epistemology and methodology. Epistemology is the theory of knowledge, including the theory of how we gain knowledge. Methodology is the theory of method, the reflection on the methods one employs to achieve a certain task. Hermeneutics is the link between the two.

Theological epistemology is concerned with the nature of revelation and with the question as to how we can know God. One's attitudes towards these issues will be determined by some fundamental theological stances, namely towards the nature and work of Christ, and how human beings appropriate this. One's epistemology will then shape one's hermeneutics, because what one believes to be the nature of religious knowledge will shape the way in which one sees religious knowledge understood and communicated. Consequently, the way in which one sees religious knowledge understood and communicated will affect one's methodology, one's reflection on appropriate methods for the theological task at hand, be it the interpretation of a biblical text, writing a treatise on the Trinity, planning a liturgy, or preaching a sermon. Finally, from the methodology follows the method, which is the way in which one goes about the task. To close the circle, the praxis of the Church, its liturgical and sacramental life, its proclamation, community life, and the pastoral ministry one receives will, in turn, shape one's fundamental theological views.

It is of utmost importance for theological intellectual integrity to be coherent in these areas. If theologians are incoherent, and one step does not follow from the other, they will not only damage their own integrity, but also the academic quality of their work and the credibility of their ministry.

Within this nexus, hermeneutics is in a crucial position, being situated between the more cerebral areas of fundamental theology and epistemology on the one hand and the applied areas of methodology and method on the other. It is the bridge between theory and praxis. Consequently, some hermeneutical writings will lean towards the applied side, which is usually the case in writings on biblical hermeneutics, which focus on the application of hermeneutical theory to biblical interpretation. Others will lean towards the theoretical side, by focusing on the nature of language and understanding. As we will see, the existentialist hermeneutics of the twentieth century even claimed that hermeneutics should take the place of ontology (the reflection on the very nature of being), and thus made hermeneutics the foundation of all philosophy and theology.

In this book, I try to strike a balance between the practical aspect of hermeneutics and the theoretical, keeping in mind that the purpose of this book is not to introduce biblical hermeneutics but general theological hermeneutics. However, as everything in theology is interrelated, we will not be able to avoid touching on issues of biblical hermeneutics.

The approach of this book

This book is essentially a historical introduction to theological hermeneutics. It will follow the development of the philosophical and theological assumptions with which people approached the problematic activity of reading. It is, as it were, a history of the problem of understanding. In this history, we will identify persistent problems, and how interpreters sought to solve these problems with all philosophical and philological tools that were at hand. We will trace how hermeneutics developed from the theory of textual interpretation into the universal philosophy of being. And we will discover the close relationship between philosophical and theological hermeneutics.

The presentation will take the form of a narrative from antiquity to the so-called hermeneutic school of the twentieth century and the present. This will be complemented by an introduction to alternative proposals, such as structuralist and postmodern hermeneutics as well as critical theory and related approaches, namely feminism and post-colonial hermeneutics. We will also discover how the different schools of thought do not live in isolation, but enter into dialogue, critique each other and keep each other accountable.

The choice of this structure carries with it my own bias, as my own thought is deeply indebted to the hermeneutical school. Others will be able to construct alternative narratives of the development of hermeneutics and the interaction of the various schools. However, I trust that the student will gain a broad overview of the development of hermeneutics and the current debates as a basis for further studies of this fascinating and exciting field.

Further reading

Introductions to the subject

Abrams, M. H., 1999, *A Glossary of Literary Terms*, 7th edn, Fort Worth, Tex.: Harcourt Brace College.

Bontekoe, Ronald, 1996, *Dimensions of the Hermeneutic Circle*, Atlantic Highlands, NJ: Humanities Press International.

Bruns, Gerald L., 1992, *Hermeneutics Ancient and Modern*, New Haven; London: Yale University Press.

Eagleton, Terry, 1996, *Literary Theory: An Introduction*, 2nd edn, Oxford: Blackwell.

Ferguson, Duncan S., 1987, *Biblical Hermeneutics: An Introduction*, London: SCM Press.

Grondin, Jean, 1994, *Introduction to Philosophical Hermeneutics*, *Yale Studies in Hermeneutics*, New Haven; London: Yale University Press.

Harrisville, Roy A. and Walter Sundberg, 2002, *The Bible in Modern Culture: Baruch Spinoza to Brevard Childs*, 2nd edn, Grand Rapids, Mich.: W. B. Eerdmans.

Inwood, Michael, 1998, 'Hermeneutics', in: Edward Craig (ed.), *Routledge Encyclopedia of Philosophy*, vol. IV, London; New York: Routledge, pp. 384–9.

Jasper, David, 2004, *A Short Introduction to Hermeneutics*, Louisville, Ky.: Westminster John Knox Press.

Jeanrond, Werner G., 1994, *Theological Hermeneutics: Development and Significance*, London: SCM Press.

Kaiser, Walter C. and Moisés Silva, 1994, *An Introduction to Biblical Hermeneutics: The Search for Meaning*, Grand Rapids, Mich.: Zondervan.

Oeming, Manfred, 2006, *Contemporary Biblical Hermeneutics: An Introduction*, translated by Joachim F. Vette, Aldershot: Ashgate.

Ramberg, Bjørn and Kristin Gjesdal, 2005, 'Hermeneutics', in: *The Stanford Encyclopedia of Philosophy* (website, Winter 2005), edited by Edward N. Zalta. Available from http://plato.stanford.edu/archives/win2005/entries/hermeneutics/.

Terrin, Aldo Natale, Christoph Dohmen et al., 2007, 'Hermeneutics', in: Hans Dieter Betz, Don S. Browning et al. (eds), *Religion Past and Present*, vol. IV, Leiden: Brill.

Thiselton, Anthony C., 1998, 'Hermeneutics, Biblical', in: Edward Craig (ed.), *Routledge Encyclopedia of Philosophy*, vol. IV, London; New York: Routledge, pp. 389–95.

Readers

Klemm, David E. (ed.), 1986, *Hermeneutical Inquiry: Volume 1: The Interpretation of Texts, AAR Studies in Religion*, vol. 43, Atlanta: Scholars Press.
Klemm, David E. (ed.), 1986, *Hermeneutical Inquiry: Volume 2: The Interpretation of Existence, AAR Studies in Religion*, vol. 44, Atlanta: Scholars Press.
Mueller-Vollmer, Kurt (ed.), 1989, *The Hermeneutics Reader: Texts of the German Tradition from the Enlightenment to the Present*, New York: Continuum.
Ormiston, Gayle L. and Alan D. Schrift (eds), 1990, *The Hermeneutic Tradition: From Ast to Ricoeur*, Albany, NY: State University of New York Press.

Notes

1   John Maynard Keynes, 1936, *The General Theory of Employment, Interest and Money*, London: Macmillan, p. 383.
2   Hans-Georg Gadamer, 1959, 'Hermeneutik', in: Joachim Ritter (ed.), *Historisches Wörterbuch der Philosophie*, vol. 3, Darmstadt: Wissenschaftliche Buchgesellschaft, col. 1061.
3   Martin Heidegger, 1962, *Being and Time*, translated by John Macquarrie and Edward Robinson, Oxford: Basil Blackwell, p. 195.

1

Hermeneutics in Antiquity

Introduction

Hermeneutical reflection began when the old myths about the gods did not make sense any more. The great myths, especially Homer's *Iliad* and *Odyssey*, were the authoritative texts of ancient Greek culture, but already in the classical period, beginning in the sixth century BC, aspects of these texts had become problematic.[1] Although the final form of these epics was comparatively recent, they reflected the social reality and religion of a long bygone age. Thus the way in which these texts depicted moral behaviour did not meet the norms of the readers; the attitude towards state and society in the texts was seen as backward and outdated compared with developing political theory. Furthermore, the perception of the gods as presented in the epics did not correspond to the theology of the time. The gods of the old myths had physical bodies, which could even be wounded, their moods changed, and they were often driven by inferior motives. In short, they behaved very much like the aristocracy of an age long past.

The philosophers from the sixth century onwards disagreed on the precise nature of the divine, and whether it could be manifest in many gods or only in one, but they all agreed that the divine could not be moved or changed or affected by external influence, not to mention that the divine could not occur within human-like bodies. The anthropomorphism of Homer and Hesiod was discarded.[2]

Thus the old myths contradicted the social experience in the developing city states and the morality that was required for this new social order, as well as growing theological insights. A radical solution to this problem was suggested by Plato, who in his most important work, *The Republic*, suggested that these harmful myths should simply be forbidden:

> But the narrative of Hephaestus binding Hera his mother, or how on another occasion Zeus sent him flying for taking her part when she was being beaten, and all the battles of the gods in Homer – these tales must not be admitted into our State, whether they are supposed to have an allegorical meaning or not.[3]

A significant number of thinkers, namely of the Stoic school of philosophy, chose not to follow Plato's suggestion, but the alternative which he implies: allegorical interpretation. Allegorical interpretation assumes, in short, that the text may say one thing, but it really means something quite different.[4] This way of reading soon became the dominant way of dealing with difficult passages or even whole texts in antiquity and throughout the Middle Ages.

Language and meaning

Before we examine the ancient authors' approach to textual interpretation, it is worthwhile to look at the purpose of the exercise: what did the ancient authors think they were doing when they read texts? What was their aim when reading, and what did they expect to find within texts? As far as we can establish, philosophers from Plato onwards reflected on the way in which language is meaningful.

In his dialogue *Ion*, Plato suggested that 'no one can become a good rhapsode [singer] who does not understand the meaning of the poet. For the rhapsode ought to interpret the thought (*dianoia*) of the poet to his hearers, but how can he interpret him well unless he knows what he means?'[5] For Plato, the interpreter who performs an epic or poem before an audience, conveys the mind or the thought of the author. Thus the recovery of the thought (*dianoia*) of the author is the task of interpretation.

In a similar vein, Aristotle suggests that

> spoken words are the symbols of mental experience and written words are the symbols of spoken words. Just as all people have not the same writing, so they have not the same speech sounds, but the mental experiences, which these directly symbolize, are the same for all, as also are those things of which our experiences are the images.[6]

For Aristotle, all humans have basic mental experiences in common, which can be expressed in language. Consequently, interpretation is the recovery of the mental experience from the spoken or written words.

The classical philosophers saw the mind or thought (*dianoia*) as linguistically constituted. When we think, we think in language. Thus Plato can describe the mind as the inner conversation of the soul: 'Are not thought (*dianoia*) and speech (*logos*) the same, with this exception, that what is called thought is the silent conversation of the soul with itself?'[7]

Thus there is, according to ancient philosophy, an inner conversation, or an inner word, which is thought, and this can be expressed in speech, in an external word. With this insight in mind, the Stoic philosophers introduced the distinction between the *logos endiathetos* (the inner word, that what is meant, i.e. the thought) and the *logos prophorikos* (the external, spoken word).[8] We hear speech (the external word, the *logos prophorikos*), and by interpreting it, we can comprehend the meaning of the utterance (the thought, inner word or *logos endiathetos*). Thus there is congruence between speech and thought, which assumes that the thought is contained in speech completely, and that we can understand the thought or the mental experience contained in the utterance without loss.

It is important to emphasize this attitude of classical Greek and Roman philosophy, because, as we will see below, the congruence between inner and external word is quite problematic. Yet it was only much later that Augustine of Hippo realized that there may be a loss of meaning in the transition from thought to speech and vice versa (see pp. 45–7).

Graeco-Roman antiquity

Allegorical interpretation

Probably the most significant hermeneutical innovation of the ancient philosophers is allegorical interpretation. This strategy is based on the assumption that the text may say one thing, but it really means something quite different. It was developed in Graeco-Roman antiquity, but adopted and applied in many other contexts. It came to be widely used within the Christian Church, and was almost generally accepted until the end of the Middle Ages.

As early as the sixth century BC, interpreters began to read Homer applying allegorical interpretation. They felt that Homer and Hesiod, the two (supposed) authors of the foundational texts of Greek civilization, needed to be defended when their stories and genealogies of gods did not match current religious thought any more. Thus, we find the first attempts of allegorical interpretation in writers such as Hecarus (*c.*550–476 BC) and Theagenes of Rhegium (flourished *c.*525 BC).[9] Theagenes, for example, interpreted the battle of the gods in the *Iliad* (Il. 20) as the struggle of the elements and natural qualities of the world. So he wrote that the gods Apollo, Helios and Hephaestus really represented fire, Poseidon and Scamander stood for water, etc., and thus that the narrative really represented the natural opposites in the world.[10] Although none of Theagenes' writings is preserved, and all we know about him is through other authors, he represents the earliest known example of the allegorical interpretation of the ancient myths.

Another strategy, which we find first applied in the writings of Anaxagoras (500–428 BC), is to interpret the true content of the myths as ethical: he is reported to have said that the events in Homer's writings are about virtue and righteousness.[11] This strategy of honouring the ancient texts as authoritative, while at the same time interpreting them in a way that removes the offence of their archaic content, proved highly successful and popular. Already at the time of Plato (i.e. in the early and mid fourth century BC) allegorical interpretation seems to have achieved widespread popularity.

Plato, as we have seen above, did not approve of allegorical interpretation of myths. All truth was accessible for him only through dialectical thinking, a particular way of using one's reason. Thus any attempt to bring some deeper, acceptable meaning into the texts seemed to him not worth the effort.[12] Why should one try to interpret these texts if the truth is accessible in a much more straightforward way? As a result, Platonic philosophers and the grammarians at the great library in Alexandria, who were deeply influenced by Platonism, rejected allegorical interpretation until the emergence of neo-Platonism in the third century AD.

The Stoic philosophers, however, made great use of allegorical interpretation. They developed a number of new techniques, such as the etymological interpretation of names.[13] This technique identifies the origin (often somewhat far-fetched) of a name and derives the allegorical meaning from it. So Pherekydes, who lived in the mid sixth century BC, could explain the god Kronos as the concept of time, as the name Kronos seems to be derived from the Greek word *chronos* (time).[14] Through the influence of the Stoic hermeneutics, the use of allegorical interpretation became not only widespread, but also influenced first-century Judaism and Christianity.

Thus allegorical interpretation is best understood as a sophisticated critical device for the interpretation of texts that were seen as authoritative, but which could not be interpreted literally any more since the literal sense had become meaningless or even offensive. As we will see shortly, as its use was adopted in early Christianity, it remained the main critical tool until the Reformation. Thus it was in use for some 2,000 years and, once it was discarded, it would be difficult to find a suitable critical device to replace it (see section 'Enlightenment', pp. 79–81).

Historical grammatical interpretation

We have already seen that allegorical interpretation was not without its critics. Plato rejected it out of hand, and in this he was followed by the grammarians at the great library of Alexandria in Egypt, who were influenced by Platonic philosophy. This is ironic in the light of the later reputation of Alexandria as the centre of allegorical interpretation. But this reputation was based on Philo of Alexandria (20 BC–AD 50) and, later, on neo-Platonic theologians such as Cyprian and Origen. The Alexandrian grammarians, however, developed a sophisticated historical and grammatical method of interpretation. Their interpretation of texts was built on the grammatical explanation of linguistically difficult passages and the exploration of the historical background of texts. Thus they sought to elucidate the literal meaning of texts. They even developed critical methods, such as textual criticism, which is employed to reconstruct the original text of a possibly corrupted writing.[15]

Other methods, such as comparison of style and vocabulary, were used to judge if a text was written by the author to whom it was ascribed. Using these methods, the Alexandrian grammarians were able to determine that Homer had not written a number of poems ascribed to him, and the grammarian Aristophanes of Byzantium was even able to show that the ending of Homer's *Odyssey* was not by the same author as the rest of the work. Finally, ancient interpreters criticized the content of a text in the light of the advanced knowledge of their time.

Thus interpretation in antiquity was far from being uncritical. On the contrary, Hellenistic grammarians were using a number of critical tools in their exegesis, that is, in their interpretation of texts, as a matter of course. These were employed to elucidate and, if necessary, to judge the literal meaning of texts.

Judaism

To describe and discuss the principles of ancient Jewish hermeneutics is a difficult undertaking. Since the discovery of the Dead Sea Scrolls our knowledge of ancient Jewish literature has grown rapidly. The scholarly literature on the subject is vast and continues to grow. Consequently, it will not be possible to offer a comprehensive overview of ancient Jewish hermeneutics. Instead I will focus on five areas, identified by James Dunn as characteristic for ancient Jewish exegesis. These areas include Targum, Midrash, Pesher, typology and allegory.[16] In addition to these, I will discuss briefly the hermeneutical function of the developing tradition. The order in which these issues are discussed is systematic, rather than chronological. The developing tradition, and Targumim (i.e. translations), do not presuppose a literally fixed canon of sacred Scripture, while Pesher, Midrash and allegorical interpretation do presuppose a fixed canon. Typology, as we will see, works under both sets of presuppositions, and is therefore discussed in between the two groups.

A developing tradition

Until the reformation of Judaism after the destruction of the temple, the Jewish sacred texts were by no means fixed. A number of different versions of the texts were in use, and the tradition still in flux. Thus, in order to apply the traditional texts to changing circumstances and theological preferences, the tradition could be developed further: texts could be corrected by additional texts, which would present a new angle on a question, or the wording could be altered.

We can find various examples for this strategy. The differences between the Greek and the Hebrew versions of the Jewish Scriptures show that there was a continuing development in some areas of literature, such as in wisdom literature. In the Septuagint, the supposedly divinely inspired Greek translation of the Hebrew Scriptures, there are some additional wisdom books, namely *Ben Sira* (*Wisdom of Jesus Son of Sirach*, also known as *Ecclesiasticus*) and the *Wisdom of Solomon*, which are not part of the Hebrew canon. *Ben Sira* was most likely written in the second century BC,[17] while *Wisdom of Solomon* was most likely written in the first century BC.[18] These two books represent important further development in the genre of wisdom literature, which begins with Proverbs and the wisdom psalms, and continues with Job and Ecclesiastes. In these books, we can identify a development of thought within the Jewish Scriptures. *Ben Sira* and *Wisdom of Solomon* offer a further development of theology, applied to the circumstances of the second and first centuries BC. In a similar vein, we find additional books such as *Jubilees*, a theological interpretation of biblical material, creatively rewriting this material and adding to it. Thus the author of *Jubilees* interpreted the biblical material, including historical and legal texts, for the new, changed circumstances. This form of interpretation, which we also find in a number of Qumran documents, such as the *Damascus Document* and the *Temple Scroll*, went 'to extreme lengths to bring the text of that Mosaic Law into line with its "correct" meaning'.[19]

Translations (Targumim)

We find the same need to update the biblical law for a different era in the Targumim. A Targum is an Aramaic translation of the Hebrew Bible. Aramaic was the common language of most people in Palestine in the first centuries BC and AD, and thus their access to biblical texts would have been through these translations. But they went further than literally translating the texts – they were intended 'to interpret the biblical message for the common people'.[20] They took account of the current understanding of the Jewish law and altered their material accordingly. Thus they were 'an up-to-date version of the Scriptures, on which perforce had to agree with current law and customs'.[21]

The same applies to the Greek translation of the Jewish Scriptures. The Septuagint, as this translation is known, was translated in the Hellenistic environment of second-century BC Egypt. Its translation of the Hebrew text is often extremely free, adjusting texts for the social and philosophical context in which Egyptian Jews found themselves. The authority of this translation, which became the basis for Greek-speaking Judaism and for early Christianity, was explained by a story of its divine inspiration. Seventy-two Jewish elders were supposed to have translated the Jewish Scriptures within 72 days, and the result was found to be authentic and authoritative. This story is highly unlikely, as the Septuagint (the name comes from the Greek *septuaginta*, meaning 'seventy', referring to the number of the elders) reflects an adaptation of the Hebrew material for the Hellenistic context. However, it demonstrated the high esteem in which this translation was held.

Typology

Typology is a hermeneutical device which assumes that the present is prefigured (*typos*, in Greek, means 'prefiguration') by events in the past. The correspondence between the past and present does not require written text, but functions at the level of the event – even though the historical event may be a construction of the present.[22]

For instance, Deutero-Isaiah sees the Exodus as a prefiguration of the expected return of the Jewish people from the exile.

Thus says the Lord, who makes a way in the sea, a path in the mighty waters, who brings out chariot and horse, army and warrior; they lie down, they cannot rise, they are extinguished, quenched like a wick:

Do not remember the former things, or consider the things of old. I am about to do a new thing; now it springs forth, do you not perceive it? I will make a way in the wilderness and rivers in the desert. The wild animals will honour me, the jackals and the ostriches; for I give water in the wilderness, rivers in the desert, to give drink to my chosen people, the people whom I formed for myself so that they might declare my praise. (Isa. 43.16–21)

Thus some traditional material, in this case the Exodus from Egypt, is used as an archetype of the expected salvation of Israel from the exile. It is interesting to note that much of the Exodus material of the Pentateuch was written during this period. We can identify an interesting double movement: the Exodus is the prefiguration of the expected salvation, and, at the same time, the Exodus tradition is shaped with its current application in mind.

Typology therefore constructs meaning for the present from narratives of the past, which, in turn, are shaped by the present need. Underlying typology is the assumption that God's expected action in the present must have a precedent in God's action in the past. Consquently, authors take up relevant traditions and develop them in order to make sense of the present. Their belief in the continuity of God's action gives them the freedom to use their traditions in such a free and imaginative way.

Midrash

Once a canon of sacred Scripture has been established and closed, strategies like juxtaposing older traditions with newer ones, or adapting older material for changing circumstances, do not work any more. Instead, interpreters have to focus on the interpretation of the established material and make it relevant for the present.

One of these strategies is the Midrash. In its broader sense, Midrash can entail all ways of textual interpretation that make a text relevant for the present.[23] In its narrower sense, Midrash refers to a particular type of Rabbinic exegesis. Its aim was to make the sacred texts of the Jewish Scriptures relevant for one's own situation. It was built on the assumption that every element of the text, down to the individual letter, was significant and a bearer of God's will.[24] This led to an imaginative approach to biblical texts, allowing for some (to our understanding) extravagant intertextual connections. The style of such approaches can be seen in the following excerpts from the Genesis Rabba.

The Torah was to God, when He created the world, what the plan is to an architect when he erects a building.

The א [aleph], being the first letter of the Hebrew Alphabet, demurred at her place being usurped by the letter ב [beth], which is second to her, at the creation; the history of which commences with the latter instead of with the former. She was, however, quite satisfied when told that in the history of giving the Decalogue, she would be placed at the beginning in the word אנכי, for the world has only been created on account of the Torah, which, indeed, existed anterior to creation; and had the Creator not foreseen that Israel would consent to receive and diffuse the Torah, creation would not have taken place.[25]

Light is mentioned five times in the opening chapter of the Bible. This points to the five books of Moses. 'God said let there be light' refers to the book of Genesis, which enlightens us as to how creation was carried out. The words 'And there was light' bear reference to the book of Exodus, which contains the history of the transition of Israel from darkness to light. 'And God saw the light that it was good': this alludes to the book of Leviticus, which contains numerous statutes. 'And God divided between the light and between the darkness': this refers to the book of Numbers, divided as that book is between the history of those who came out of Egypt and that of those who were on their way to possess the promised land. 'And God called the light day': this bears reference to the book of Deuteronomy, which is not only a rehearsal of the four earlier books, but contains Moses' eloquent dying charge to Israel and many laws not mentioned in the preceding books.[26]

The Hebrew word for 'forming' is, in connexion with the formation of man, spelled exceptionally וייצר with two '', which is not its proper spelling. This is to be taken as a hint that man was formed out of two elements – spirit and matter. This is also manifested in man's life. His material part has need of matter to sustain him, and of the other laws of nature; he grows, flourishes, decays and dies. But, on the other hand, he resembles spiritual beings by walking upright, by his power of speech and thought, and by being able in some degree to see behind him without need of turning his head round; which facility is given to man alone and not to the lower animals.[27]

This style of exegesis is based on the supposition that every word, even every letter of the Jewish Scriptures, is inspired and meaningful, but also that the use of these texts is not confined to historical and legal knowledge; the Scriptures are also for the edification of both the individual and the Jewish people communally.[28]

Rabbinic legal interpretation was more prescriptive, in so far as it was recognized that it had to be based on rules. There was no single set of rules, but various collections which were commonly attributed to the great rabbis. These rules facilitated the delineation of existing laws from biblical law and the creation of new laws on the basis of the interpretation of the biblical law. Thus the application of the biblical law was sufficiently flexible to account for the needs of the present.[29]

Overall, it is a mark of this kind of exegesis that the overruling concern is the present needs of the community. As the text is God's own word for the community, it must be relevant and true, even if it is not so at the literal level. Instead of rewriting the text, however, the interpreter comments on the sacred text, finding relevant meaning in it.

Pesharim

The community at Qumran developed a distinct approach to biblical texts. The basic assumption of their exegesis was that they were living in the end time, and that God's promised saving actions would take place soon. Consequently, they applied prophecies and other apocalyptic texts to their own situation by establishing point-to-point correspondences between their situation and the text.[30]

So, for example, the Pesher Habakkuk, which contains an interpretation of the prophet of the same name, can present this interpretation of a passage from the Prophet Habakkuk: 'For this he continually unsheathes his sword to slaughter peoples without pity. Its interpretation concerns the Kittim (i.e. Romans) who will cause many to die by the edge of the sword.'[31] In the original context, the passage appears to refer to the Chaldeans, that is, the Babylonians, and thus to the political situation at the time of Habakkuk. The interpreter, however, takes this to refer to his own time, which he saw as the end of days, in which the final judgement was imminent.

Interpreters used this technique, going through the text verse by verse, deciphering the hidden meaning of the text, or, as a critical modern reader might say, reading their own situation into the text. This was seen as a legitimate way of reading, because God inspired the interpreter to find this hidden meaning, which God had intended but hidden until the end time had arrived. Again, the relevance of the text for the present was the guiding principle of the interpretation. Modern notions of authenticity and historical truth did not occur to the interpreter.

Allegorical interpretation

The Jewish community of Alexandria in Egypt found itself in a very different situation. It did not see itself as involved in the struggles that would precede God's final judgement, but as an integral part of the society of the greatest metropolis of the Hellenistic world. In this environment, learned Jews lived in close contact with educated Greek and Egyptian people. In assuming the values and even the Platonic philosophy of its Hellenistic environment, some core contents of the Jewish Scriptures were perceived as offensive.

Jewish theologians and philosophers began to use allegorical interpretation in the second century BC. Aristobulus, who lived in the mid second century BC in Alexandria, applied allegorical interpretation in his commentary to the Pentateuch, the first five books of the Bible.[32] The *Letter of Aristeas* used allegorical interpretation in order to defend the Jewish food laws against Hellenistic critics:

> So, to prevent our being perverted by contact with others or by mixing with bad influences, he hedged us in on all sides with strict observances connected with meat and drink and touch and hearing and sight, after the manner of the Law. In general everything is similarly constituted in regard to natural reasoning, being governed by one supreme power, and in each particular everything has a profound reason for it, both the things from which we abstain in use and those of which we partake. For illustration I briefly give you one or two examples. Do not take the contemptible view that Moses enacted this legislation because of an excessive preoccupation with mice and weasels or suchlike creatures. The fact is that everything has been solemnly set in order for unblemished investigation and amendment of life for the sake of righteousness. The birds which we use are all domesticated and of exceptional cleanliness, their food consisting of wheat and pulse – such birds as pigeons, turtledoves, locusts, partridges, and, in addition, geese and others of the same kind. As to the birds which are forbidden, you will find wild and carnivorous kinds, and the rest which dominate by their own strength, and to find their food at the expense of the aforementioned domesticated birds – which is an injustice; and not only that, they also seize lambs and kids and outrage human beings dead or alive. By calling them impure, he has thereby indicated that that is the solemn binding duty of those for whom the legislation has been established to practice righteousness and not to lord it over anyone in reliance upon their own strength, nor to deprive him of anything, but to govern their lives righteously, in the manner of the gentle creatures among the

aforementioned birds which feed on those plants which grow on the ground and do not exercise a domination leading to the destruction of their fellow creatures.[33]

The *Wisdom of Solomon*, a book that is contained in the Greek canon of the Old Testament but not in the Hebrew, is evidently influenced by the Stoic practice of allegorical interpretation, when, for example, it interprets the feeding of Israel with Manna in the desert (cf. Exodus 16) in a rather spiritual way:

Instead of these things you gave your people food of angels, and without their toil you supplied them from heaven with bread ready to eat, providing every pleasure and suited to every taste. For your sustenance manifested your sweetness toward your children; and the bread, ministering to the desire of the one who took it, was changed to suit everyone's liking. Snow and ice withstood fire without melting, so that they might know that the crops of their enemies were being destroyed by the fire that blazed in the hail and flashed in the showers of rain; whereas the fire, in order that the righteous might be fed, even forgot its native power. For creation, serving you who made it, exerts itself to punish the unrighteous, and in kindness relaxes on behalf of those who trust in you. Therefore at that time also, changed into all forms, it served your all-nourishing bounty, according to the desire of those who had need, so that your children, whom you loved, O Lord, might learn that it is not the production of crops that feeds humankind but that your word sustains those who trust in you. For what was not destroyed by fire was melted when simply warmed by a fleeting ray of the sun, to make it known that one must rise before the sun to give you thanks, and must pray to you at the dawning of the light; for the hope of an ungrateful person will melt like wintry frost, and flow away like waste water. (Wisd. 16.20–29)

Furthermore, the inclusion of the Song of Songs into the Hebrew Scriptures was only possible because it was interpreted allegorically, as its literal meaning is quite plainly that of a love poem, which, literally understood, would have been unacceptable. However, as it was generally understood as referring to the relationship between God and Israel, and later between God and the Church, it was not only acceptable but considered of great spiritual value.

The apex of allegorical interpretation in Judaism, however, was the Jewish philosopher Philo of Alexandria (*c.*20 BC–AD 50). For him, in order to gain access to the full meaning of the text, we must leave the literal sense behind and focus on the allegorical:

> But they who follow only what is plain and easy [i.e. those who are content with the literal sense], . . . I would exhort not to be content with stopping at this point, but to proceed onward to look at the passage in a figurative way, considering that the mere words of the scriptures are, as it were, but shadows of bodies, and that the meanings which are apparent to investigation beneath them, are the real things to be pondered upon.[34]

This passage is only one of many in which Philo develops a theory of allegorical interpretation. Behind every text is a deeper meaning, which either discloses ethical or cosmological meaning. This deeper meaning of the text is not for everyone – it is for the few, who are interested in the soul and not in the body.[35] According to Philo's theory of allegorical interpretation, there are certain hints in the text that the literal sense has to be given up in favour of the allegorical. This is chiefly if the literal sense is offensive, either by saying something about God that we know is not true, such as describing God anthropomorphically, that is, by ascribing human attributes to God, or by contradicting other passages, the knowledge of the time, or universal morality.[36] Although Philo's allegorical interpretation seems to be restricted in theory, in practice he interprets every biblical text allegorically. So it is no surprise that he had to defend himself against those who, using his methods of interpretation, gave up on the literal meaning of the Torah altogether and claimed they did not have to follow it.[37]

In order to get a flavour of Philo's method, it may be worthwhile to quote a longer passage from his commentary on Genesis 2.13, which is a description of the rivers flowing out of Paradise:

> 'And a river goes forth out of Eden to water the Paradise. From thence it is separated into four heads: the name of the one is Pheison. That is the one which encircles the whole land of Evilat. There is the country where there is gold, and the gold of that land is good. There also are the carbuncle and the sapphire stone. And the name of the second river is Gihon; this is that which encircles the whole land of Ethiopia. And the third river is the Tigris. This is the river which flows in front of the Assyrians. And the fourth river is the Euphrates.' In these words Moses intends to sketch out the particular virtues. And they also are four in number, prudence, temperance, courage, and justice. Now the greatest

river from which the four branches flow off, is generic virtue, which we have already called goodness; and the four branches are the same number of virtues. Generic virtue, therefore, derives its beginning from Eden, which is the wisdom of God; which rejoices and exults, and triumphs, being delighted at and honoured on account of nothing else, except its Father, God, and the four particular virtues, are branches from the generic virtue, which like a river waters all the good actions of each, with an abundant stream of benefits. Let us examine the expressions of the writer: 'A river', says he, 'goes forth out of Eden, to water the Paradise.' This river is generic goodness; and this issues forth out of the Eden of the wisdom of God, and that is the word of God. For it is according to the word of God, that generic virtue was created. And generic virtue waters the Paradise: that is to say, it waters the particular virtues. But it does not derive its beginnings from any principle of locality, but from a principle of pre-eminence. For each of the virtues is really and truly a ruler and a queen. And the expression, 'is separated', is equivalent to 'is marked off by fixed boundaries'; since wisdom appoints them settled limits with reference to what is to be done. Courage with respect to what is to be endured; temperance with reference to what is to be chosen; and justice in respect of what is to be distributed.

'The name of one river is Pheison. This is that river which encircles all the land of Evilat; there is the country where there is gold. And the gold of that land is good; there also are the carbuncle and the sapphire stone.' One of the four virtues is prudence, which Moses here calls Pheison: because the soul abstains [pheison from pheidomai, to spare, or abstain from] from, and guards against, acts of iniquity. And it meanders in a circle, and flows all round the land of Evilat; that is to say, it preserves a mild, and gentle, and favourable constitution. And as of all fusible essences, the most excellent and the most illustrious is gold, so also the virtue of the soul which enjoys the highest reputation, is prudence. And when he uses the expression, 'that is the country where there is gold', he is not speaking geographically, that is, where gold exists, but that is the country in which that valuable possession exists, brilliant as gold, tried in the fire, and valuable, namely, prudence. And this is confessed to be the most valuable possession of God.[38]

Philo's hermeneutical approach thus enabled him to take the ancient authoritative texts seriously and, at the same time, remove the offence they might cause to the educated reader. Moreover, he is able to read these texts in a way that is relevant for the Hellenistic environment in which he lives, and which resonates with the Platonic thought of this environment. This would give him lasting influence over the way in which the early Church was to interpret its Bible.

Christianity

New Testament

The earliest Christians saw themselves as the community in which the promises of God had been fulfilled. Therefore, in a similar vein to the approach of the Pesharim, early Christian interpreters would relate the prophecies of the Jewish Scriptures to the present salvation. Consequently, texts, which in their original context refer to events at the time of the author, could be applied to Jesus of Nazareth. Thus, when Luke's Gospel tells of Jesus reading Isaiah 61.1–2 in the synagogue (Luke 4.16–21), he reads the text as if it referred to himself.

> When he came to Nazareth, where he had been brought up, he went to the synagogue on the sabbath day, as was his custom. He stood up to read, and the scroll of the prophet Isaiah was given to him. He unrolled the scroll and found the place where it was written: 'The Spirit of the Lord is upon me, because he has anointed me to bring good news to the poor. He has sent me to proclaim release to the captives and recovery of sight to the blind, to let the oppressed go free, to proclaim the year of the Lord's favour.' And he rolled up the scroll, gave it back to the attendant, and sat down. The eyes of all in the synagogue were fixed on him. Then he began to say to them, 'Today this scripture has been fulfilled in your hearing.'

Any critical reading of Isaiah 61 will show that this text cannot refer to Jesus, but to events related to the end of the exile. However, early Christians read this text as if it related to Jesus, even if somewhat out of context. Thus a relation between the Old Testament and the New Testament was established.

Luke's use of Isaiah 61 is not an isolated instance. The writers of the three synoptic gospels saw Isaiah 40.3 as fulfilled in the coming of John the Baptist. Matthew took the miraculous conception of Jesus as fulfilling the prophecy of Isaiah 7.14. Matthew also saw a number of small features of Jesus' ministry to be the fulfilment of Old Testament prophecies, such as the fact that Jesus speaks in parables as relating to Isaiah 6.9

(Matt. 13.13–16, Mark 4.11–13), and Jesus' desire not be made known (Matt. 12.15–21) as the fulfilling of Isaiah 42.1–4. It is noticeable that most of these proof texts are taken out of context, and then applied to events of Jesus' ministry as depicted in the New Testament.

Another exegetical tool of the early Church was typological interpretation. In its Christian use, typological interpretation reads a passage in the Old Testament as a prefiguration, not a prophecy, of a Christian belief. There are many examples of this interpretative strategy, such as Paul's treatment in 1 Corinthians 10 of Exodus 13.21–22, 14.19–30 and Exodus 17:

> I do not want you to be unaware, brothers and sisters, that our ancestors were all under the cloud, and all passed through the sea, and all were baptized into Moses in the cloud and in the sea, and all ate the same spiritual food, and all drank the same spiritual drink. For they drank from the spiritual rock that followed them, and the rock was Christ. Nevertheless, God was not pleased with most of them, and they were struck down in the wilderness. Now these things occurred as examples for us, so that we might not desire evil as they did. (1 Cor. 10.1–6)

Paul thus reads these events as prefiguring Christian beliefs – the cloud that led the Israelites passing through the Red Sea becomes a prefiguration of baptism, and the water-giving rock a prefiguration of Christ with strong eucharistic overtones. And, according to 1 Corinthians 10.6, all this happened as example (*typos*) for Christians. Another example is the interpretation in John's Gospel (John 3.14) of the story of the bronze serpent on the pole in Numbers 21.6–9, which is understood as a prefiguration of the crucifixion of Jesus Christ. These are only a few examples of a great number of instances of typological interpretation in the New Testament.

Christian writers also employed traditional allegorical interpretation. Paul, in Galatians 4.21ff, interprets the story of Sarah and Hagar (Gen. 21.8–14) as referring to the relation between law and gospel. In Romans 4.9–25 Paul reads the counting of Abraham's faith as righteousness in Genesis 15.6 as referring to his own theological concept of justification by faith, and uses the statement that Abraham will be the father of many nations in Genesis 17.5 as evidence for this interpretation. Interestingly, the author of the Letter of James (2.21–24) takes issue with Paul's interpretation of this material, and, interpreting Genesis 15.6 in the light of the story of the sacrifice of Isaac in Genesis 22, comes to the opposite conclusion from Paul, namely, that we are justified by works. Thus both authors use texts from Genesis for a theological debate with which the texts have nothing to do. But by reading the texts allegorically, they are able to make them relevant as proof texts for their own concerns.

But what is the purpose of these ways of treating the Jewish Scriptures? From today's reader's point of view, the strategies depicted above seem arbitrary and, from a critical perspective, untenable. Having said this, we have seen before that allegorical interpretation was a widely recognized approach to texts, and thus the early Church could use it to solve the problem at hand.

The theologians of the early Church found themselves in a situation similar to that of the Greek thinkers of the fourth century BC, in so far as they recognized the Hebrew Scriptures as authoritative, yet these Scriptures did not warrant the new faith in a straightforward way. Thus, in order to maintain the authority of the Hebrew Scriptures, at the same time allowing them to be relevant as the Christian Old Testament, a connection between the Old and the New Testaments had to be constructed. This was done by applying the scheme of prophecy and fulfilment, typological and allegorical interpretation. Thus the early Christians used the best hermeneutical methods available in their time to solve a hermeneutical problem at hand.

The Apologists

Strictly speaking, the period of the New Testament writers and the early Church forms a continuity and any firm distinction between them is arbitrary. There is a wealth of early Christian literature from the first and early second century, and before the end of the second century it was far from clear which writings were authoritative Christian Scriptures and which were not. Only in its response to the so-called Gnostic crisis of the second century AD did the early Church define (however loosely to begin with) an authoritative canon of Scriptures.

There was, however, one canon that was generally considered to be authoritative, that of the Old Testament, especially in the form of the supposedly divinely inspired Greek translation, the Septuagint. The early Christian authors continued to interpret the Old Testament along the lines of the New Testament authors, using the same techniques and strategies in interpretation.[39] The new development in biblical interpretation was the development of the canon of the New Testament and the resulting need for the interpretation of the texts of the New Testament.

Before the definition of the canon of the New Testament we find that different Christian communities developed their own traditions. Those churches that went back to the mission of Paul, for example, used Pauline letters, and possibly one of the gospels, in their liturgy. In the Pastoral Letters, which were included in the canon, we see how the Pauline tradition is continued and developed further in response to the needs of the churches. We find this continued in the letters of the Apostolic Fathers of the late first and early second centuries.

In Justin Martyr (died c.162–8) we find a wide range of references to the synoptic gospels, which he assumes to be the 'memoirs' of the Apostles.[40] Interestingly, he can also refer to the 'memoirs' of Peter, which may be a reference to a gospel that, when the canon was defined later in the century, was not included.[41] At any rate, it is interesting to note that Justin uses quotations from the gospels rather freely and inaccurately. On the basis of this evidence, it has also been assumed that Justin is not using any of the canonical gospels, but a harmony of the gospels.[42] In short, Justin does not seem to assume an authoritative canon of New Testament Scriptures, which, being divinely inspired, would need to be interpreted in the same way as the Old Testament. Instead, he seems to rely on the witness of 'memoirs', that is, the gospels or a harmony of gospels, to provide reliable information about the circumstances of Jesus' ministry, death and resurrection. He uses these in order to show how Old Testament prophecies have been fulfilled in Jesus Christ, and sees no further need for interpretation.[43]

It is evident from Justin's writings that he is familiar with the Acts of the Apostles and a number of epistles of the New Testament, but he never quotes them verbatim as authoritative texts or sees any need to interpret them. In fact, Justin refers to the epistles by way of allusion, and not direct quotation, and uses them as guides to the correct interpretation of the Christian tradition.[44]

Thus it appears that Justin does not assume that there is a canon of sacred Scriptures of the New Testament which needs to be interpreted, but a number of writings by authoritative figures, who bear witness to Jesus' life and death and who give guidance in the interpretation of Scripture, namely, the Old Testament, and of the Christian tradition. In short, there is no notion of a canon of sacred scriptures of the New Testament, but a continuing tradition in which Justin stands in the same way as the Apostles.

Origen

The need to interpret a normative canon of New Testament Scriptures arose only with the definition of the canon at the end of the second century. This brought with it certain problems, such as textual variations in different copies of the same book as well as contradictions or tensions between the canonical texts. Thus it became necessary to interpret the Scriptures of the New Testament just as the Old Testament was already being interpreted. The first great theorist and practitioner of the interpretation of the Bible as a whole, that is, Old and New Testaments, is the Alexandrian theologian Origen (c.185–c.251 AD).

First of all, there was a need for a reliable text. Controversies with Jewish theologians had shown that it was essential for Christian apologists to have a reliable text on the basis of which they could argue with their Jewish opponents – in short, Christians needed to agree on the actual wording of their sacred Scriptures.[45] Origen embarked on a major text-critical exercise, by comparing the wording of all the versions of the Old Testament that were available to him. These were the Hebrew text, the Hebrew text transliterated into Greek, the Septuagint and the Greek translations by Aquila of Sinope, Symmachus the Ebionite and Theodotion. He arranged these texts in six columns, so that the wording could be compared easily. Then he used the critical methods of the grammarians at Alexandria and attempted to establish a critically annotated text of the Greek Old Testament. The Hexapla, as this critical master work was known, was kept in the library at Caesarea. Sadly, it was destroyed in the sixth century.[46]

Origen's enterprise is remarkable, as it is the first critical attempt at the text of the Old Testament by a Christian. The need to establish a reliable text arose in the context of the polemical controversy between Christian and Jewish scholars. It provided the basis for all subsequent work of this kind.[47] Having established a reliable text, Origen then makes use of philological and archaeological research in order to elucidate its literal meaning.[48]

Interestingly, Origen never applied his critical method to the New Testament, which he quotes often in a cavalier manner, giving the same text in a variety of forms. In some places, he seems to be quoting inaccurately from memory, in others the variance in the text can be explained by his use of a number of different manuscripts.[49] One explanation for this might be that accurate use of the New Testament was not essential, compared to the Hebrew Scriptures, as there was no controversy at the time that required a reliable critical text of the New Testament.

For our hermeneutical reflections, we can see in Origen an early example of the need to adopt methods from one's environment, in this case the grammarians at Alexandria, and to use them in order to solve a problem at hand.

However, Origen did not become famous for his interpretation of the literal meaning of the text. In fact, he is known for his extensive use of allegorical interpretation and its application to the New Testament. As we have seen, allegorical and typological interpretation of some Old Testament texts was very common in the early Church. Yet Origen went beyond the common usage of allegory in both theory and practice. Moreover, Origen saw allegorical or typological interpretation as universal, in other words, *every* text has a higher, spiritual meaning. Thus Origen, in the footsteps of his fellow Alexandrian Philo, was able to find a higher meaning in every biblical text.

Origen moved beyond the common usage of allegorical interpretation by assuming that the New Testament is a prefiguration of the kingdom to come.[50] This enabled Origen to interpret the texts of the New Testament allegorically, and to search within its words for deeper, spiritual meaning. This approach to the New Testament had some significant implications: it means that Origen assumed that the New Testament is divinely inspired sacred Scripture. This is very different from Justin Martyr's assumption that the gospels contained reliable witness, and that the epistles contained some authoritative interpretation of the Christian faith (see p. 26). Thus we see how a fixed canon of sacred Scripture of the New Testament developed, which, with increasing temporal distance to the time of its writing, was regarded with increasing veneration.

Origen assumed that biblical texts contained three senses (in this he is the precursor of the medieval fourfold meaning of Scripture (see section 'Medieval interpretation', pp. 52–4)): the literal, the moral and the spiritual. Origen compared these to the three parts of the human being in ancient Christian understanding: body, soul and spirit.[51] The literal sense refers to the superficial, straightforward literal reading of the text, which he could call also the historical or the corporeal sense.[52] As we have seen above, Origen made a great exegetical effort to elucidate the literal sense by all critical means available to him. Yet he thought that this sense of Scripture was intended primarily for the simple and uninstructed. Nevertheless, it should not be discarded, as it could be of great benefit for those who believe because of it.[53]

The second layer of meaning is the moral meaning, which corresponds to the human soul. This meaning is for the more advanced in the mysteries of faith. Finally, there is the spiritual sense of Scripture, which is accessible for those who are perfect in the faith,[54] those who 'can identify the heavenly realities'.[55] At this level, the Scriptures refer to the deep mysteries of Christianity, such as the Heavenly Jerusalem,[56] the Last Judgement,[57] or other contents of the Christian faith, even if they do not refer to them on the literal level.

Origen could approach the Bible in this way because he believed that the whole Bible was literally inspired by the Holy Spirit, who endowed the Scriptures with multiple levels of meaning in order to convey the fullness of God's revelation. Thus, when we interpret these texts, we need to move beyond the simple literal sense. Otherwise a whole dimension of the meaning of the Bible will be lost. Origen wrote:

Since the (Spirit's) primary goal was to present the logical system of spiritual realities by means of events that happened and things that were to be done, the Word used actual historical events wherever they could be accommodated to these mystical (meanings), hiding the deeper sense from the multitude. But where the recorded actions of a specific person did not fit the account of the inner coherence of intelligible realities in terms of the deeper mystical meaning, Scripture has woven into the historical narrative some features which did not happen; sometimes the event is an impossibility; sometimes, though possible, it actually did not happen. Sometimes only a few phrases which are not true in the bodily sense are inserted, sometimes more. We must assume an analogous situation in regard to the law. Frequently one can find commandments which are useful in themselves and appropriate for the time of legislation. Sometimes, however, their usefulness is not self-evident. At other times, even impossible things are commanded; such instances challenge the more skilful and inquisitive to devote themselves to a painstaking examination of the text and become seriously convinced that a sense worthy of God needs to be sought in these commandments.

But the Spirit made such arrangements not only with regard to the period before the advent of Christ; being the same Spirit and coming from the one God, he acted similarly when dealing with the Gospels and Apostles. Even they did not present the historical narrative completely free of additions which did not actually happen; nor did they always transmit the legal prescription and commandments in such a way that they seem reasonable in themselves.[58]

Thus Origen was able to hold together two insights: on the one hand, the Bible is inspired by God, while, on the other hand, it contains historical inaccuracies and impossibilities and in places even contradicts our knowledge of the nature and will of God. Origen's approach to the interpretation of Scripture combined the critical need of the scholar with the spiritual need of the Church in a coherent system of interpretation. Although his excessive use of allegorical interpretation did not become the standard of the medieval Church, Origen's theory of allegorical interpretation would influence the Church's reading of the Bible for centuries to come, in the form of a more moderate approach to allegory proposed by Augustine of Hippo (see p. 44).

The Antiochene School

Such a highly critical and philosophically informed approach at the forefront of hermeneutical reflection as Origen's could not stay without its critics. Thus, from the mid third century AD an exegetical school formed that rejected the Alexandrian use of allegorical interpretation and focused on historical-grammatical exegesis. After its centre in Antioch it is known as the Antiochene School. It was founded by Lucian of Antioch (died 312 – sometimes known as Lucian of Samosata, which is misleading as there is a pagan author of the same name who died in 180).[59] Eustathius of Antioch (died before 357), who explicitly attacked Origen and the allegorical interpretation in one of his works,[60] and Ephrem the Syrian (died c.378) were early proponents of this school. It flourished with Diodore of Tarsus (died 390), Theodore of Mopsuestia (died c.428), John Chrysostom (died 407) and Theodoret of Cyrus (died 457).

The Antiochene theologians all rejected allegorical interpretation, but, somewhat inconsistently, admitted typological interpretation of the Old Testament. This was permissible in their eyes because this technique had also been applied by the authors of the New Testament. But their use of typology was not restricted to those parts of the Old Testament that had been interpreted in this way by the authors of the New Testament, but also included a range of other texts.[61] Obviously, different theologians of this school would apply typological interpretation in different degrees, but in principle its legitimacy was beyond dispute. Thus, even those theologians who regarded the literal meaning of the text as its primary meaning had to acknowledge in their work that this was not possible in the face of the difficulties, tensions and contradictions of the text. In other words, they could not interpret the text without resorting to allegory as a critical method.

Conclusion

In our investigation of the development of hermeneutical thought we have now reached the end of antiquity. We established that the one fundamental problem occurring at every stage is the challenge of allowing authoritative traditional texts to remain authoritative, although they do not make immediate sense any more under the circumstances of ever-changing culture. We saw this at work in philosophical exegesis of Homer, as well as in the interpretation of Jewish and Christian Scriptures. Authors may have differed on the treatment of texts in such situations – Plato, probably the most radical among ancient interpreters, suggested that they be discarded altogether; the Stoics, Philo, Paul and the Church Fathers tended to interpret them allegorically. Within this field, we find differences in the degree to which allegory may be applied – Origen and the Alexandrians thought that it should be used everywhere, while the Antiochenes believed that it could be applied only to the Old Testament, and there only sparsely and only in the form of typological interpretation. However, it was beyond dispute that these texts had to be interpreted beyond their literal sense in order to maintain both their authority and their relevance.

Thus we can draw a first conclusion, which is that hermeneutics is engaged in the removal of obstacles to understanding. It analyses what hinders understanding, and then develops strategies to overcome these hindrances. Thus hermeneutics is closely related to the practicalities of interpreting texts, and this is one of its functions. But what would happen if the obstacles to understanding reside at a different level, not only at that of the interpretation of difficult texts, but at the level of the translation from thought to speech, from the inner word to the external word? The philosophy of Augustine of Hippo, which we are going to discuss in the next chapter, will highlight this problem. And so we need to turn to Augustine and the transition from ancient to medieval hermeneutical thinking.

Further reading

Graeco-Roman antiquity

Aristotle, 1928, *The Works of Aristotle translated into English*, translated by W. D. Ross, 12 vols, Oxford: Clarendon Press.

Arnold, Edward Vernon, 1911, *Roman Stoicism: Being Lectures on the History of the Stoic Philosophy with Special Reference to its Development within the Roman Empire*, Cambridge: Cambridge University Press.

Burkert, Walter, 1987, *Greek Religion: Archaic and Classical*, Oxford: Basil Blackwell.

Cohen, S. Marc, 2003, 'Aristotle's Metaphysics', in: *The Stanford Encyclopedia of Philosophy* (website, Winter 2003), edited by Edward N. Zalta. Available from http://plato.stanford.edu/archives/win2003/entries/aristotle-metaphysics.

Johnston, Sarah Iles (ed.), 2004, *Religions of the Ancient World: A Guide*, Cambridge, Mass.: Harvard University Press.

Joosen, J. C., and J. H. Waszink, 1950, 'Allegorese', in: Theodor Klauser (ed.), *Reallexikon für Antike und Christentum: Sachwörterbuch zur Auseinandersetzung des Christentums mit der antiken Welt*, vol. I, Stuttgart: Anton Hiersemann, cols 283–93.

Pépin, Jean and Karl Hoheisel, 1988, 'Hermeneutik', in: Ernst Dassmann (ed.), *Reallexikon für Antike und Christentum*, vol. XIV, Stuttgart: A. Hiersemann, cols 722–71.

Plato, 1953, *The Dialogues of Plato*, edited by Benjamin Jowett, 4th edn: Clarendon Press.

Schreckenberg, H., G. Mayer et al., 1966, 'Exegese', in: Theodor Klauser (ed.), *Reallexikon für Antike und Christentum: Sachwörterbuch zur Auseinandersetzung des Christentums mit der antiken Welt*, vol. VI, Stuttgart: A. Hiersemann, cols 1174–229.

Stenudd, Stefan, 'Theagenes', in: *Cosmos of the Ancients* (website, accessed 15 November 2006). Available from http://www.stenudd.com/myth/greek/theagenes.htm.

Zeller, Eduard and Oswald Joseph Reichel, 1870, *The Stoics, Epicureans and Sceptics*, London: Longmans.

Judaism

Charles, R. H. (ed.), 1913, *The Letter of Aristeas*, Oxford: The Clarendon Press. Available from http://www.ccel.org/c/charles/otpseudepig/aristeas.htm.

Charlesworth, James H. and P. Dykers, 1976, *The Pseudepigrapha and Modern Research*, *Septuagint and Cognate Studies Series*, vol. 7, Missoula, Mont: Scholars Press for the Society of Biblical Literature.

Charlesworth, James Hamilton, 1983, *The Old Testament Pseudepigrapha*, 2 vols, Garden City, NY: Doubleday.

Davies, Philip R., 2003, 'Biblical Interpretation in the Dead Sea Scrolls', in: Alan J. Hauser and Duane Frederick Watson (eds), *A History of Biblical Interpretation*, Grand Rapids, Mich.: William B. Eerdmans, pp. 144–66.

DeSilva, David Arthur, 2002, *Introducing the Apocrypha: Message, Context, and Significance*, Grand Rapids, Mich.: Baker Academic.

Dimant, Devorah, 1992, 'Pesharim, Qumran', in: David Noel Freedman, Gary A. Herion et al. (eds), *The Anchor Bible Dictionary*, vol. 5, New York: Doubleday, pp. 244–51.

García Martínez, Florentino, 1994, *The Dead Sea Scrolls Translated: The Qumran Texts in English*, translated by Wilfred G. E. Watson, Leiden, New York: E. J. Brill.

Joosen, J. C. and J. H. Waszink, 1950, 'Allegorese', in: Theodor Klauser (ed.),

Reallexikon für Antike und Christentum: Sachwörterbuch zur Auseinander-setzung des Christentums mit der antiken Welt, vol. I, Stuttgart: Anton Hiersemann, cols 283–93.

McNamara, Martin, 2003, 'Interpretation of Scripture in the Targumim', in: Alan J. Hauser and Duane Frederick Watson (eds), *A History of Biblical Interpretation*, Grand Rapids, Mich.: William B. Eerdmans, pp. 167–97.

Pépin, Jean and Karl Hoheisel, 1988, 'Hermeneutik', in: Ernst Dassmann (ed.), *Reallexikon für Antike und Christentum*, vol. XIV, Stuttgart: A. Hiersemann, cols 722–71.

Porton, Gary G., 1992, 'Midrash', in: David Noel Freedman, Gary A. Herion et al. (eds), *The Anchor Bible Dictionary*, vol. 4, New York: Doubleday, pp. 818–22.

Rapaport, Samuel, 1907, *Tales and Maxims from the Midrash*, London: Routledge. Available from http://www.sacred-texts.com/jud/tmm/index.htm.

Schreckenberg, H., G. Mayer et al., 1966, 'Exegese', in: Theodor Klauser (ed.), *Reallexikon für Antike und Christentum: Sachwörterbuch zur Auseinander-setzung des Christentums mit der antiken Welt*, vol. VI, Stuttgart: A. Hiersemann, cols 1174–229.

Smolar, Leivy, Moses Aberbach et al., 1983, *Studies in Targum Jonathan to the Prophets*, Library of Biblical Studies, New York: Ktav Pub. House: Baltimore Hebrew College.

Yonge, Charles Duke (ed.), 1854–90, *The Works of Philo Judaeus*, London: H. G. Bohn. Available from http://www.earlychristianwritings.com/yonge/.

Christianity

Daniélou, Jean, 1955, *Origen*, New York: Sheed and Ward.

Dunn, James D. G., 2006, *Unity and Diversity in the New Testament: An Inquiry into the Character of earliest Christianity*, 3rd edn, London: SCM Press.

Froehlich, Karlfried, 1984, *Biblical Interpretation in the Early Church, Sources of Early Christian Thought*, Philadelphia: Fortress Press.

Joosen, J. C. and J. H. Waszink, 1950, 'Allegorese', in: Theodor Klauser (ed.), *Reallexikon für Antike und Christentum: Sachwörterbuch zur Auseinander-setzung des Christentums mit der antiken Welt*, vol. I, Stuttgart: Anton Hiersemann, cols 283–93.

Osborn, Eric Francis, 1973, *Justin Martyr, Beiträge zur historischen Theologie* 47, Tübingen: J. C. B. Mohr (Paul Siebeck).

Pépin, Jean and Karl Hoheisel, 1988, 'Hermeneutik', in: Ernst Dassmann (ed.), *Reallexikon für Antike und Christentum*, vol. XIV, Stuttgart: A. Hiersemann, pp. 722–71.

Schreckenberg, H., G. Mayer et al., 1966, 'Exegese', in: Theodor Klauser (ed.), *Reallexikon für Antike und Christentum: Sachwörterbuch zur Auseinander-setzung des Christentums mit der antiken Welt*, vol. VI, Stuttgart: A. Hiersemann, pp. 1174–229.

Shotwell, Willis A., 1965, *The Biblical Exegesis of Justin Martyr*, London: SPCK.

Simonetti, Manlio, Anders Bergquist et al., 1994, *Biblical Interpretation in the*

Early Church: An Historical Introduction to Patristic Exegesis, Edinburgh: T & T Clark.

Young, Frances M., 2003, 'Alexandrian and Antiochene Exegensis', in: Alan J. Hauser and Duane Frederick Watson (eds), *A History of Biblical Interpretation*, Grand Rapids, Mich.: William B. Eerdmans, pp. 334–54.

Notes

1 Walter Burkert, 1987, *Greek Religion: Archaic and Classical*, Oxford: Basil Blackwell, pp. 120–5.

2 Burkert, *Greek Religion: Archaic and Classical*, pp. 305–11; Jon Mikalson, 2004, 'Greece', in: Sarah Iles Johnston (ed.), *Religions of the Ancient World: A Guide*, Cambridge, Mass.: Harvard University Press, pp. 217–18.

3 Plato, *The Republic*, II. 378d, in: Plato, 1953, *The Dialogues of Plato*, edited by Benjamin Jowett, 4th edn: Clarendon Press, vol. II, p. 223.

4 In the Greek, the first part of the word comes from *allos*, different, and *agoreuein*, to express. Thus the text means something different than it says.

5 Plato, *Ion*, 530c, in: Plato, *The Dialogues of Plato*, vol. I, p. 103.

6 Aristotle, *On Interpretation (Peri Hermeneia)*, I, in: Aristotle, 1928, *The Works of Aristotle translated into English*, translated by W. D. Ross, 12 vols, Oxford: Clarendon Press, vol. 1, 16a (translation slightly updated). After this, Aristotle remarks that he has already dealt with this issue in his treatise on the soul. *On the Soul* (*Peri Psyches*), however, does not contain anything on this topic. Classicists have been speculating a great deal on this issue, and the most likely solution is that Aristotle elaborated on the relation between thought and speech in another work on the subject. The distinction of thought (word in the soul) and speech (external word) is presupposed in the *Posterior Analytics*, I.X.

7 Plato, *Sophist*, 263e, in: Plato, *The Dialogues of Plato*, vol. III, p. 421 (translation slightly updated).

8 Edward Vernon Arnold, 1911, *Roman Stoicism: Being Lectures on the History of the Stoic Philosophy with Special Reference to its Development within the Roman Empire*, Cambridge: Cambridge University Press, p. 146; Jean Pépin and Karl Hoheisel, 1988, 'Hermeneutik', in: Ernst Dassmann (ed.), *Reallexikon für Antike und Christentum*, vol. XIV, Stuttgart: A. Hiersemann, cols 728–9; Eduard Zeller and Oswald Joseph Reichel, 1870, *The Stoics, Epicureans and Sceptics*, London: Longmans, p. 72 n 1. Zeller points out that this is essentially the same as Aristotle's distinction of the word or discourse in the soul (*logos en ten psychen*) and the external word or discourse (*ho exo logos*) in the *Posterior Analytics*, I.X.

9 J. C. Joosen and J. H. Waszink, 1950, 'Allegorese', in: Theodor Klauser (ed.), *Reallexikon für Antike und Christentum: Sachwörterbuch zur Auseinandersetzung des Christentums mit der antiken Welt*, vol. I, Stuttgart: Anton Hiersemann, cols 283–4.

10 Stefan Stenudd, 'Theagenes', in: *Cosmos of the Ancients*. Available from http://www.stenudd.com/myth/greek/theagenes.htm (accessed 15 November 2006).

11 Joosen and Waszink, 'Allegorese', p. 284.

12 Joosen and Waszink, 'Allegorese', p. 285.

34

13   Joosen and Waszink, 'Allegorese', p. 285.

14   H. Schreckenberg, 1966, 'Exegese I (heidnisch, Griechen u. Römer)', in: Theodor Klauser (ed.), *Reallexikon für Antike und Christentum*, vol. VI, col. 1175.

15   Schreckenberg, 'Exegese I', col. 1178–80.

16   James D. G. Dunn, 2006, *Unity and Diversity in the New Testament: An Inquiry into the Character of Earliest Christianity*, 3rd edn, London: SCM Press, pp. 82–7.

17   David Arthur DeSilva, 2002, *Introducing the Apocrypha: Message, Context, and Significance*, Grand Rapids, Mich.: Baker Academic, p. 153.

18   DeSilva, *Introducing the Apocrypha: Message, Context, and Significance*, pp. 132–3.

19   Philip R. Davies, 2003, 'Biblical Interpretation in the Dead Sea Scrolls', in: Alan J. Hauser and Duane Frederick Watson (eds), *A History of Biblical Interpretation*, Grand Rapids, Mich.: William B. Eerdmans, p. 155.

20   Martin McNamara, 2003, 'Interpretation of Scripture in the Targumim', in: Alan J. Hauser and Duane Frederick Watson (eds), *A History of Biblical Interpretation*, p. 173.

21   Leivy Smolar, Moses Aberbach et al., 1983, *Studies in Targum Jonathan to the Prophets*, *Library of Biblical Studies*, New York: Ktav Pub. House: Baltimore Hebrew College, p. 61 (quoted in McNamara, 'Interpretation of Scripture in the Targumim', p. 173).

22   Dunn, *Unity and Diversity in the New Testament*, p. 86.

23   Gary G. Porton, 1992, 'Midrash', in: David Noel Freedman, Gary A. Herion et al. (eds), *The Anchor Bible Dictionary*, vol. 4, New York: Doubleday, pp. 181–2.

24   Porton, 'Midrash', p. 820.

25   Gen. Rabba 1, Samuel Rapaport, 1907, *Tales and Maxims from the Midrash*, London: Routledge, pp. 57–8. Available from http://www.sacred-texts.com/jud/tmm/index.htm.

26   Gen. Rabba 3, Rapaport, *Tales and Maxims from the Midrash*, p. 59.

27   Gen. Rabba 14, Rapaport, *Tales and Maxims from the Midrash*, p. 66.

28   G. Mayer, 1966, 'Exegese II (Judentum)', in: Theodor Klauser (ed.), *Reallexikon für Antike und Christentum*, vol. VI, col. 1202–3.

29   Mayer, 'Exegese II', col. 1196–8. In Hebrew, the first word of the book of Genesis is $b^e r\bar{e}'\check{s}\hat{\imath}t$ (in the beginning), while the Ten Commandments begin with $'\bar{a}n\bar{o}k\hat{\imath}$ (I am).

30   Devorah Dimant, 1992, 'Pesharim, Qumran', in: David Noel Freedman, Gary A. Herion et al. (eds), *The Anchor Bible Dictionary*, vol. 5, New York: Doubleday, pp. 248–9.

31   1 QpHab 6.8–10, in: Florentino García Martínez, 1994, *The Dead Sea Scrolls Translated: The Qumran Texts in English*, translated by Wilfred G. E. Watson, Leiden; New York: E. J. Brill, p. 199.

32   All that remains of Aristobulus' writings are a few fragments quoted by Eusebius of Caesarea (died AD 340). For information on his life, see James H. Charlesworth and P. Dykers, 1976, *The Pseudepigrapha and Modern Research*, *Septuagint and Cognate Studies Series*, vol. 7, Missoula, Mont.: Scholars Press for the Society of Biblical Literature, pp. 81–2.

33 *The Letter of Aristeas*, §§142–8, in: James Hamilton Charlesworth, 1983, *The Old Testament Pseudepigrapha*, 2 vols, Garden City, NY: Doubleday, vol. 2, p. 22. An older translation can be found in: R. H. Charles (ed.), 1913, *The Letter of Aristeas*, Oxford: The Clarendon Press. Available from http://www.ccel.org/c/charles/otpseudepig/aristeas.htm.

34 Philo of Alexandria, *On the Confusion of Tongues*, XXXVIII, 190, in: Charles Duke Yonge (ed.), 1854–90, *The Works of Philo Judaeus*, London: H. G. Bohn. Available from http://www.earlychristianwritings.com/yonge/.

35 J. Grondin, 1994, *Introduction to Philosophical Hermeneutics*, Yale University Press, pp. 34–5.

36 Mayer, 'Exegese II', col. 1206.

37 Joosen and Waszink, 'Allegorese', col. 287.

38 Philo of Alexandria, *Allegorical Interpretation of Genesis* II.III, XIX, 63–XX, 67, in: Yonge (ed.), *The Works of Philo Judaeus*.

39 For example, Shotwell points out that Justin Martyr is directly indebted to the authors of the New Testament in both understanding of Scripture and in methodology (Willis A. Shotwell, 1965, *The Biblical Exegesis of Justin Martyr*, London: SPCK, pp. 63–4).

40 Shotwell, *The Biblical Exegesis of Justin Martyr*, p. 23.

41 Shotwell, *The Biblical Exegesis of Justin Martyr*, p. 24.

42 Eric Francis Osborn, 1973, *Justin Martyr, Beiträge zur historischen Theologie*, vol. 47, Tübingen: J. C. B. Mohr (Paul Siebeck), pp. 125–34.

43 Shotwell, *The Biblical Exegesis of Justin Martyr*, p. 25.

44 Shotwell, *The Biblical Exegesis of Justin Martyr*, p. 23.

45 Jean Daniélou, 1955, *Origen*, New York: Sheed and Ward, p. 133.

46 Daniélou, *Origen*, pp. 133–5.

47 Daniélou, *Origen*, p. 135.

48 Daniélou, *Origen*, p. 133.

49 Daniélou, *Origen*, p. 137.

50 Daniélou, *Origen*, p. 170.

51 W. E. Gerber, 1966, 'Exegese III (NT u. Alte Kirche)', in: Theodor Klauser (ed.), *Reallexikon für Antike und Christentum*, vol. VI, Stuttgart: A. Hiersemann, col. 1218.

52 The fact that Origen is still assuming a literal sense and a historical reference of the text has led some scholars to distinguish Origen's 'typological' interpretation from a supposedly pagan 'allegorical' interpretation (Daniélou, *Origen*, pp. 139–99). This is not only a highly artificial distinction, but also not fully accurate. Origen assumes a literal or historical sense of the Scriptures, but he is perfectly happy to discard it if it contradicts our understanding of God, or does not make sense in any other way. Thus not every passage has a literal meaning, whereas every passage does have a spiritual meaning. Thus this distinction between Christian 'typological' and pagan 'allegorical' interpretation has been discarded. Frances M. Young, 2003, 'Alexandrian and Antiochene Exegesis', in: Alan J. Hauser and Duane Frederick Watson (eds), *A History of Biblical Interpretation*, pp. 335–8.

53 Origen, *On First Principles*, IV, 2, 6 (quoted from: Karlfried Froehlich, 1984, *Biblical Interpretation in the Early Church, Sources of Early Christian Thought*, Philadelphia: Fortress Press, p. 59).

54   H. Schreckenberg, G. Mayer et al., 1966, 'Exegese', in: Theodor Klauser (ed.), *Reallexikon für Antike und Christentum*, vol. VI, col. 1218.

55   Origen, *On First Principles*, IV, 2, 6 (Froehlich, *Biblical Interpretation in the Early Church*, p. 59).

56   Origen, *On First Principles*, IV, 3, 8 (Froehlich, *Biblical Interpretation in the Early Church*, p. 69).

57   Origen, *On First Principles*, IV, 3, 10 (Froehlich, *Biblical Interpretation in the Early Church*, pp. 70–1).

58   Origen, *On First Principles*, IV, 2, 9 (Froehlich, *Biblical Interpretation in the Early Church*, pp. 62–3).

59   Manlio Simonetti, Anders Bergquist et al., 1994, *Biblical Interpretation in the Early Church: An Historical Introduction to Patristic Exegesis*, Edinburgh: T&T Clark, pp. 59–69.

60   Joosen and Waszink, 'Allegorese', cols 290–1.

61   Gerber, 'Exegese III', col. 1220ff.

2

Augustine of Hippo

Introduction and biography

Augustine of Hippo (Aurelius Augustinus, 354–430) belongs to the period that marked the transition from antiquity to the Middle Ages. The theologians and philosophers of this age both preserved elements of ancient theological and philosophical thought and laid the foundation for later Latin theology. Among this group of writers, Augustine is arguably the most influential. We can see in him the father of Western hermeneutical thinking. All Western hermeneutical thinking is, knowingly or not, influenced by one aspect or another of his thinking. During the Middle Ages, his advice on literal and allegorical interpretation was generally heeded. During the Reformation the Lutherans took up his notion of the incarnation of the thought in the spoken word, while the Calvinists emphasized his theory of signs. Augustinian thinking influenced existentialism, semiotics and even approaches to the Bible making use of literary theory. In short, whether we like it or not, he is always with us. It is for these reasons that Gerhard Ebeling called Augustine's *On Christian Doctrine* the most influential work of hermeneutics.[1]

Augustine contributed to virtually every field of theology. A brief indication of his great impact on Western theological thinking would include his formulation of the doctrine of the Trinity. Augustine introduced the concept of the double procession of the Holy Spirit from the Father and the Son, which has influenced Western theological thinking up to the present day and which continues to be a major divisive issue between the Western and the Eastern Church. Augustine's doctrine of salvation and election became highly influential, though often controversial, in Western Christianity. The Reformers would return to his thought on the issue. Theological reflection on the nature of the Church in its Western form also goes back to Augustine.

Augustine tells the story of his life in his intellectual and spiritual memoirs, the *Confessions* (*Confessiones*). He was born at Thagaste in Northern Africa in 354 and received a classical education at Thagaste, nearby Mauros, and later in Carthage. He worked as a teacher of rhetoric in Carthage, Rome and Milan. During this time, he was influenced by

Manichaeism, Stoicism and neo-Platonism. This intellectual background is important to keep in mind when we discuss his hermeneutical thinking, as Augustine draws on ideas from his intellectual environment, and engages with them critically.

At the age of 32 Augustine converted to Christianity. He lived in an ascetic lay community, where he was able to pursue theological studies for some years, before he was ordained priest in Hippo, also in Northern Africa, and subsequently became bishop of the city.

Augustine was a prolific writer and never afraid of a controversy. In the years between his conversion and ordination, he published a number of philosophical works. During his ministry as bishop he concentrated on theological works, often apologetic or controversial.

In Augustine's lifetime, the Roman Empire went through a deep crisis, which eventually led to the disintegration of its western half. In 430, during the dying days of the western empire, the Vandals besieged Hippo and Augustine died during the siege.

Sources

Augustine's thoughts on hermeneutical themes are scattered throughout his whole work. We find important insights in some of his early writings, in *On Dialectic* (*De dialectica*)[2] and in the beautiful dialogue between Augustine and his son Adeodatus in *The Teacher* (*De magistro*).[3] In these works, Augustine develops a theory of signs, which we will discuss below. Augustine develops the theory of signs further in the second book of his work *On Christian Doctrine* (*De doctrina Christiana* 396–426),[4] in which he also proposes a methodology for the proper treatment of unknown and ambiguous signs. Here, Augustine engages in a deeply hermeneutical activity – the removal of obstacles to understanding. These three works were all written within ten years of Augustine's conversion to Christianity, in the period between 387 and 396.

While working on his book *On the Trinity* (*De Trinitate*),[5] which occupied Augustine from 404 to 420, he also wrote a series of *Lectures or Tractates on the Gospel according to St. John* (*Tractatus in Iohannis Evangelium*)[6] between 407 and 417. These studies led him to a renewed recognition of the importance of the description of the incarnation in John's Gospel: 'And the Word became flesh' (John 1.14). Augustine developed his thought on the basis of this theological concept. He saw that it could be applied to language in general, and, in Book 15 of *On the Trinity*, concluded that the thought is incarnate in the spoken word.

Words and signs

The best known of Augustine's contributions to hermeneutical thinking is his theory of signs. Some of the issues that Augustine discusses in this context may appear as commonplace to the modern reader, for example that a sign always points to a thing beyond itself. But it was Augustine who first developed these ideas, which only after his death became common currency in European thinking. Therefore, it is only with hindsight that we perceive them as commonplace.

Augustine begins with his assumption that we speak in order to teach (*The Teacher* 1.1–2). This means that we speak in order to convey information. Even a command, such as 'You shall not kill!' is, for Augustine, a statement of fact, meaning 'It is wrong to kill'. This basic attitude towards language as exclusively propositional (making statements) is worth keeping in mind – we will discuss it later, when we come to Martin Heidegger's existentialist understanding of language and H.-G. Gadamer's view of language as dialogue (see p. 121 on Heidegger and pp. 139–40 on Gadamer).

We convey information by using signs. Signs always point away from themselves at what they signify. Augustine defines the sign as 'a thing which of itself makes some other thing come to mind, besides the impression that it presents to the senses'.[7] Therefore, a sign always points away from itself, and signifies something else. Augustine continues: 'So when we see a footprint, we think that the animal whose footprint it is has passed by; when we see smoke we realize that there is fire beneath it; when we hear the voice of an animate being we note its feeling; and when the trumpet sounds soldiers know they must advance or retreat or do whatever else the state of the battle demands.'[8]

Augustine distinguishes two types of signs, natural and conventional signs.[9] Natural signs are those which occur in nature, and which do not rely on any agreed definition; in this way smoke points to fire. Conventional signs are signs that signify a meaning which is not intrinsic to them (unlike fire to smoke), but which is agreed by convention. The word 'fire' signifies a 'natural agency or active principle operative in combustion' by convention in English, and when I hear someone use the word 'fire', then I can fairly assume that the sign refers to the thing that is commonly associated with it. Other cultures may use completely different words for it, such as *ignis* (Latin) or *brann* (Norwegian). People use these signs 'in order to show, to the best of their ability, the emotions of their mind, or anything that they have felt or learnt'.[10] For the sake of his argument, Augustine restricts himself to the discussion of verbal signs, which can be spoken or written.

Signs point away from themselves to something else that we have in mind, an emotion or something we have learnt. One might have assumed that words refer to something outside the mind, to a thing or a state of affairs or to a fact, but this is not Augustine's view. In order to understand this, we must look at Augustine's thoughts on this subject. Augustine distinguishes between the word (*verbum*, the utterance, the sound of the syllables we speak), the thought of the speaker (*dicibile*, what we have in mind when we speak; or the knowledge of the thing, *cognitio rei*), the responding thought of the listener (*dictio*, the association caused in the mind when we hear the word; or knowledge of the sign, *cognitio nominis*) and the thing (*res*).[11]

What 'thing' means is straightforward; it is the object about which we speak outside our mind, for example, a horse. 'Word' is the utterance 'horse', the sound made by the spoken word or the shape the letters take on paper. The *dicibile* (literally: what can be said) is our knowledge of the horse, which we express when we use the word 'horse'. In other words, it is what we are trying to say. The *dictio* (literally: what is said) is the image of the horse in our mind, which is caused when we hear 'horse', or, as it were, what we hear when we listen. So we have two groups of terms, those outside the mind, thing and word, and those within the mind, knowledge of the thing (*dictio*) and knowledge of the word (*dicibile*).

In simpler terms, language does not refer to things, but to our mental images of things. So when I tell a funny story that happened to me with a horse, then this story, this word, to use Augustine's terminology, does not refer to the event itself, but to my mental image of the event. So the hearer does not gain knowledge about the event itself, but of my mental image of it. He or she will form a mental image, which is recovered from my narrative.

We will see later, in the discussion of Heidegger's existentialist hermeneutics, that the mental image is not a mere image of the event, but it is my interpretation of the event, which adds another dimension to the process of understanding (see p. 121). This expansion of Augustine's theory is, however, beyond the scope of his own thought.

Memory

What we have in mind about things, horses or anything else, comes from our memory. Augustine returned to his theory of memory over and over again during his literary life. There is a section on memory (*memoria*) in *The Teacher*, and nearly all of Book 10 of his *Confessions* is dedicated to this subject.[12] This concept causes some difficulties for Augustine, as he tries to import neo-Platonic concepts into Christianity without their pagan connotations. In Platonic thought, we never learn anything new, but only remember. For Plato and his followers, the teacher is only the midwife of remembrance. We know everything, but this knowledge is not conscious. So we need a teacher who helps us to give birth to the knowledge that is hidden in our memory.[13] But how does knowledge get into our memory? Plato introduces the concept of reincarnation so that all knowledge can reside in the memory. The soul has seen all truth before our birth. When it enters a human body, it forgets that it knows, but does not forget the knowledge itself. Thus, with some help, knowledge can be recovered.

Augustine cannot allow the concept of reincarnation into his thinking, as this would contradict core Christian beliefs. Instead, Augustine defines memory as the place where all our perceptions and emotions which we have had in our life are stored.[14] This leaves him with the problem of truths of reason, mathematical truths.[15] Augustine assumes that all this knowledge is already in the memory, and when we learn truths of reason, we gather them up from the various places in the memory where they are stored and bring them into the present.[16] As pre-natal memory is impossible, Augustine assumes in *The Teacher* that Christ, who dwells in the inner person, teaches us all these things.[17] In the *Confessions*, he explicitly avoids the question: 'From where and how did these things enter my memory? I don't know. Because when I first learned them, I did not believe another mind, but recognized them in my own.'[18] Thus, in establishing the origin of knowledge, Augustine leaves an unsatisfactory gap at a key stage of his argument.

However, the origin of knowledge for Augustine is the memory. If we want to speak of a truth that we have in mind, such as a past event or a philosophical truth, we have this in our memory. This content of the intended utterance is the *dicibile*, which we then express in words. When listeners hear our words, images will be brought into their mind from their memory. This thought, which is provoked by our words, is the *dictio*.

Using signs

In order to convey the thought, the *dicibile*, we use signs. There is a multitude of possible signs we can use, such as words, traffic signs, trumpet signals, gestures, etc. However, Augustine restricts the discussion to verbal signs, to words, written or spoken. We use words, combining them to form statements, such as sentences or larger units. Within these, the individual signs complement each other, qualify each other and thus convey the meaning.

It is the interpreter's task to decipher the signs, attribute their proper meaning, understand how they relate to each other and qualify each other, and thus gain knowledge of the meaning of the text. In *On Christian Doctrine*, Augustine seems to imply that, in principle, reading is straight-forward and leads to a proper understanding of the text. If one reads the biblical books, with which Augustine is mainly concerned in this context, then one will understand a number of issues which are clearly stated in them, such as ethical precepts or articles of belief. And the 'greater a person's intellectual capacity, the more of these one finds. In clearly expressed passages of scripture one can find all the things that concern faith and moral life.'[19] Therefore, all that is necessary can be learned from the clear passages of Scripture.

There are, however, obscure passages within the Bible, but the problems they pose can be overcome by following the rules that Augustine develops in Books 2 and 3 of *On Christian Doctrine*. For obvious reasons, Augustine is mainly concerned with the interpretation of Christian Scripture, but his rules can also be applied to other texts. In the beginning of Book 3, Augustine gives a brief outline of his suggestions for successful interpretation.

> The student who fears God earnestly seeks his will in the holy scriptures. Holiness makes him gentle, so that he does not revel in controversy; a knowledge of languages protects him from uncertainty over unfamiliar words or phrases, and a knowledge of certain essential things protects him from the ignorance of the significance and detail of what is used by way of imagery. Thus equipped, and with the assistance of reliable texts derived from the manuscripts with careful attention to the need for emendation, he should now approach the task of analysing and resolving the ambiguities in the scriptures.[20]

Thus we need a good knowledge of the original language, of the linguistic conventions of the time, and we also need reliable manuscripts – Augustine suggests textual criticism here. Would this mean that, to the modern interpreter, he would also recommend the other methods of historical criticism?

For Augustine the task of critical interpretation is to eliminate obstacles to understanding. Understanding of the text is hindered by signs being either unknown or ambiguous. The problem of unknown signs is best overcome by learning the language better.[21] Where knowledge of the language does not illuminate meaning, it may be that signs are used metaphorically. In order to understand metaphors, not only knowledge of signs is important, but also knowledge of the things to which they refer; then the interpreter can see the analogy between the thing signified by the sign and the thing to which it is attributed. For example, when Jesus tells his disciples to be as wise as serpents, we need to know about serpents and then decide which attributes of serpents are to be attributed to the disciples.[22]

The ambiguity of passages could be the result of ambiguous punctuation, as manuscripts did not contain punctuation marks in antiquity. Readers had to find out where to put them themselves. Augustine gives examples of texts in which a comma can be set in different places to change the meaning significantly.[23] In such cases, readers should first try to understand the sentence in the light of the rule of faith, that is, in the light of the received Christian doctrine. Then they should read the passage in the light of clearer passages, and failing this, they should refer to the authority of the Church.[24] If there are still a number of possible interpretations, readers may decide for themselves.

A further means of interpretation is the interpretation of allegory, which we have already encountered above, in the discussion of the Alexandrian School and Origen (see pp. 27–30). Augustine does not explain how we derive the spiritual meaning from the text; this seems to be generally known. However, Augustine gives rules for readers so that they may establish properly if a passage is to be understood literally or figuratively. The signal that a text is to be read allegorically is that 'anything in the divine discourse that cannot be taken either to good morals or to the true faith should be taken as figurative'.[25] Thus, Augustine has restricted the use of allegory significantly, by limiting it to those texts that cannot be understood properly if interpreted literally.

Augustine makes a number of assumptions about the interpretation of Scripture. When interpreting the Bible it is important to note that the Bible consists of individual books, which are made up of individual signs. But the Bible as a whole is a sign in itself, and this sign points to God. Therefore, interpretation of the Bible can and must be holistic; we can use clear passages in one book to elucidate obscure ones in another. The task of interpretation is given; it is the quest for God and God's will, which can be known through diligent study of the Scriptures. In this context, it is also important to approach the reading with the right attitude, which is faith, love and hope.[26] The subject of the text, which is God, must make himself known to the reader, otherwise all the effort will be in vain.

As we have seen, there are two aspects to Augustine's hermeneutical theory so far: first, an analysis of the principles of understanding, based on a theory of signs, and second, a rule-based methodology for the interpretation of texts. These two elements belong together, understanding of how understanding works and the practice of interpretation.

The inner word in the spoken word

Augustine developed the theory of signs within ten years of his conversion. It is fair to assume that his thought developed further during his lifetime, and in particular during his ecclesiastical ministry. Often Augustine would work on several books at a time. For example, between 404 and 420 Augustine wrote *On the Trinity*, a major dogmatic treatise on this key tenet of Christian belief. During part of this time, Augustine also engaged deeply with John's Gospel, and wrote a series of lectures or treatises on the subject, the *Lectures or Tractates on the Gospel according to St. John* (*Tractatus in Iohannis Evangelium*) from 407 to 417. The leitmotif going through this work is 'the word became flesh', and it would be surprising if his studies had not influenced his theological thinking. And indeed, when Augustine discusses the incarnation in Book 15 of *On the Trinity*, he introduces a modified version of *logos* Christology, based on the incarnation of the word of God.

In this section, Augustine explores how we can speak of Jesus Christ as the word of God without seeing him subordinate to the God the Father. In his argument, he discusses a new development in his hermeneutical thinking, before he applies the insights gained to the Trinity and the incarnation. Underlying Augustine's thought is the Stoic distinction between the inner word (*logos endiathetos/verbum interius*) and the spoken word (*logos prophorikos/verbum externum*) (see pp. 10–11). Before we speak, we have the word in our mind (heart); it is 'the word which we speak in the heart'.[27] This is the *verbum interius*, the thought before it reaches any lingual form, before it is articulated.

> It is possible therefore to understand the meaning of a word, not before it is uttered aloud, but even before the images of its uttered sounds are rehearsed in thought; for there is a 'word' which belongs to no tongue. . . . When we speak the truth, that is, say what we know, there must be born out of the knowledge held in our memory a word which corresponds in all respects to the knowledge of which it is born. The thought which has received form from the object of our knowledge is the word

spoken in the heart – a word that is neither Greek nor Latin nor any other tongue. Only when we need to convey it to the knowledge of those to whom we speak, do we employ some token by which to signify it.[28]

The thought, the inner word, which emerges from the memory, is pre-lingual, as it were, it has no lingual form yet. When we want to utter the thought, the inner word, then we need to translate it into language. When we do so, the inner word is embodied, incarnate in the spoken word.

> We may compare the manner in which our own word is made a bodily utterance, as it were, through assuming that utterance as a means of displaying itself to human senses, with that in which the Word of God was made flesh, through assuming that flesh as a means of displaying itself to human senses. Even as our word is made utterance yet not changed into utterance, so the word of God was made flesh, but most assuredly not changed into flesh.[29]

The significance of this thought can hardly by overestimated; just as the eternal word of God became incarnate in Jesus Christ, so our thought becomes incarnate in our spoken word. The inner word, our thought which we try to communicate, is contained in our utterance, yet not exhausted in it. The utterance is not the same as the thought, but it is the thought 'in the manner in which it may be seen or heard thought the medium of the body'.[30] The task of understanding is therefore to 'arrive at the human word which is . . . a word neither producing itself in sound nor object of thought in a likeness of sound, . . . but the word that precedes all the tokens by which it is signified'.[31]

Therefore, there is a complex movement from thought to thought via the spoken word. There is something on our mind that we want to express. This thought, the inner word (or, to use the terminology of *On Dialectic*, the *dicibile*) is then translated into the spoken word. Listeners hear the spoken word, and need to arrive at the inner word, the thought that is contained within it.

It is worth noting that in this train of thought, the spoken word does not point at a thought that is beyond it, but the thought is contained in the utterance, it is incarnate in the spoken word. Therefore, language does not point at a meaning which is beyond it, but it contains meaning. I do not believe that Augustine was fully aware of the implications of this thought, and it was not until the Reformation that it was fully understood. It was Luther who drew out the consequences of Augustine's insights. We will return to this at various points of our investigation (see pp. 70–4).

There are certainly differences between God's inner word and its incarnation on the one hand and human thought and language on the other. Unlike humans, God is perfectly self-conscious; God has God's own memory continuously before God's mind. Therefore, God's inner word contains God's whole mind. And when God utters the word, in the incarnation, then this is a perfect expression of the inner word.[32] Humans, however, do not have their whole memory consciously in their mind, but only parts of it. We are temporal beings, and thus the images in our memory can pass through our mind only successively. Therefore, even our thought can only contain part of our memory, and when we express this in spoken words, we cannot fully express what we mean – our language is imperfect, our spoken word (*verbum externum/logos prophorikos*) does not perfectly contain the thought (*verbum interius/logos endiathetos*).[33] With this, Augustine has left the confines of the Stoics' naïve optimism about language and identified not only an uncertainty in the realm of understanding, but a fundamental obstacle.

Because of this imperfection, namely that human thought cannot be adequately expressed in language, Augustine understands that we cannot utter our thought straight away. The word needs developing. So when thought emerges from our memory, we try to capture it in language, we begin an inner dialogue, which is our conscious thought, in order to bring this thought into words. This is a process of mind, in which 'darting hither and thither with a kind of passage, as we turn our thought from one object to another in the course of discovery and presentation'.[34] Augustine seems to have in mind the passage from Plato's dialogue *The Sophist*, in which thought is called the 'silent inner conversation of the soul with itself'.[35] Because of the insufficiency of our ability to express a thought adequately, we engage in the inner dialogue of the soul with itself, we ruminate and think the thought through over and over again, until we feel that we can utter it. In this, Augustine differs from Plato, because the latter did not assume the loss in the transition from the inner to the external word. Consequently, for Augustine the inner conversation has the additional dimension that it serves to translate the thought into language, and then to refine the linguistic expression of the thought.

And even then Augustine assumes that misunderstanding is the normal result and that we can never fully comprehend each other. The listener or reader will never arrive at the speaker's or author's thought, but can only approximate it. Therefore, hermeneutics is a never-ending task.

Conclusion

We have identified three strands in Augustine's hermeneutical thinking: the theory of signs, the rule-based methodology for faithful interpretation and the incarnation of the inner word in the spoken word. Each of these three strands will be influential in the history of hermeneutical thinking, although different thinkers will emphasize different strands. Lutherans and existentialists will emphasize the incarnation of the thought in the spoken word, while Calvinists and interpreters following Karl Barth will stress the theory of signs. Others again will stress the rule-based methodology of interpretation. We will encounter all these schools in the course of this investigation, and it may be worthwhile to keep in mind that Augustinian thinking is behind their ideas.

When the German philosopher Hans-Georg Gadamer was asked what the universal aspect of hermeneutics consisted in, he answered briefly 'In the *verbum interius*.' Augustine was probably not aware of the enormous philosophical problem he raised with his teaching of the inner and the spoken word. But he was aware of the problem of the universality of misunderstanding – and he saw hope. In the chapter on the beatific vision in *The City of God*, Augustine tells us that when we finally behold God in his glory, then our thoughts shall be fully transparent to each other.[36] In the heavenly Jerusalem we may not have a hermeneutical problem any more, but as long as we live in this transitory world, we will have to live with misunderstanding and with continuing hermeneutical investigation. Augustine shows us that hermeneutics is an expression of human temporality and thus mortality.

Further reading

Augustine, 1953, *Earlier Writings*, translated by J. H. S Burleigh, Philadelphia: Westminster Press.

Augustine, 1955, *Later Works*, translated by John Burnaby, Philadelphia: Westminster Press.

Augustine, 1956, *Homilies on the Gospel of John; Homilies on the first Epistle of John; Soliloquies, A Select Library of the Nicene and post-Nicene Fathers of the Christian Church*. First Series, vol. 7, Grand Rapids: Eerdmans.

Augustine, 1975, *De dialectica*, translated by Belford Darrell Jackson, *Synthese historical library*, vol. 16, Dordrecht, Holland; Boston: D. Reidel Pub. Co.

Augustine, 1995, *De doctrina Christiana*, translated by R. P. H. Green, *Oxford Early Christian Texts*, Oxford and New York: Clarendon Press.

Augustine, 1997, *On Christian Teaching*, Oxford and New York: Oxford University Press.

Augustine, 2002, *On the Trinity: Books 8–15*, translated by Stephen McKenna, edited by Gareth B. Matthews, *Cambridge Texts in the History of Philosophy*, Cambridge: Cambridge University Press.

Augustine, 2003, *Concerning the City of God against the Pagans*, translated by H. R. Bettenson, Harmondsworth: Penguin.

Brown, Peter, 2000, *Augustine of Hippo: A Biography*, London: Faber.

Cary, Phillip, 2000, *Augustine's Invention of the Inner Self: The Legacy of a Christian Platonist*, Oxford and New York: Oxford University Press.

Chadwick, Henry, 1986, *Augustine*, *Past Masters*, Oxford and New York: Oxford University Press.

Fitzgerald, Allan and John C. Cavadini, 1999, *Augustine through the Ages: An Encyclopedia*, Grand Rapids, Mich.: W.B. Eerdmans.

Rist, John M., 1994, *Augustine: Ancient Thought Baptized*, Cambridge and New York: Cambridge University Press.

TeSelle, Eugene, 1970, *Augustine the Theologian*, London: Burns & Oates.

Notes

1   Gerhard Ebeling, 1959, 'Hermeneutik', in: Kurt Galling (ed.), *Die Religion in Geschichte und Gegenwart*, vol. 3, 3rd edn, Tübingen: J. C. B. Mohr (Paul Siebeck), col. 249.

2   *De dialectica* is available on the Internet under http://ccat.sas.upenn.edu/jod/texts/dialectica.html (the Latin text and a good modern English translation). There is only one modern edition: Augustine, 1975, *De dialectica*, translated by Belford Darrell Jackson, *Synthese Historical Library*, vol. 16, Dordrecht, Holland; Boston: D. Reidel Pub. Co.

3   There is no English version of *The Teacher* available on the Internet. The Latin text can be downloaded from http://www.stormloader.com/cactus/all.htm. A printed version is available in Augustine, 1953, *Earlier Writings*, translated by J. H. S Burleigh, Philadelphia: Westminster Press.

4   A somewhat dated English translation is available at http://ccat.sas.upenn.edu/jod/augustine/ddc.html. A good English translation can be found in Augustine, 1997, *On Christian Teaching*, Oxford and New York: Oxford University Press. There is also a good bilingual edition (containing the same English text): Augustine, 1995, *De doctrina Christiana*, translated by R. P. H. Green, *Oxford Early Christian texts*, Oxford and New York: Clarendon Press.

5   An English version is available online at http://www.ccel.org/fathers2/NPNF1-03/. The Latin can be found under http://phil.flet.mita.keio.ac.jp/person/nakagawa/texts.html. A printed version, containing all the relevant sections, is Augustine, 2002, *On the Trinity: Books 8–15*, translated by Stephen McKenna, edited by Gareth B. Matthews, *Cambridge Texts in the History of Philosophy*, Cambridge: Cambridge University Press. The same section of the text is also available in Augustine, 1955, *Later Works*, translated by John Burnaby, Philadelphia: Westminster Press.

6   http://www.ccel.org/fathers2/NPNF1-07/. The only printed version of which I am aware contains the same text: Augustine, 1956, *Homilies on the Gospel of John; Homilies on the first Epistle of John; Soliloquies, A Select Library of the Nicene and post-Nicene Fathers of the Christian Church. First Series*, vol. 7, Grand Rapids: Eerdmans.

7   *On Christian Doctrine* 2.1.1.

8   *On Christian Doctrine* 2.1.1.

9   *On Christian Doctrine* 2.1.2.

10   *On Christian Doctrine* 2.2.3.

11   *The Teacher* 9.27, *On Dialectic* 5.

12   Martin Heidegger regarded this book as so important that he dedicated a whole lecture course to its interpretation. Martin Heidegger, 1995, 'Augustinus und der Neuplatonismus', *Phänomenologie des religiösen Lebens*, *Gesamtausgabe*, vol. 60, Frankfurt am Main: Klostermann.

13   Plato develops this in his dialogue *Meno*.

14   *The Teacher* 12.39, *Confessions* 10.8.

15   *Confessions* 10, 10.17–12.19.

16   *Confessions* 10.11.18.

17   *The Teacher* 11.38.

18   *Confessions* 10.10.17.

19   *On Christian Doctrine* 2.9.14, quoted from: Augustine, *De doctrina Christiana*, p. 133.

20   *On Christian Doctrine* 3.1.1.

21   *On Christian Doctrine* 2.11.16.

22   *On Christian Doctrine* 2.5.9.

23   *On Christian Doctrine* 3.3.5.

24   *On Christian Doctrine* 3.2.2.

25   *On Christian Doctrine* 3.10.14.

26   *On Christian Doctrine* 1.39.

27   *On the Trinity* 15.10.19.

28   *On the Trinity* 15.10.19, translation from Augustine, *Later Works*.

29   *On the Trinity* 15.11.20 (translation slightly modernized).

30   *On the Trinity* 15.11.20.

31   *On the Trinity* 15.11.20.

32   *On the Trinity* 15.13.22.

33   *On the Trinity* 15.13.22.

34   *On the Trinity* 15.15.25.

35   Plato, *Sophist*, 263e.

36   A somewhat dated English translation is available at http://www.ccel.org/fathers/NPNF1-02/. The Latin text can be found at http://phil.flet.mita.keio.ac.jp/person/nakagawa/texts.html. There is a good Penguin Classics edition: Augustine, 2003, *Concerning the City of God against the Pagans*, translated by H. R. Bettenson, Harmondsworth: Penguin.

3

The Middle Ages

Jerome's translation

Augustine is the towering figure at the end of antiquity and the beginning of the Middle Ages. Not far behind him in terms of influence comes Jerome (Eusebius Sophronius Hieronymus, died *c*.420), who was able to make his mark in a unique way – he was responsible for the authoritative Latin text of the Bible, which was the commonly used text in the Western Church until the Reformation, and in the Roman Catholic Church until the Second Vatican Council (1962–5).

Eastern Christianity had a more or less fixed Greek text of the Bible, in what today we call the Majority Text of the New Testament and in the Septuagint as the authoritative version of the Old Testament. In the West, however, there was an abundance of Latin translations of the Bible, which were of diverse quality.[1] Thus Jerome was asked by Pope Damasus to revise the text of the available translations in order to produce a unified high quality text of the Bible, which would later become known as the *Vulgate*. It is not certain which books of the New Testament he revised (or rather retranslated) for the *Vulgate*, and which are older Latin translations. Jerome certainly translated the four Gospels, but which of the epistles and other writings he revised is still subject to controversy.[2] For those books he did translate, however, he embarked on a major critical exercise, trying to establish the most reliable text in the original language, that is, Greek for the New and Hebrew for the Old Testament. However, where the text of the Hebrew deviated from the Greek in the Old Testament, he followed the authoritative text of the Church, thus subordinating his critical judgement to the traditions of the Church.[3] Whatever the details of his work, it is important for us to note that with Jerome's *Vulgate* (Latin for *common*) translation of the Bible the Latin West had a commonly accepted text as the basis for theology, until it was rejected by the Humanist scholars and Reformers of the sixteenth century (see pp. 64–7).

Jerome also exercised some considerable influence through his biblical commentaries. He wrote widely on many books of the Old and New Testament, combining great scholarly erudition in the interpretation of the literal-historical sense with impressive allegorical interpretation. With both he would profoundly influence medieval exegesis.

After Jerome and Augustine we can definitely say that classical antiquity is over, and that the Middle Ages have begun, at least in the Western part of the Roman Empire. When Augustine died, the Western Roman Empire was rapidly declining, and it would only take another 46 years until it formally ceased to exist.

The legacy of these two theologians would dominate the Middle Ages. They laid the foundations for all medieval approaches to texts. As Beryl Smalley puts it, 'St. Jerome gave the medieval scholar his text and his learned apparatus; St. Augustine told him what his aim should be.'[4]

Medieval interpretation

The commonly agreed principles of medieval exegesis were the acceptance of allegorical interpretation as a critical tool and an appeal to the rule of faith, that is, the Church's magisterium (teaching office), in case of doubt. Smalley puts the fundamental assumptions of medieval interpreters in a nutshell:

> The Word is incarnate in Scripture, which like man has a body and soul. The body is the words of the sacred text, the 'letter' and the literal meaning. The soul is the spiritual sense. . . . If, in rare moments of scepticism, a medieval scholar questioned the truth of Scripture, he never doubted that it had letter and spirit; he only feared that the spirit might be bad. Naturally, then, he understood the relationship between letter and spirit in the same way as he did the relationship between body and soul. This depended on his philosophy of life and on his way of living.[5]

Although the degree to which allegorical interpretation was to be employed may have been disputed, its basic legitimacy was virtually universally agreed. In short, on the basis of the hermeneutical assumptions of late antiquity, medieval interpreters were able to make sense of biblical and other texts, and this basic attitude would not be challenged until the Reformation. Thus the hallmark of medieval exegesis is continuity, and we do not find any significant innovations in hermeneutical reflection.

Medieval hermeneutical theory assumes that there are four senses of Scripture, one literal sense and three spiritual senses. The spiritual senses are the allegorical sense (in the narrower sense of the word), moral sense and anagogical sense. The allegorical sense in this context refers to contents of belief, that is, that passages of no obvious doctrinal content can be interpreted as referring to contents and mysteries of the Christian dogma. The moral sense refers to Christian morality, and the anagogical sense to the mysteries of the life in the world to come after the final judgement. This fourfold sense of Scripture was generally accepted in the Middle Ages, and what we would call allegorical interpretation (in its wider sense) was understood to consist of the three spiritual senses. A well-known aid to memory, which was made popular by Nicholas of Lyra (*c.*1330) but was probably composed by Augustine of Dacia around 1260, helped the medieval student in learning these:

Littera gesta docet, quid credas allegoria,
Moralis quid agas, quo tenda anagogia.
The letter teaches events, allegory what you should believe,
Morality teaches what you should do, anagogy what mark you should be aiming for.[6]

The most influential theoretical considerations on the theory and practice of the interpretation of text, especially the Bible, can be found in Thomas Aquinas' (died 1274) monumental *Summa Theologiae*. Here Thomas explains under the heading, 'Can one passage of Scripture bear several senses?'

St. Gregory declares that holy Scripture transcends all other sciences by its very style of expression, in that one and the same discourse, while narrating an event, transmits a mystery as well . . .

That God is the author of holy Scripture should be acknowledged, and he has the power, not only of adapting words to convey meanings (which men can also do), but also of adapting things themselves. In every branch of knowledge words have meaning, but what is special here is that the things meant by the words also themselves mean something. That first meaning whereby the words signify things belong to the sense first mentioned, namely the historical or literal. That meaning, however, whereby the things signified by the words in their turn also signify other things is called the spiritual sense; it is based on and presupposes the literal sense.

Now this spiritual sense is divided into three. For, as St Paul says, the Old Law is the figure of the New, and the New Law itself, as Dionysius says, is the figure of the glory to come. Then again, under the New Law the deeds wrought by our Head are signs of what we ourselves ought to do.

Well then, the allegorical sense is brought into play when the things of the Old Law signify the things of the New Law; the moral sense when the things done in Christ and in those who prefigured him are signs of what we should carry out; and the anagogical sense when the things that lie ahead in eternal glory are signified.

Now because the literal sense is that which the author intends, and the author of the holy Scripture is God who comprehends everything all at once in his understanding, it comes not amiss, as St. Augustine observes, if many meanings are present even in the literal sense of one passage of Scripture.[7]

This passage sums up the medieval hermeneutical theory with regard to biblical texts. Because God is the author not only of the Bible, but also of the world and all that takes place within it, even the events described in the Bible are signs of the deeper truths of Christian faith. Thus the medieval fourfold sense of Scripture is based on the belief in the sovereignty of God. Allegorical interpretation had thus developed from a concept that was born out of the embarrassment with the content of the authoritative texts of Hellenic culture, the *Iliad* and the *Odyssey*, to one that was an expression of faith in the sovereignty of God.

Ways of speaking of God

Medieval hermeneutical reflection did not stop with the theory and praxis of textual interpretation. Another problem medieval thought had to address was the question of how human language can speak of God, who dwells beyond this world, and at the same time penetrates its very fabric; who is beyond human comprehension, and, at the same time, is to be found in the depths of the human mind, as Augustine had taught.

Equivocity

One way of solving this problem was *via negativa*, by negation. According to this doctrine, human language is incapable of expressing God's nature, as God is beyond this world and therefore beyond human language. So in speaking of God, the theologian must deny divine properties. So we cannot say that God is good, because God's goodness is completely different from human goodness.

This way of thinking goes back to the neo-Platonic way of thinking within Christian theology, and is particularly connected with the influence of pseudo-Dionysius the Areopagite. Behind this name hides a Greek theologian of the late fifth century AD who wrote a number of treatises, claiming that he was the member of the Areopagus in Athens who, according to Acts 17.34, was one of the few converts after Paul's speech there. The fact that his writings were unknown until the early sixth century, however, as well as that the theology presented in his writings is clearly influenced by the neo-Platonist philosopher Proclus (c.AD 411–85), indicate that this description cannot be true in the modern sense.

Pseudo-Dionysius holds that God is utterly unutterable, that we cannot say anything about God, apart from what God has revealed. So he writes:

> Here too let us hold on to the scriptural rule that when we say anything about God, we should set down the truth 'not in the plausible words of human wisdom but in demonstration of the power granted by the Spirit' (1 Cor. 2.4) to the scripture writers, a power by which, in a manner surpassing speech and knowledge, we reach a union superior to anything available to us by way of our own abilities or activities in the realm of discourse and intellect. This is why we must not dare to resort to words or conceptions concerning that hidden divinity which transcends being, apart from what the sacred scriptures have divinely revealed. Since the unknowing of what is beyond being is something above and beyond speech, mind or being itself, one should ascribe to it an understanding beyond being . . . Just as the senses can neither grasp nor perceive the things of the mind, just as representation and shape cannot take in the simple and shapeless, just as corporeal form cannot lay hold of the intangible and incorporeal, by the same standard of truth beings are surpassed by the infinity beyond being, intelligences by that oneness which is beyond intelligence. Indeed, the inscrutable One is out of the reach of every rational process. Nor can any words come up with the inexpressible Good, this One, this Source of all unity, this supra-existent Being. Mind beyond mind, word beyond speech, it is gathered up by no discourse, by no intuition, by no name. It is and it is as no other being is. Cause of all existence, it alone could give an authoritative account of what it really is.[8]

So we cannot apply any attributes to God. We cannot say that God is good, for God is beyond human goodness, of which he is the source. Divine goodness is so different from human goodness that we cannot say 'God is good.' We can either deny God's goodness or, better still, say that God is super-good, beyond goodness; not that God exists, but that

God is super-existent; not that God is substance, but that God is super-substantial.[9]

If human language is thus incapable of expressing the divine, then the question remains as to how we can meaningfully speak of God. Would we not be reduced to silence, and all theology impossible? Indeed, silence is in the end all that remains for pseudo-Dionysius. He actually views this in a positive light, because if we proceed to deny all attributes of God, then this will lead to mystical union with the divine.

> If God cannot be grasped by mind or sense perception, if he is no particular being, how do we know him? This is something we must enquire into.
>
> It might be more accurate to say that we cannot know God in his nature, since this is unknowable and is beyond the reach of mind or of reason. But we know him from the arrangement of everything, because everything is, in a sense, projected out of him, and this order possesses certain images and semblances of his divine paradigms. We therefore approach that which is beyond all as far as our capacity allows us and we pass by way of the denial and the transcendence of all things and by way of the cause of all things. God is therefore known in all things and as distinct from all things. He is known through knowledge and through unknowing. Of him there is conception, reason, understanding, touch, perception, opinion, imagination, name, and many other things. On the other hand he cannot be understood, words cannot contain him, and no name can lay hold of him. He is not one of the things that are and he cannot be known in any of them. He is known to all from all things and he is known to no one from anything.
>
> This is the sort of language we must use about God, for he is praised from all things according to their proportion to him as their Cause. But again, the most divine knowledge of God, that which comes from unknowing, is achieved in a union far beyond mind, when mind turns away from all things, even from itself, and then it is made one with the dazzling rays, being then and there enlightened by the inscrutable depth of Wisdom.[10]

The mystical union with God is the end of theology, which consists in the denial of all divine attributes, and the end of all human knowledge. For this reason, this type of theology, which is commonly called negative or *apophatic* theology, is traditionally connected with the mystical tradition within Christianity. However, the understanding of theological language as apophatic does not make theological language redundant.

On the contrary, there is an important function for language and definition within this tradition.

Apophatic language comes into its own when theology is seen as based on experience. This may be the experience of mystical union, as the Areopagite suggests, but it may also be the communal experience of the presence of Christ and of redemption in worship, or any other foundational experience that one may see as underlying Christianity. This experience cannot be put into words comprehensively or exhaustingly. Consequently, there is no need to formulate any clear-cut expression of the communal experience, as this is a lived experience, which is shared in action. Certainly, people will speak of this experience, in poetic terms, in narrative terms or in metaphors. Dogmatic language only becomes necessary if someone proposes a description of the experience that contradicts the shared experience. The Greek Orthodox theologian Christos Yannaris gives an illuminating example for this understanding of theological language:

> Let us suppose that someone appears who claims that *maternal love* means relentless strictness and wild daily beating of a child. All of us who have a different experience of maternal love will protest about this distortion and will oppose to it a *definition* of our own experience: For us maternal love is affection, tenderness, care, all combined with a judicious and constructive strictness.[11]

Thus the definition of maternal love only becomes necessary if someone produces a description that the majority sees as wrong. Otherwise, no one would see the need to define something as self-evident as maternal love. It also means that the definition does not replace the experience. If one has not experienced maternal love, then one will never know it, however many definitions and descriptions one hears or reads.

Apophatic theological language works analogously to this. It defines the boundaries of acceptable descriptions of shared experience. A good example for this is the Definition of Chalcedon, which has at its core a paradox and four negative statements. It asserts that Jesus Christ is two natures in one person (two *physeis* in one *hypostasis* – the common translation of *physis* and *hypostasis* as 'nature' and 'person' can be misleading, because it obscures the origin of this terminology in ancient metaphysics). According to the rules of ancient metaphysics, which is the background to this statement, this is paradox and nonsensical. This paradox, however, is not solved. The definition does not say how one person can be of two natures, it only says how it does not: the two natures are in one person unmixed, unchanged, undivided and not separated. In doing so, the council rejected the opposite positions of Nestorianism and Monophysitism as inadequate expressions of the Christian faith, but offered no positive explanation. Thus the experience of salvation was safeguarded against inappropriate descriptions and explanations, while space was left for theological exploration within these two boundaries.

Apophatic theological language does not only work by denying knowledge, but also by defining the limits of theological language with regard to the communal Christian experience. We will need to return to this understanding of apophatic language later, when we develop an overall picture of theological hermeneutics in a later chapter (see section 'A hermeneutical theology', p. 212).

Analogy

The obvious alternative to apophatic theological language would be that human language can directly refer to God, that it is used univocally. This, however, would pose the problem of God's transcendence, that God is not part of this world but beyond it. In the early Middle Ages, some theologians proposed the univocal use of language with regard to God. This, however, was out of unease with the apophatic approach, and, at least partially, for lack of a viable alternative. For univocal use of language with regard to God poses too many problems.

The viable alternative was developed in the thirteenth century as a result of the rediscovery of Aristotle's philosophy. This alternative view was the use of analogical language.

If we use analogical language when speaking of God, that is, if we use terms from within creation and attribute them to God, then, according to the definition of the Fourth Lateran Council of 1215, 'between the Creator and the creature there cannot be a likeness so great that the unlikeness is not greater'.[12] This means that, although there is some similarity between divine and human attributes, there is even greater dissimilarity. So one can say that God is just, but one needs to keep in mind that God's justice is very different from human justness.

We must be careful to distinguish metaphor in language regarding God from analogy. In metaphorical language, we can compare God to something worldly, and see certain similarities. So on the one hand, we can say that God is a fortress, because God shares certain attributes with a fortress. At the same time, however, we can also affirm that God is obviously not a fortress, because God is not a building. So in metaphorical language, we can both affirm and deny the same thing without contradiction. On the other hand, one cannot both affirm and deny that God is just. To deny that God is just would contradict our understanding of God, even if we recognize that God's justice is qualitatively different from human justice. So those attributes that we can only affirm and not deny are, according to medieval understanding, analogies.

According to Thomas Aquinas, we can speak of God by means of analogy because there is a causal relation between God and creation. So we can attribute goodness to God because God is the cause of goodness in the world. When we speak of causes, however, we must not confuse this with the way in which we use the word today. In our modern understanding, there is only one cause, which is the one that brings about an effect. So if I drop my pen, then it falls down because of my negligence and because of gravity. So gravity and my negligence (and probably some more things) are the cause of the pen falling down. According to Aristotelian physics, which is the philosophical background of Thomas' thought, causes are something completely different.[13] There are four causes for everything: the material cause, the formal cause, the final cause and the efficient cause. So the copy of Thomas' *Summa Theologiae* on my table is caused by its matter, i.e. the material stuff it is made from. The formal cause is its inner being, its 'bookness' as it were. The final cause is its purpose, which is to be read. The efficient cause is that what brings it about – the librarian who gave the book to me, the printer, Thomas Aquinas as the author, the translator, etc. So, unlike in the modern understanding, it is not the physical process that is the efficient cause, but the substance that causes it.

In addition, there will always be something of the being of the efficient cause in what is caused – which is where the book as example fails. So if God causes goodness, then God's goodness, which is part of God's own being, is in the goodness God causes. So if we say that God is good, we can say so because God's goodness is contained in the goodness we see around us. Or, in Thomas' words, 'words of this sort [i.e. good] do not only say how God is a cause, they also say what he is. When we say he is good or wise we do not simply mean that he causes wisdom or goodness, but that he possesses these perfections transcendently.'[14] Because for Thomas analogy is based on the correlation of God's being and that of creation, we call this form of thought *analogia entis*, analogy of being.

While the analogy of being is a useful hermeneutical tool to speak of God meaningfully while safeguarding God's transcendence, it is obvious that it is dependent on certain philosophical presuppositions, namely Aristotelian metaphysics. This means that, once Aristotelian metaphysics is replaced by different philosophical presuppositions, then the whole concept becomes redundant. Thus wherever Thomist philosophy and theology are abandoned, analogical language with reference to God based on the analogy of being becomes impossible. It was only much later, in the twentieth century, that the Swiss theologian Karl Barth would develop another way of analogical language with regard to God, the *analogia fidei*, the analogy of faith. This will be discussed in a later chapter (see the section 'Analogy of faith', pp. 181–2).

Univocity

The Franciscan theologians of the later thirteenth century attacked the very foundations of Thomism in a number of ways. In particular the thought of John Duns Scotus (*c.*1266–1308) would be instrumental in the undoing of the theology of Thomas Aquinas. In the context of this hermeneutical investigation, Scotus' teaching of the univocity of being is of particular relevance. We recall that univocity means that a term is used in exactly the same way when applied to two objects. Scotus' innovation was that he gave a firm philosophical basis to the univocal understanding of language with reference to the divine. Thus he is able to apply the term 'being' univocally to God and creation. In other words, he does not see a qualitative difference between God's being and that of created beings.

We have seen above that in negative theology, we cannot legitimately say that God is, or that God exists, because God is so completely different from everything within creation that we cannot apply such concepts to God. We must either say that God is not, which is the same as that God does not exist, or we may say that God super-exists, that God is above being (see pp. 55–6). If we are using analogical language, we may say that God exists, but that God's existence is, despite certain similarities to human existence, still more different. Duns Scotus, apparently ignorant of Thomas' teaching on analogy, asserted in opposition to the theologian and philosopher Henry of Ghent (*c.*1217–93) that the concept of being could be applied to God and creation univocally.[15] This, however, brought with it the danger of undermining the transcendence of God, God's qualitative difference from creation. Scotus avoided this problem by means of exceedingly subtle distinctions.[16] (His name of honour among the Doctors of the Church is *Doctor Subtilis* – the subtle doctor – for a reason!) However, once this principle was established, it was open to the interpretation that God exists just as a given human being exists, in the sense that both occur within the realm of being. Even though Scotus was able to avoid this conclusion, his work opened the possibility of this interpretation. This would play a very important part in the development of modern notions of the existence of God and the relation between God and the world, which would eventually lead to modern atheism. But this is a strand we cannot pursue within this hermeneutical study.

Conclusion

In this chapter, we have explored two issues that medieval thought contributes to the problem of understanding, the further development and use of allegorical interpretation and the problem of the application of human language to God. Despite the popular impression that pre-modern interpretation was uncritical, we have seen that medieval scholarship inherited allegorical interpretation as its critical tool from antiquity. This tool would aid the interpreter when the literal meaning of the text caused insurmountable difficulties, or even prove to be a more broadly applied tool of textual interpretation, in particular of the Bible, but also of other texts.

Furthermore, we have seen how medieval theologians struggled with the problems of speaking of the God who is greater than creation, and, at the same time, penetrating every part of it. This aspect of medieval thought raised problems that would re-occur at various times of history, and to which different answers would be suggested.

We will see in the course of this study that the questions that the medieval theologians and philosophers raised or inherited from their forebears in antiquity will not go away, but persist and demand a considered answer from every generation, even if the answer may look very different from the approach taken by the medieval thinkers.

Further reading

Anselm of Canterbury, 1974, *Basic Writings*, edited by S. N. Deane, 2nd edn, La Salle, Ill.: Open Court.

Aquinas, Thomas, 1964, *Summa Theologiae: Latin Text and English Translation, Introductions, Notes, Appendices and Glossaries*, London and New York: Blackfriars and McGraw-Hill.

Ashworth, E. Jennifer, 2004, 'Medieval Theories of Analogy', in: *The Stanford Encyclopedia of Philosophy* (website, Winter 2004), edited by Edward N. Zalta. Available from http://plato.stanford.edu/archives/win2004/entries/analogy-medieval/.

Brown, Dennis, 2003, 'Jerome and the Vulgate', in: Alan J. Hauser and Duane Frederick Watson (eds), *A History of Biblical Interpretation*, Grand Rapids, Mich.: William B. Eerdmans, pp. 355–79.

Giannaras, Christos, 1991, *Elements of Faith: An Introduction to Orthodox Theology*, Edinburgh: T & T Clark.

Halsall, Paul (ed.), 2006, 'The Internet Medieval Sourcebook' (website, accessed 17 August 2006). Available from http://www.fordham.edu/halsall/sbook.html.

King, Peter, 2002, 'Scotus on Metaphysics', in: Thomas Williams (ed.), *The Cambridge Companion to Duns Scotus*, Cambridge and New York: Cambridge University Press, pp. 15–68.

Lubac, Henri de, 1998, *Medieval Exegesis*, Grand Rapids, Mich.; Edinburgh: W. B. Eerdmans; T & T Clark.

Menn, Stephen P., 2003, 'Metaphysics: God and Being', in: Arthur Stephen McGrade (ed.), *The Cambridge Companion to Medieval Philosophy*, Cambridge: Cambridge University Press, pp. 147–70.

Pseudo-Dionysius, 1987, *Pseudo-Dionysius: The Complete Works*, translated by Colm Luibhéid and Paul Rorem, *The Classics of Western Spirituality*, New York: Paulist Press.

Smalley, Beryl, 1983, *The Study of the Bible in the Middle Ages*, 3rd edn, Oxford: Basil Blackwell.

Notes

1   Dennis Brown, 2003, 'Jerome and the Vulgate', in: Alan J. Hauser and Duane Frederick Watson (eds), *A History of Biblical Interpretation*, Grand Rapids, Mich.: William B. Eerdmans, pp. 358–9.

2   Brown, 'Jerome and the Vulgate', pp. 359–62.

3   Brown, 'Jerome and the Vulgate', p. 363.

4   Beryl Smalley, 1983, *The Study of the Bible in the Middle Ages*, 3rd edn, Oxford: Basil Blackwell, p. 23.

5   Smalley, *The Study of the Bible in the Middle Ages*, p. 1.

6   Henri de Lubac, 1998, *Medieval Exegesis*, Grand Rapids, Mich.; Edinburgh: W. B. Eerdmans; T & T Clark, p. 1 (for the Latin, note 1, p. 271).

7   Thomas Aquinas, *Summa Theologiae*, Ia. I, 10 (Thomas Aquinas, 1964, *Summa Theologiae: Latin Text and English Translation, Introductions, Notes, Appendices and Glossaries*, London and New York: Blackfriars and McGraw-Hill, vol. 1, pp. 37–9. Italics in the original).

8   Pseudo-Dionysius, *The Divine Names*, I. 1 (translation taken from: Pseudo-Dionysius, 1987, *Pseudo-Dionysius: The Complete Works*, translated by Colm Luibhéid and Paul Rorem, *The Classics of Western Spirituality*, New York: Paulist Press, pp. 49–50).

9   E. Jennifer Ashworth, 2004, 'Medieval Theories of Analogy', in: *The Stanford Encyclopedia of Philosophy* (website, Winter 2004), edited by Edward N. Zalta. Available from http://plato.stanford.edu/archives/win2004/entries/analogy-medieval/.

10   Pseudo-Dionysius, *The Divine Names*, VII, 3 (Pseudo-Dionysius, *Complete Works*, pp. 108–9).

11   Christos Giannaras, 1991, *Elements of Faith: An Introduction to Orthodox Theology*, Edinburgh: T & T Clark, p. 16.

12   Twelfth Ecumenical Council: Lateran IV 1215, in: 'The Internet Medieval Sourcebook', 2006, edited by Paul Halsall. Available from http://www.fordham.edu/halsall/sbook.html (accessed 17 August 2006).

13   For a more comprehensive description, S. Marc Cohen, 2003, 'Aristotle's Metaphysics', in: *The Stanford Encyclopedia of Philosophy* (website, Winter 2003), edited by Edward N. Zalta. Available from http://plato.stanford.edu/archives/win2003/entries/aristotle-metaphysics.

14   Thomas Aquinas, *Summa Theologiae*, Ia. 13, 6 (vol. 3, p. 71).

15   Stephen P. Menn, 2003, 'Metaphysics: God and Being', in: Arthur Stephen McGrade (ed.), *The Cambridge Companion to Medieval Philosophy*, Cambridge: Cambridge University Press, pp. 162–4.

16   For the argument see Peter King, 2002, 'Scotus on Metaphysics', in: Thomas Williams (ed.), *The Cambridge Companion to Duns Scotus*, Cambridge; New York: Cambridge University Press.

4

Humanism and the Reformation

Humanism

Ad fontes!

Based on the hermeneutical assumptions outlined in the previous chapter, medieval theology developed over about a thousand years with remarkable continuity. Augustine and Jerome were the guides to the proper interpretation of Scripture; they aided the interpreter by providing critical tools, as well as the methods of allegorical interpretation. They also established the interpreter's reliance on the Church's teaching office, which guarded the true faith which the interpretation must not contradict.

In the course of the Middle Ages, scholars began to compile authoritative interpretations of biblical passages from the writings of Church Fathers and early medieval theologians. This became an authoritative compendium of quotations, called the *Glossa Ordinaria*. The quotations were attached to relevant passages of the Bible, thus providing a running commentary on the text of the *Vulgate*. The *Glossa Ordinaria* was based on such a compilation by Anselm of Laon in the twelfth century and developed and broadened throughout the late Middle Ages. The *Glossa* itself became the authoritative commentary on the Bible, eventually being studied more than the text itself. This development was not restricted to theology, but was also found in jurisprudence, where a *Glossa Ordinaria* on the *Corpus Iuris Canonici*, that is, the canon or Church law, as well as on the *Corpus Iuris Civilis*, the civil or secular law, became authoritative. In all these instances, the *Glossa* became the lens through which the text was to be read, and determined its meaning for the reader. Thus increasing attention was paid to authoritative interpretation at the expense of the text itself. The interpretation eclipsed the text.

This movement, which was intimately connected with the development of scholastic theology, was countered from the fourteenth century onwards by Renaissance humanism. This was a broad cultural movement that was based on the rebirth of classical scholarship. Humanist scholars rediscovered and studied the classical Latin and Greek authors of antiquity and revived the use of classical Latin, as opposed to medieval ecclesiastical Latin. The newly found ability to access the ancient authors directly resulted in the discovery that the medieval translations and interpretations of these texts were often inaccurate. Consequently, the humanists wanted to go behind the medieval corruption of classical learning; they wanted to return *ad fontes*, that is, to the sources, back to the original texts. Adherents of the new learning also found a new purpose of interpretation. Instead of the dogmatic interest of the scholastics, they saw the ancient texts as containing the lived experience of the ancients, and thus they read and interpreted texts in order to regain the experience of the original writers.[1]

This movement had important implications for Church and theology, of which two are particularly relevant in our study of the history of hermeneutics. First, when theologians went back *ad fontes*, to the sources, it meant that they returned to the Bible and to the Church Fathers and studied them directly, not through the lens of scholastic glosses and commentaries. The new approach was deliberately undogmatic and open to new readings of the sacred Scriptures. Second, the commonly used text of the Bible, Jerome's *Vulgate*, was found to be lacking and inaccurate in comparison with the Greek and Hebrew originals. Thus the humanists felt a need either to study the texts in their original language, or at least to provide more accurate translations.

Thus, in the eyes of the humanists, the theology of the Middle Ages was discredited, because it was based on an inaccurate text of the Bible, which, as they thought, had then been subjected to a fanciful dogmatic interpretation. Thus the humanists threw overboard medieval scholasticism and perceived dogmatism and promoted their own fresh approach to the texts, which they encountered with renewed immediacy. Such an approach was necessarily a great challenge to the dogmatic systems and subtleties of the late medieval period, and would have a major impact on the Reformation of the sixteenth century.

Two literal senses of Scripture

The new focus on the literal sense of the text posed new problems for the interpreter with regard to the Old Testament. Was the Old Testament not a Jewish writing, and so, if one interpreted it literally, would it not lead to a Jewish theology? In order to avoid this problem, humanists developed the concept of two literal senses of Scripture. Thus they distinguished between the straightforward literal sense, called the historical literal sense, and the prophetic literal sense, which assumed that certain passages in the Old Testament really referred to Christ, even if a straightforward literal reading might not suggest so.[2] The prophetic literal sense could be found in the writings of the prophets, in the Psalms, and in other prophetic passages. Thus a typological interpretation of the Old Testament continued to be legitimate, although under the guise of a prophetic literal sense. The Reformers would make use of this distinction, and, although they abolished allegorical interpretation in principle, they would continue to interpret parts of the Old Testament typologically.

Erasmus

The towering figure of Northern European Renaissance humanism was Desiderius Erasmus, often known as Erasmus of Rotterdam (c.1463–1535). Erasmus laid important foundations for early modern hermeneutics, while he was, in many ways, deeply rooted in medieval hermeneutical theory and practice.

Erasmus laid foundations for the further development of hermeneutical thought mainly through his critical scholarship. Following the Renaissance motto *ad fontes!*, he made available critical editions of many Church Fathers, among them Augustine, Ambrose, Jerome and others. During the Middle Ages, theologians did not have access to complete texts of patristic writings, but usually only to isolated sound bites, called 'sentences'. Thus, when Erasmus and other humanist scholars provided a wide range of patristic texts for a broader readership, it gave scholars access to a completely new dimension of theology. Furthermore, Erasmus published a critical edition of the Greek New Testament, which is known as the *textus receptus*, the received or the agreed text. Even though this edition's accuracy did not meet Erasmus' own standards, it was replaced as the basis of biblical scholarship only in the nineteenth century. However, it provided a text of the New Testament that was much more reliable than Jerome's *Vulgate*.

In his interpretation of the Bible, Erasmus did not follow the dogmatic tradition of the Middle Ages. Instead, he read it as a guide to a simple Christian lifestyle, within a theological framework which he called the *philosophia Christi*, the philosophy of Christ. This approach overcame medieval dogmatism and promoted what he saw as a simple biblical theology. This position is beautifully summarized in his argument with Martin Luther, when he writes that

> there are other things which God has willed to be most plainly evident, and such are the precepts for the good life. This is the Word of God,

which is not to be bought in the highest heaven, nor in distant lands overseas, but it is close at hand, in our mouth and in our heart. These truths must be known by all, but the rest are more properly committed to God, and it is more religious to worship them, being unknown, than to discuss them, being insoluble.[3]

Some of these remaining things, which Erasmus thought we should worship in ignorance, are mentioned earlier in the passage. They include the the doctrines of the Trinity and of the natures of Christ, as well as a number of other issues which remain, for Erasmus, obscure. This anti-dogmatic and moralizing stance prefigures already a later, modern theology.

Yet at the same time Erasmus was deeply rooted in medieval thought and practice. He happily accepted the legitimacy of allegorical interpretation for biblical interpretation, although he did not think it proper to use it as the basis for theological statements. In his arguably most influential religious writing, the *Enchiridion militis christiani* (which can be translated as Handbook or Dagger of the Christian Soldier), he used allegorical interpretation extensively. Later in his life, however, Erasmus made much less use of the spiritual sense of Scripture. He came to see that the full meaning was contained within the literal sense of the text, and could be established by using the critical methods developed by the humanist scholars.[4] However, he never denied the legitimacy of allegorical interpretation, and continued to make use of the tropological or moral sense, which suited his theological agenda, seeing the Bible as the guide to the good moral life of the Christian.

Reformation

Sola scriptura

There are a number of issues on which all mainstream Reformers would agree, two of which are relevant for our inquiry. These are the principle of *sola scriptura*, Scripture alone, and the fundamental clarity of Scripture in its literal sense, even if this may include the prophetic literal sense outlined above.

Sola scriptura, however, did not imply that the Scriptures were to be interpreted without any aid or guide. On the contrary, the Reformers of the Magisterial Reformation, which included the Lutheran, Reformed and Anglican Reformation, maintained that the Bible must be read in the light of the traditional interpretation, which they took to be that of the

Church Fathers. In their eyes, this tradition had been corrupted by medieval scholastic theology. So the Reformers followed the humanists back to the sources, *ad fontes*, back to the text of the Bible and to the writings of the Church Fathers. In opposition to this conservative approach, the Radical Reformation suggested that each believer could read the Bible without recourse to the tradition, and that the inspiration of the Holy Spirit would suffice as interpretative tool. The Magisterial Reformers rejected this, because they saw it, not without reason, as a recipe for anarchy and chaos.

Thus the mainstream Reformation did not reject the positive part tradition had to play in the interpretation of Scripture. Instead, the polemic was directed against a particular understanding of tradition that had evolved during the Middle Ages. The medieval Church had developed a doctrine of an oral tradition which, independently of Scripture, was supposed to have been passed down from the Apostles and preserved within the Church. This tradition was valued even as a second source of revelation besides the Scriptures. It was this notion which the Reformers rejected, and the call *sola scriptura* thus means that Scripture, interpreted on the basis of a (purified) tradition, was the basis of Christian faith and theology.

This is illustrated by the fact that Luther even allowed for interpreting a biblical passage beyond the literal meaning if 'it is forced on us by the evident nature of the context, the absurdity of the literal sense as conflicting with one or another of the articles of faith'.[5] The articles of faith are the traditional interpretation of the Bible, as established by the Church Fathers and the definitions of the councils. This purified tradition guides the reader, so that if a passage contradicts the tradition, the articles of faith, then it has to be interpreted beyond the literal sense.

Thus, accepting the value of tradition for the interpretation of the Bible, the Reformers positioned themselves within the ecclesiastical tradition of biblical interpretation. For them, interpreting the Scriptures was a communal endeavour of the Church, not only within the scholarly community of a particular time, but of the universal Church of all times and ages. In order to ensure that individual study of the Scriptures would be within the parameters of this traditional reading, lay people were given catechisms which they would usually have to memorize before their confirmation. These catechisms provided the theological framework that would ensure that the Bible was read in the 'correct' way. Within Lutheranism this was the *Small Catechism* of Martin Luther, within Reformed Christianity it was the *Heidelberg Catechism*, and within the English Reformation it was the Catechism of the *Book of Common Prayer*. These short and accessible compendia of theology would guide the lay reader of the Bible towards a reading that would be in conformity with the tradition of the Church as each Reformed Church had received it.

When the Reformers insisted that the tradition of the Church was a guide in the interpretation of Scripture, they assumed that the tradition of the Church, namely, Church Fathers, medieval theologians, councils and synods, was a reliable summary of the content of the Bible. However, where the tradition disagreed with Scripture, it had to be rejected. Furthermore, the Reformers saw that the Bible was not a quarry of proof texts. Instead, they insisted that individual texts had to be read in context, and that the widest possible context was the Bible as a whole. Against this background they accepted that some individual texts could be at odds with the meaning of Scripture in its totality.

The role the Reformers attribute to the tradition can be understood as an acknowledgement of the circular nature of interpretation, of the hermeneutic circle (see the section 'The hermeneutical circle', pp. 4–5). This means that we understand the whole text if we understand all its individual parts, while we can only understand the individual parts in the light of the whole. The way to enter this circle was, for the Reformers, the guidance of the tradition, which is based on the consensus on the meaning of the Bible, shared by the Church throughout the ages. Guided by this, the reader will understand the individual parts, and gain a better and deeper understanding of the whole. Thus the Bible could be understood in its literal sense, but one had to approach it and to enter the hermeneutic circle in the appropriate way, that is, guided by the rule of faith and the purified tradition of the Church.

These hermeneutical insights are illustrated by Luther's German translation of the Bible. Critics of Luther's translation pointed out that he had taken too many freedoms. Luther had indeed rendered the text rather freely and creatively – to the extent that it has been said that Luther 'created the text for a second time in German'.[6] Luther justifies this in *On Translating*. Here, Luther points out that his translations of individual texts are governed by his understanding of the whole. So when he justifies his rendering of Romans 3.28 as 'For we hold that a person is justified without the works of the law by faith alone'[7] ('alone' is not in the Greek text) he argues that this is an accurate representation of what Paul means here within the framework of his theology, and that he, Luther, had put this into German as clearly as possible, even if it meant inserting a word into the text. His understanding of the whole of Paul's theology allowed Luther to take some liberty in the detail. This liberty enabled Luther to present a translation in accessible German, sometimes retelling more than translating accurately. Bernhard Lohse rightly points out that 'Luther's translation of the Bible was intended to make the divine word relevant to his own historical situation. To put it very pointedly, God, who once spoke through the biblical authors in Greek and Hebrew, now communicated the same message in German through Luther's translation.'[8]

The key to the Scriptures

All mainstream Reformers agreed that it was necessary to have an adequate understanding of the word of God as hermeneutical key to the Scriptures, which would enable the reader to unlock their literal meaning. The Reformers also agreed that the literal meaning of the Bible could be established by everyone prepared to study the text. In order to have faith in this meaning, however, the reader needed to be inspired by God through the Holy Spirit. Inspiration was thus not necessary in order to establish the literal meaning of the Bible. However, in order to recognize that this is really the word of God, and to believe and trust in it, the reader would need the illumination of the Holy Spirit.[9]

Despite these broad agreements, there were also substantial and deep theological disagreements among the different currents within the Reformation, most chiefly between the Reformed (Zwinglian and Calvinist) camp and the Lutherans. Of particular interest for us are their conflicting understandings of the word of God and its relation to the human word of the Bible. Lutherans and Calvinists agreed that the word of God needed to be preached, and both held a high view of the preacher's office. The preacher was God's instrument in bringing the word of God to the congregation, and the word of proclamation was intimately connected with the word of God. However, the nature of this relationship was hotly disputed.

Martin Luther understood the gospel,[10] the good news which is the word of God, to be a living proclamation, which brings Christ himself to the hearer:

When you open the book containing the gospels and read or hear how Christ comes here or there, or how someone is brought to him, you should therein perceive the sermon or the gospel through which he is coming to you, or you are brought to him. For the preaching of the gospel is nothing else than Christ coming to us, or we being brought to him. When you see how he works, however, and how he helps everyone to whom he comes or who is brought to him, then rest assured that faith is accomplishing this in you and that he is offering your soul exactly the same sort of help and favor through the gospel. If you pause here and let him do you good, that is, if you believe that he benefits and helps you, then you really have it. Then Christ is yours, presented to you as a gift.[11]

Thus the word of God is an address through which Christ comes to the hearer or reader. The word of God is contained in the human word of the Bible, and wherever Christ is proclaimed, he is present within the proclamation itself. Human language is therefore able to contain the word of God, and meaning in general. In order to understand the thrust of this point better, we need to look at the alternative as it is presented by John Calvin.

For Calvin, the word of God is not a promise or an address, but the proclamation of a fact:

> The atonement whereby sins are cleared, that the curse and judgement of death should no longer weigh upon us, is to be sought precisely in His sacrificial death. Righteousness, salvation and eternal felicity are based on his rising again. Thus the Gospel is the solemn proclamation of the presence of the Son of God revealed in the flesh to renew a fallen world, to restore men from death into life.[12]

Thus for Calvin, it is not through the language of the text that Christ is brought to the hearer – Christ is present already, and language only points at the thing, in this case at Christ's saving presence. This is further illustrated in Calvin's commentary on 2 Corinthians 5.19, where he explains the role of Christ as the mediator:

> My answer is that we were loved from the beginning of the world, but not apart from Christ. But I do agree that the love of God was first in time and in order also as regards God; but, as regards us, his love has its foundation in the sacrifice of Christ. For when we think of God apart from a mediator we can only conceive of Him as being angry with us, but when a mediator is interposed between us, we know that He is pacified towards us.[13]

Thus the love of God has always been there, but the human person who thinks of God apart from the mediator, that is, apart from Christ, can only perceive a wrathful God. So what is changed is human perception, not the fundamental relation between God and the human being – which cannot be changed anyway, as for Calvin God predestined all human beings either to salvation or damnation before the world began. Consequently, God's relation to the human person was defined in the act of predestination before creation, and what needs to be corrected is the human attitude. The proclamation is then only a witness and testimony to what has already happened: 'Ministers of the Church are ambassadors for testifying and proclaiming the blessing of reconciliation . . .'[14]

We can therefore observe a fundamental difference in the hermeneutics of Luther and Calvin. For Luther, the spoken language, the *verbum externum*, contains what it means – the *verbum interius* is incarnate in it. In other words, the sign itself brings about what it signifies, it is an effective sign. Thus Luther takes up, consciously or not, Augustine's insight of the incarnation of the inner word in the spoken word (see p. 45). Calvin, on the other hand, takes language to be merely a sign that points away from itself to a reality beyond itself, thus using Augustine's theory of signs (see p. 42), yet without reference to his teaching on the incarnation of the word. For him, the sign is not effective, only demonstrative.

Both Luther's and Calvin's hermeneutics are rooted in their Christology, their understanding of the doctrine of the person and work of Christ. Luther, on the one hand, taught that in the incarnation the eternal *logos* entered and is present in the flesh, yet without being exhausted in it.[15] Calvin, on the other hand, taught that 'even if the Word in his immeasurable essence united with the nature of man into one person, we do not imagine that he was confined therein'.[16] Thus for Calvin, the *logos* does not enter the flesh, but is merely united with the flesh into one person. We can see this attitude again in a discussion of the ascension, where Calvin keeps the divine and the human attributes of Christ as far apart as possible:

> We always have Christ according to the presence of majesty; but of his physical presence it was rightly said to his disciples, 'You will not always have me with you' (Matt. 26.11). For the church had him in his bodily presence for a few days; now it holds him by faith, but does not see him with the eyes.[17]

Luther argues to the contrary:

> Christ's body is at the right hand of the Father, as it is commonly known. The right hand of God, however, is everywhere [. . .] therefore it is as well in bread and wine on the table. Yet, where God's right hand is, Christ's body and blood must be.[18]

Luther's position can be illustrated in his discussion of the theology of Nestorius, a fifth-century theologian, in which Luther insists that the human and divine nature of Christ are so intimately united in one person that we can properly say of the eternal word of God what we say of the man Jesus of Nazareth and vice versa:

> We Christians must describe all the idiomata [attributes] of the two natures of Christ, both persons, equally to him. Consequently Christ is God and man in one person because whatever is said of him as man must be said of him as God, namely Christ has died, and Christ is God; therefore God died – not the separated God, but God united with humanity.[19]

In short, for Luther the eternal word of God entered the human flesh, yet without being completely absorbed in it, as Luther's distinction between 'God united with humanity' and 'the separated God' indicates. This has important implications for Luther's understanding of the sacraments, especially the Eucharist. Luther asserts in this context: 'All right, Christ walks on earth, and the entire Godhead is in him in person and in essence on earth.'[20]

Thus Luther is able to hold together the apparent contradiction that God can be within the flesh and at the same time be above all and outside all created things. This paradoxical statement, that God is in the elements of the Lord's Supper and at the same time infinitely above them, which attempts to hold together the eternal and the temporal without collapsing them into each other, is an important feature of Lutheran theology. This attitude has important hermeneutical implications, when we consider the meaning of an utterance, the *verbum interius*, as transcendent, and the utterance as material. Then, for Luther, the meaning of the utterance is embodied, is present within the utterance itself. For Calvin, on the other hand, the meaning of the utterance is not present in it. Language points to something that is outside itself.

We can observe at this point that hermeneutical theory is intimately connected with Christology, in particular with the relation between the divine and human nature of Christ. This has a great bearing on the doctrine of the sacraments, in particular on the question as to if and how Christ can be present within the elements of the Eucharist, and also on the hermeneutical question if language can contain what it means, or if it merely points at it. Luther developed his Christology out of the needs of his eucharistic theology, and this had, consciously or not, important implications for his understanding of language and meaning. For him, the words of the Bible and of proclamation are the bearers of the word of God, which would address the reader or hearer with the promise of salvation in Jesus Christ. The hearer, in turn, would then trust in this promise.

Calvin's very different Christological assumptions lead him to his understanding of the relation between time and eternity, between immanence and transcendence, as well as language and meaning. Anything temporal cannot contain the eternal, anything inner-worldly cannot contain the transcendent, the human word cannot contain the divine *logos*. Or, in the words of the later Calvinist theologians, *finitum non est capax infinitum* – the finite cannot contain the infinite.

We will see this question of Lutheran and Calvinist Christology and its implications for hermeneutics arise again when we discuss the hermeneutical developments of the twentieth century, as Lutheran theologians such as Rudolf Bultmann, Gerhard Ebeling and those who follow their approach still base their hermeneutics on Martin Luther's Christological position (see pp. 127–8), while Reformed theologians following Karl Barth base theirs on the Calvinist position (see pp. 181–2).

This Christological basis is even relevant for non-Christians participating in the hermeneutical debate. Although non-Christians will usually not hold any Christological position, they will nevertheless have a fundamental philosophical understanding of the relation between time and eternity, immanence and transcendence, even if this is not explicitly articulated. Thus the issues that were articulated in Christological terms during the time of the Reformation also apply to the general debate. In fact, the Christological terminology may even be helpful to articulate issues that would otherwise be hard to identify.

Conclusion

Humanism and the Reformation brought about a sea change in hermeneutical thinking, and consequently in the way in which texts were approached. Critical tools were developed, the literal meaning of the text elevated, and the fundamental clarity of Scripture established. But we have also seen that in many ways the Reformers advocated a conservative approach to Scripture, insisting that it had to be read in the light of the Church's tradition, albeit a purified tradition. Thus scriptural interpretation was safeguarded against an arbitrary individualistic approach to the text.

The Reformation was one very important influence on the development of modern hermeneutics, both by its own contribution to hermeneutical thinking as well as by the questions it raised for coming generations. Thus the insistence on the literal understanding of the, in principle, clear and accessible text is one of the foundations of modern interpretation theory. However, this also poses problems, because the difficulties within Scripture, for which allegorical interpretation had been developed, did not go away. Thus a new way of dealing with the obscure passages was needed, and this led to the development of the historical-critical methods of textual interpretation. This would preoccupy theologians over the next few hundred years.

There are many things we can learn from studying the hermeneutics of the Reformers. However, we need to be careful not to import modern questions into their thinking. The Reformers did not know of historical-critical interpretation, and questions relating to its use were therefore not within their horizon. Thus to ask if Luther's theology or that of Calvin or Melanchthon would support or prohibit historical-critical interpretation is an anachronism. Having said this, we can find starting points within Reformation theology that enabled and aided the development of historical-critical thinking. This development will be the subject of the following sections.

Further reading

Augustijn, C., 1991, *Erasmus: His Life, Works and Influence*, Erasmus Studies, 10, Toronto: University of Toronto Press.

Calvin, Jean, 1960, *Institutes of the Christian Religion*, edited by John Thomas McNeill and Ford Lewis Battles, *The Library of Christian Classics*, vols 20–1, Philadelphia: Westminster Press.

Calvin, Jean, 1964, *The Second Epistle of Paul the Apostle to the Corintians and the Epistles to Timothy, Titus and Philemon*, translated by T. A. Smail, edited by David W. Torrance and Thomas Forsyth Torrance, *Calvin's Commentaries*, vol. 10, Grand Rapids, Mich.: W. B. Eerdmans.

Calvin, Jean, 1972, *A Harmony of the Gospels, Matthew, Mark and Luke*, edited by David W. Torrance and Thomas Forsyth Torrance, 3 vols, *Calvin's Commentaries*, vols 1–3, Grand Rapids, Mich.: W. B. Eerdmans.

Dickens, A. G. and Whitney R. D. Jones, 1994, *Erasmus the Reformer*, London: Methuen London.

Erasmus, Desiderius, 1965, *Essential Works of Erasmus*, New York: Bantam.

Erasmus, Desiderius, 1975, *The Collected Works of Erasmus*, Toronto: University of Toronto Press.

Hoffmann, Manfred, 1994, *Rhetoric and Theology: The Hermeneutic of Erasmus*, Erasmus Studies, 12, Toronto; London: University of Toronto Press.

Jensen, Alexander S., 2002, 'Martin Luther's "sin boldly" Revisited: A Fresh Look at a Controversial Concept in the Light of Modern Pastoral Psychology', *Contact: The Interdisciplinary Journal of Pastoral Studies* 137, pp. 2–13.

Lohse, Bernhard, 1987, *Martin Luther: An Introduction to his Life and Work*, Edinburgh: T & T Clark.

Luther, Martin, 1955, *Luther's Works*, edited by Jaroslav Pelikan and Helmut T. Lehman, Philadelphia: Concordia; Fortress Press.

Luther, Martin, 1959, 'A Brief Introduction on what to Look for and Expect in the Gospels', in: E. Theodore Bachmann (ed.), *Luther's Works*, vol. 35, Philadelphia: Fortress Press, pp. 113–24.

Luther, Martin, 1959, 'On Translating: An Open Letter', in: E. Theodore Bachmann (ed.), *Luther's Works*, vol. 35, Philadelphia: Fortress Press, pp. 177–202.

Luther, Martin, 1961, 'That these Words of Christ, "This is My body," etc., Still Stand Firm against the Fanatics', in: Robert H. Fischer (ed.), *Luther's Works*, vol. 37, Philadelphia: Fortress Press, pp. 13–150.

Luther, Martin, 1966, 'On the Councils and the Church', in: Eric W. Gritsch (ed.), *Luther's Works*, vol. 41, Philadelphia: Fortress Press, pp. 9–178.

Luther, Martin and Desiderius Erasmus, 1969, *Luther and Erasmus: Free Will and Salvation*, edited by E. Gordon Rupp and Philip S. Watson, *The Library of Christian Classics*, vol. 17, Philadelphia: Westminster Press.

Lutheran World Federation and The Catholic Church, 1999, 'Joint Declaration on the Doctrine of Justification' (website, accessed 7 November 2006). Available from http://www.vatican.va/roman_curia/pontifical_councils/chrstuni/documents/rc_pc_chrstuni_doc_31101999_cath-luth-joint-declaration_en.html1.

McGrath, Alister E., 1987, *The Intellectual Origins of the European Reformation*, Oxford and New York: B. Blackwell.

McGrath, Alister E., 1999, *Reformation Thought: An Introduction*, 3rd edn, Oxford and Malden, Mass.: Blackwell Publishers.

Melanchthon, Philipp and Martin Bucer, 1969, *Melanchthon and Bucer*, *The Library of Christian Classics*, vol. 19, edited by Wilhelm Pauck, Philadelphia: Westminster Press.

Pannenberg, Wolfhart, 1959, 'Christologie II: Dogmengeschichtlich', in: Kurt Galling (ed.), *Die Religion in Geschichte und Gegenwart*, vol. 1, 3rd edn, Tübingen: J. C. B. Mohr (Paul Siebeck), pp. 1762–77.

Notes

1   Alister E. McGrath, 1999, *Reformation Thought: An Introduction*, 3rd edn, Oxford, UK; Malden, Mass.: Blackwell Publishers, p. 45.

2   Alister E. McGrath, 1987, *The Intellectual Origins of the European Reformation*, Oxford, UK; New York: B. Blackwell, pp. 157–8.

3   Martin Luther and Desiderius Erasmus, 1969, *Luther and Erasmus: Free Will and Salvation*, edited by E. Gordon Rupp and Philip S. Watson, *The Library of Christian Classics*, vol. 17, Philadelphia: Westminster Press, pp. 39–40.

4   McGrath, *The Intellectual Origins of the European Reformation*, p. 155.

5   Luther and Erasmus, *Luther and Erasmus*, p. 221 (Weimarer Ausgabe [WA] XVIII, 700).

6   Bernhard Lohse, 1987, *Martin Luther: An Introduction to his Life and Work*, Edinburgh: T & T Clark, p. 113.

7   Martin Luther, 1959, 'On Translating: An Open Letter', in: E. Theodore Bachmann (ed.), *Luther's Works*, vol. 35, Philadelphia: Fortress Press.

8   Lohse, *Martin Luther: An Introduction to his Life and Work*, p. 115.

9   Luther and Erasmus, *Luther and Erasmus*, p. 159 (WA XVIII, 652–3).

10   It may be worthwhile pointing out here that the term 'gospel' in this context refers to the good news of Christian proclamation itself. The four books of the Bible called the Gospels are seen by the Reformers as containing the gospel, which is also contained in the letters and other writings of the New Testament.

11   Martin Luther, 1959, 'A Brief Introduction on what to Look for and Expect in the Gospels', in: E. Theodore Bachmann (ed.), *Luther's Works*, vol. 35, Philadelphia: Fortress Press, p. 121 (WA X, 13–14).

12   Jean Calvin, 1972, *A Harmony of the Gospels, Matthew, Mark and Luke*, edited by David W. Torrance and Thomas Forsyth Torrance, 3 vols, *Calvin's Commentaries*, vols 1–3, Grand Rapids, Mich.: W. B. Eerdmans, p. xi.

13   Jean Calvin, 1964, *The Second Epistle of Paul the Apostle to the Corinthians and the Epistles to Timothy, Titus and Philemon*, translated by T. A. Smail, edited by David W. Torrance and Thomas Forsyth Torrance, *Calvin's Commentaries*, vol. 10, Grand Rapids, Mich.: W. B. Eerdmans, pp. 78–9.

14   Calvin, *Second Corinthians, Timothy, Titus and Philemon*, p. 79.

15   Wolfhart Pannenberg, 1959, 'Christologie II: Dogmengeschichtlich', in: Kurt Galling (ed.), *Die Religion in Geschichte und Gegenwart*, vol. 1, 3rd edn, Tübingen: J. C. B. Mohr (Paul Siebeck), cols. 1774–5.

16   Jean Calvin, 1960, *Institutes of the Christian Religion*, edited by John Thomas McNeill and Ford Lewis Battles, *The Library of Christian Classics*, vols 20–1, Philadelphia: Westminster Press, Book II, Ch. XIII: 4, p. 481.

17   Calvin, *Institutes of the Christian Religion*, Book II, Ch. XVI: 14, p. 523.

18   Martin Luther, 1961, 'That these Words of Christ, "This is My body," etc., Still Stand Firm against the Fanatics', in: Robert H. Fischer (ed.), *Luther's Works*, vol. 37, Philadelphia: Fortress Press, p. 63 (WA XXIII, 143).

19   Martin Luther, 1966, 'On the Councils and the Church', in: Eric W. Gritsch (ed.), *Luther's Works*, vol. 41, Philadelphia: Fortress Press, p. 103 (WA L, 589).

20   Luther, 'That these Words of Christ, "This is My body," etc., Still Stand Firm against the Fanatics', p. 61 (WA XXIII, 139).

5

Rationalism and Enlightenment

A new context

Two hundred years after the Reformation, the world had changed completely. Great discoveries had been made, which redrew the maps of the earth and the universe. New continents and previously unheard of people had been discovered, and the new astronomy had shown that the earth was not the centre of the universe, but one planet among many within the solar system. But most dramatically, God had ceased to be the centre of reality, and had been replaced with the rational human self. This development held dramatic implications for philosophy and theology, and, more important in our context, for the understanding of texts, both sacred and profane.

Already at the time of the Reformation, Nicolaus Copernicus (1473–1543) published his work *On the Revolutions of the Heavenly Spheres*, in which he argued, on the basis of astronomical observations and mathematical calculations, that the earth was actually orbiting the sun, and not vice versa. Due to the upheaval of the Reformation, the Church did not ban this book, as it would otherwise have done, and thus it was widely available until the early seventeenth century, when it was finally banned. By then, however, it was too late to limit its influence. Other astronomers and mathematicians had already adopted the new view of the world. Johannes Kepler (1571–1630) refined Copernicus' system, and Galileo Galilei (1564–1642) found observational evidence and publicized these new ideas widely, until he was silenced by the Church. The new world-view conflicted with that presented in the authoritative texts, the Bible, Aristotle, Ptolemy (who lived in the second century AD) and the later writers who drew on their work. Thus the ancient authorities came under increasing suspicion, and their authority was gradually replaced by that of human reason in conjunction with empirical science.

The ancient authorities came under attack from various other directions: the discoveries of new lands that the ancient authorities did not mention, and new peoples who were not listed in the (supposedly comprehensive) list of peoples in the Bible (cf. Gen. 10). Isaac La Peyrère (1596–

1676) drew the consequence of these discoveries when he published his thesis of the *Pre-Adamites*. La Peyrère assumed that Adam was not the first man, but merely the tribal ancestor of Israel.[1] The growing body of doubts was summed up and brought into the public arena when Baruch Spinoza (1632–77) questioned the historical reliablility of the Pentateuch and argued that Moses was not the author of these books.[2]

In the same period, Sir Francis Bacon (1561–1626) laid the foundation for the development of the scientific method and for the empirical sciences. The scientist was now supposed to gather facts by observation and experiment, and knowledge would be gained if these facts were arranged in a way so that hypothetical universal laws could be deduced. These hypotheses could then be verified or falsified by further observations and experiments.[3] This led not only to the demystification of the world and natural explanation for things that previously had been attributed to supernatural activity, but also to an empiricist understanding of reality; true is what can be measured, and what cannot be verified by observation or experiment is not true.

The French philosopher René Descartes (1596–1650) crowned this development by laying the foundation of rationalism, a philosophy which assumes that the rational human self is the ultimate authority and the centre of reality. Thus all other authorities, including that of God and the sacred Scriptures, are to be judged by human reason. It would take Church and theology some centuries to adjust to these changes, and arguably they are still struggling with these fundamental changes in the human understanding of the world.

Enlightenment

The new way of thinking obviously had important implications for the interpretation of texts. If reason is the source of all knowledge, then texts cannot say anything the human reason could not find out by itself. Thus texts are guides to the application of reason in various areas; they are mainly pedagogical. We find this approach even in literature, where, for example, the plays of Gotthold Ephraim Lessing (1729–81) or the writings of Daniel Defoe (1661–1731) have a mainly pedagogical purpose. Defoe's *Robinson Crusoe*, for example, may be an adventure story at one level, but on another it is a pedagogical story about the rational ordering of society. With this attitude, it is not surprising that the ancient writers and their works, including the Bible, were met with distrust, as their authors were under suspicion of being influenced by unenlightened prejudice. The enlightened theologian Johann Martin Chladenius (1710–59) puts this new attitude trenchantly:

> In philosophy, there is little need for the art of interpretation. Here, every individual must rely on the strength of his own ability to think. A proposition in a philosophical work at which we can only arrive after much interpretation does not do us a particular service because we then ask whether it is true and how one should prove it – which really belongs to the art of philosophy.[4]

The new doctrine that truth is not mediated, but to be discovered by reason, has important consequences for the interpretation of the Bible. Historical events, including those which were traditionally assumed to be revelatory, such as the events described in the Bible, cannot convey any truth that could not also be reached by the use of reason alone. Lessing phrased this pointedly when he wrote that 'accidental truths of history can never become the proof of necessary truths of reason'[5] – this strict separation has become known as Lessing's 'ugly, broad ditch' after a phrase used elsewhere in the same text.[6]

As a result of rationalist philosophy, new problems arose for the interpretation of biblical texts. There are many texts that contain events and teachings that are not in accord with reason, such as the sacrifice of Isaac, the occurrences of demons and of miracles. For many Enlightenment thinkers, the easiest solution was to discard the Bible altogether as a source of truth; just as Plato had done with the foundational texts of Hellenism over two millennia before. Similarly, the German philosopher Immanuel Kant (1724–1804), whose work marks the end of the Age of Enlightenment, could proclaim in his book *The Conflict of the Faculties* (1798) that philosophy was the only source of reliable truth, while theology could not contribute anything to human knowledge at all. Consequently, Kant would only permit it to continue as the study of religion, which could only teach what had been identified as true by philosophy.

Another approach was to harmonize Christian religion with human reason. Spinoza, for example, purged revealed religion – he was from a Jewish background, but his ideas were readily applied to Christianity – of all that was opposed to reason, of all that he saw as a pollution of the true essence of religion, which is rational religion. True religion could be summarized by the double commandment 'Fear God' and 'Love your neighbour.' As far as the Bible conforms to this, it is true. Where it does not, it must be rejected.[7] This position was popularized by John Toland (1670–1722), who wrote in his work *Christianity not Mysterious*:

[We] hold that *Reason* is the only Foundation of all Certitude; and that nothing reveal'd, whether as to its *Manner* or *Existence*, is more exempted from its Disquisitions, than the ordinary Phenomena of Nature. Wherefore, we likewise maintain, . . . that *there is nothing in the Gospel contrary to Reason, nor above it; and that no Christian Doctrine can be properly call'd a Mystery.*[8]

Thus Toland discards all content of the Bible which is contrary to reason.

The natural Result of what has been said is, That to believe the Divinity of *Scripture* or the Sense of any Passage thereof, without rational Proofs, and an evident Consistency, is a blameable Credulity, and a temerarious Opinion, ordinarily grounded upon an ignorant and wilful Disposition; but more generally maintain'd out of a gainful Prospect. For we frequently embrace certain doctrines not from any convincing Evidence in them, but because they serve our Designs better than the Truth; and because other Contradictions we are not willing to quit, are better defended by their means.[9]

This rationalist criticism of the Bible was the expression of a new occurrence of an old problem: the old authoritative text did not make sense any more for enlightened thinkers of the Age of Reason. It is the same problem that we have observed in our discussion of hermeneutics in antiquity. Then philosophers had developed the allegorical method of interpretation, which was used until the Reformation. For enlightened thinkers of the seventeenth and eighteenth centuries, this was not an option any more, and so they needed to develop a modern alternative. This alternative was found in explicit criticism of the Bible, which would develop into historical criticism, not only of the Bible, but also of all important works of the past.

Another new but related issue is the new understanding of reality. As a result of the scientific revolution, reality and truth are understood empirically. Thus a narrower understanding than in the pre-modern period becomes dominant; truth, especially the truth of texts concerning history, is understood to be factual truth which can be verified empirically.

Orthodoxy

One reaction to the new way of thinking was simply to ignore it. Old Protestant orthodoxy, that is, the confessional theology of the post-Reformation period, systematized and expounded upon the Reformation inheritance without interacting with the new philosophy. The same applies to the theology of the Roman Catholic Church after the Council of Trent: it developed and deepened neo-scholastic theology, without reference to the changing environment.

The Westminster Confession of Faith, which is the main Calvinist confession in the English-speaking world, is a good example of this attitude. Written in 1646, at a time when Descartes' works were discussed all over Europe, and four years after Galileo's death, the authors stated simply:

> The authority of the Holy Scripture, for which it ought to be believed, and obeyed, depends not upon the testimony of any man, or Church; but wholly upon God (who is truth itself) the author thereof: and therefore it is to be received, because it is the Word of God.[10]

The insights of the new age are neither accepted nor rejected, but simply ignored. This attitude compares with that of the Aristotelian philosopher Cesare Cremonini, who gained notoriety as the person who refused to look through Galileo's telescope, which would have shown him evidence for the heliocentric world-view.[11] He became the model for the later invention of the clergymen who were said to have refused Galieo's invitation to observe the moons of the planet Jupiter through the telescope.

Only a few theologians engaged with the new thinking at the time, such as Christoph Wittich (1625–87) and Balthasar Bekker (1634–98) in the Low Countries (today's Netherlands).[12] They explored how theology could adopt some of the insights of Cartesian philosophy. Although they were largely marginalized in their day, they would lay the foundation for the theological work of later generations.

Scottish common-sense philosophy and modern fundamentalism

Common sense

One development, which extends beyond the period discussed in this chapter, but which is worthwhile following in this context, is that from the new scientific world-view to modern fundamentalism and conservative evangelicalism.

It is often assumed that fundamentalism and conservative evangelicalism are remnants of a pre-modern way of thinking, and thus closer to 'authentic' Christianity than modern critical theology. This view, however, does not recognize that, as we have seen above, the pre-modern approach to the Bible was far from uncritical, using allegorical interpretation to solve difficulties in the text. Literal biblicism, as we know it today, is far removed from the way in which the ancients thought. In fact, modern fundamentalism and conservative evangelicalism, which are based on a literal interpretation of the Bible, are an essentially modern world-view. Although these groups often decry the Enlightenment as the beginning of scepticism and biblical criticism, their world-view is based on Enlightenment thought, namely the realism of the Scottish Enlightenment and the scientific approach of Francis Bacon.[13]

These two elements are combined with the notion of the inerrancy of the Bible and a particular form of supernaturalism, which assumes that the world largely works according to natural laws that God instituted at the creation of the world. From time to time, however, God may suspend these natural laws in order to make space for supernatural interference in the course of the world.

As we have seen, the question of our perception of the world was far from being unproblematic in antiquity and the Middle Ages. Augustine, who laid the foundation for medieval thinking, believed that our thinking and our perception of reality are mediated by language. In order to be understood, the inner word, the thought, had to be translated into the external word, which is the conceptual thought in lingual form (see p. 45). However, Augustine assumed that in the transition from the inner word to the external word, something was lost. Moreover, we recall that Augustine taught that when we think of an object, such as an apple on the table, our thought does not refer to the physical apple, but to the mental concept of the apple. So language and thought on the one hand and reality on the other are, as it were, one removed and not directly linked.

Philosophers like Descartes and Locke had followed this ancient tradition and assumed that language refers to the mental images, to ideas of the world. The Scottish Enlightenment saw the problem very differently. Thomas Reid (1710–96), the founder of Scottish 'common-sense' philosophy, proposed a much simpler epistemology (theory of knowledge). He suggested that when we perceive an object, an apple, for instance, then it is not the mental concept that we perceive, but the apple itself. Thus we are aware of real objects directly and without mediation.[14] So when I tell someone of the apple here on the table, then my speech (if I am not deceiving the hearer) refers directly to the apple, and not to my perception of the apple. And a reader who reads my description of the apple has the real situation straight before his or her mental eye. Reid assumes that this theory of knowledge and the resulting hermeneutics are 'common sense' and immediately plausible to the 'vulgar', that is, common person. He suggested that philosophers only complicate matters unnecessarily.

The hermeneutical implications of this philosophy are obvious. In understanding the world there is no problem whatsoever – we understand reality around us without mediation and directly. The problems Augustine raised and which have occupied philosophy ever since have been sidelined, if not plainly ignored. In the area of understanding utterance, text and speech, we can access the facts that these represent, which then can be judged to be true or false.

This hermeneutical approach is rightly called 'common sense', as most people who have not reflected on the problem involved in such naïve realism would probably hold these views. In addition, the dominance of the television affirms this view – an uncritical viewer can easily believe that the images on the screen represent reality without loss. However, on the screen as well as on the page of the book, critical reflection on the processes leading to the composition of the text or the film is necessary. One obvious criticism is that, if the plain facts are accessible to every sensible person, then why do intelligent people of good will disagree about the interpretation of texts, even about the interpretation of the Bible?

Common sense, Bacon and fundamentalism

Scottish common-sense philosophy became very influential in the USA from the late eighteenth century onwards. In particular, Princeton University, which was then known as The College of New Jersey, with its close connections to Scotland, was instrumental in embedding this view firmly in American intellectual life.[15]

If common-sense realism is used in biblical interpretation, then one assumes that the text does primarily refer to events, to facts, which the reader can perceive clearly when reading attentively. These facts are collected and ordered in the fashion of Francis Bacon's scientific method. From these gathered and ordered facts doctrines can then be derived.[16] As Charles Hodge (1797–1878), principal of Princeton Theological Seminary from 1851 onwards, wrote in the introduction to his *Systematic Theology*:

> If natural science be concerned with the facts and laws of nature, theology is concerned with the facts and the principles of the Bible. If the object of the one be to arrange and systematize the facts of the external world, and to ascertain the laws by which they are determined; the object of the other is to systematize and the facts of the Bible, and ascertain the principles or general truths which those facts involve.[17]

84

An obvious prerequisite for this approach is that the facts contained in the Bible must be accurate in an empirical sense. Events must have happened as they are described, because otherwise doctrines would be false just as physical laws derived from imprecise experiments will be flawed. Thus the doctrine of the 'inerrancy' of Scripture, that is, the factual truth of every statement of Scripture, is necessary for this way of thinking. This is far removed from what the authors of the Westminster Confession had in mind when they asserted the authority of Scripture as the inspired word of God (see p. 82). Nowhere in Chapter 1 of the Confession does it mention empirical factual truth. Factual inerrancy was not an issue for the authors of the Confession, unaffected as they were by the evolving scientific world-view.

Related to this is the view that, if the facts within the Bible are this plain and easily accessible, then one does not need the support of traditional interpretation any more. We saw above that the Reformers did not envisage that believers could go and interpret the Bible for themselves (see the section 'Sola scriptura', pp. 67–70). Interpretation had to be guided by the purified tradition, which was contained in confessional writings such as the catechisms. Virtually all people, at least in the Protestant countries, would have memorized the catechism of their respective tradition, and this knowledge would guide them in their interpretation of the Bible.

The new view, however, assumed that everyone could make the right sense of the Bible. Charles Hodge put it this way: 'The Bible is a plain book. It is intelligible by the people. And they have the right and are bound to read and interpret it for themselves; so that their faith may rest on the testimony of the Scriptures, and not that of the Church.'[18] Or, in George Marsden's summary, 'any sane and unbiased person of common sense could and must perceive the same things'.[19] This flies in the face of the hermeneutical tradition from Augustine into our day that an objective interpretation is impossible. It also denies the importance of prejudices and presuppositions for interpretation, which will be discussed in a later chapter (see the section 'Understanding', pp. 118–20).

Even if one agrees with this notion, it leaves the question as to why people then disagree on the plain and self-evident meaning of Scripture, either by developing diverse doctrines or by rejecting Scripture altogether. The answer to this is surprisingly simple; those people are beset by 'invincible prejudice' or 'unreasonable dogmatism'.[20] Consequently, those who disagree with the supposed common-sense interpretation of the Bible are blinded by previous convictions that they do not let go, so that their interpretation is prejudiced sense. But why then do biblical fundamentalists

85

disagree on so many things among themselves? And who is to judge when well-meaning and intelligent people disagree on the common-sense interpretation of the Bible?

The common-sense approach to the Bible can also lead to the opposite conclusion to that of fundamentalist interpretation. It can instead lead to the rejection of the Bible as essentially false. One may say that the events and 'facts' depicted in the Bible are evidently not accurate, because they disagree with the way in which we experience the world. The biblical narratives tell of miracles and they employ pseudo-science that is evidently wrong. Consequently, one can be led to reject the Bible out of hand as being inaccurate or even plainly wrong. Common-sense realism also underlies most popular rejections of the Bible as an authoritative text.

In sum, common-sense realism has become the 'folk epistemology'. But it must be kept in mind that this is not the 'natural' and therefore 'true' way of approaching knowledge, understanding and reality, as Thomas Reid assumed. It ignores a number of epistemological and hermeneutical problems. And it ignores the basis of all hermeneutical thinking since Augustine of Hippo: that understanding itself is problematic. However, this popular approach is still influential and is the basis for much uncritical reading, including that of fundamentalist biblicism. Biblicism in itself is not a purer, more authentic approach to the Bible, but is built on outdated epistemological assumptions. It may be worthwhile recalling John Maynard Keynes' words, which we quoted in the introduction: 'practical men, who believe themselves to be quite exempt from any intellectual influences, are usually the slaves of some defunct economist.'[21] (For 'economist' one may read 'theorist' here.)

Pietism

The foundation for an alternative approach to the Bible and other texts was laid by German pietism. Although there is hardly any affinity between pietism and modern criticism, pietist interpreters developed a view of texts, especially the biblical texts, which would allow interpreters to move beyond the rationalist Enlightenment hermeneutics in the early nineteenth century and to avoid the fundamentalist hermeneutics based on Scottish common sense. Pietist hermeneutics were based on the assumption that the most significant layer of meaning in a text is not the literal sense, but the underlying 'affect' or emotion. Thus the German pietist theologian August Hermann Francke (1663–1727) taught 'that an "affect" dwells within every word that is uttered in human discourse and that emerges from the inwardness of the soul'.[22] Understanding language this way, pietist interpreters were able to move beyond the 'verbal objectivism' of old Protestant orthodoxy and to focus on an inner experience, which is mediated by the text. Francke's younger contemporary Johann Jacob Rambach (1693–1735) reinforced this point when he wrote that 'the words of an *auctoris* [author] cannot be completely understood and interpreted without knowing from which affect they have flowed'.[23] Thus the affect is not just a secondary phenomenon, but the key to the meaning of every text. Explanation and understanding of the text are only stages on the way to having one's soul touched by the text.

This approach is closely related to the focus on the affect in pietist theology and spirituality. We will see in the next chapter how Friedrich Schleiermacher used this approach in a different context and introduced it into the mainstream of hermeneutical thinking.

Conclusion

The early modern period was a time of great transformations. The medieval world-view, in which humanity was the steward and interpreter of creation, with earth and humanity in the centre of the universe, was replaced by a scientific world-view, which led to humanity's mastery over nature and human reason's pre-eminence in the determination of truth. The emerging new world-view would supersede the old, medieval world-view, and become the foundation for both rationalist criticism and fundamentalism. But it would be open to criticism itself, and eventually it would be replaced by romanticism and idealism. The pietists had already laid the foundation for what would come after the Enlightenment and rationalism, a foundation on which Friedrich Schleiermacher would build one of the most impressive theological edifices.

Further reading

Chladenius, Johann Martin, 1989, 'On the Concept of Interpretation', in: Kurt Mueller-Vollmer (ed.), *The Hermeneutics Reader: Texts of the German Tradition from the Enlightenment to the Present*, New York: Continuum, pp. 55–64.

Francke, August Hermann, 1723, *Praelectiones hermeneuticae ad viam dextre indagandi et exponendi sensum Scripturae: theologiae studiosis ostendendam, in Academia Hallensi, aliquot abhinc annis, publice habitae: Adiecta est in fine Brevis et luculenta Scripturam S. cum fructu legendi institutio, pro rudioribus scripta, et antea seorsim edita*, Halae Magdeburgicae: Litteris et impensis Orphanotrophei.

Ginsborg, Hannah, 2005, 'Kant's Aesthetics and Teleology', in: *The Stanford Encyclopedia of Philosophy* (website, Fall 2005), edited by Edward N. Zalta. Available from http://plato.stanford.edu/archives/fall2005/entries/kant-aesthetics/.

Gower, Barry, 1997, *Scientific Method: An Historical and Philosophical Introduction*, London: Routledge.

Johnson, Robert, 2004, 'Kant's Moral Philosophy', in: *The Stanford Encyclopedia of Philosophy* (website, Spring 2004), edited by Edward N. Zalta. Available from http://plato.stanford.edu/archives/spr2004/entries/kant-moral/.

Lessing, Gotthold Ephraim, 1956, 'On the Proof of the Spirit and of Power', in: Henry Chadwick (ed.), *Theological Writings: Selections in Translation*, London: Adam & Charles Black, pp. 51–6.

Lessing, Gotthold Ephraim, 1956, *Theological Writings: Selections in Translation*, edited by Henry Chadwick, London: Adam & Charles Black.

Marsden, George M., 1991, *Understanding Fundamentalism and Evangelicalism*, Grand Rapids, Mich.: W.B. Eerdmans.

Marsden, George M., 2006, *Fundamentalism and American Culture*, 2nd edn, New York: Oxford University Press.

Nadler, Steven, 2006, 'Baruch Spinoza', in: *The Stanford Encyclopedia of Philosophy* (website, Fall 2006), edited by Edward N. Zalta. Available from http://plato.stanford.edu/archives/fall2006/entries/spinoza/.

Rambach, Johann Jacob, 1725, *Institutiones hermeneuticae sacrae: variis observationibus copiossimisque exemplis Biblicis*, 2nd edn, Ienae: Ex officina Hartungiana.

Scholder, Klaus, 1990, *The Birth of Modern Critical Theology: Origins and Problems of Biblical Criticism in the Seventeenth Century*, London and Philadelphia: SCM Press; Trinity Press International.

Toland, John, 1964, *Christianity not Mysterious: Faksimile-Neudruck der Erstausgabe London 1696 mit einer Einleitung von Günter Gawlick und einem textkritischen Anhang*, Stuttgart: Friedrich Frommann Verlag.

Watkins, Eric, 2003, 'Kant's Philosophy of Science', in: *The Stanford Encyclopedia of Philosophy* (website, Winter 2003), edited by Edward N. Zalta. Available from http://plato.stanford.edu/archives/win2003/entries/kant-science/.

Yaffe, Gideon, 2005, 'Thomas Reid', in: *The Stanford Encyclopedia of Philosophy* (website, Winter 2005), edited by Edward N. Zalta. Available from http://plato.stanford.edu/archives/win2005/entries/reid.

Notes

1 Klaus Scholder, 1990, *The Birth of Modern Critical Theology: Origins and Problems of Biblical Criticism in the Seventeenth Century*, London and Philadelphia: SCM Press; Trinity Press International, p. 83.

2 Steven Nadler, 2006, 'Baruch Spinoza', in: *The Stanford Encyclopedia of Philosophy* (website, Fall 2006), edited by Edward N. Zalta. Available from http://plato.stanford.edu/archives/fall2006/entries/spinoza/.

3 Barry Gower, 1997, *Scientific Method: An Historical and Philosophical Introduction*, London: Routledge, pp. 52–5.

4 Johann Martin Chladenius, 1989, 'On the Concept of Interpretation',

in: Kurt Mueller-Vollmer (ed.), *The Hermeneutics Reader: Texts of the German Tradition from the Enlightenment to the Present*, New York: Continuum, p. 62.

5   Gotthold Ephraim Lessing, 1956, 'On the Proof of the Spirit and of Power', in: Henry Chadwick (ed.), *Lessing's Theological Writings: Selections in Translation*, London: Adam & Charles Black, p. 53.

6   Lessing, 'On the Proof of the Spirit and of Power', p. 55.

7   Nadler, 'Baruch Spinoza'.

8   John Toland, 1964, *Christianity not Mysterious: Faksimile-Neudruck der Erstausgabe London 1696 mit einer Einleitung von Günter Gawlick und einem textkritischen Anhang*, Stuttgart: Friedrich Frommann Verlag, p. 6 (italics in the original).

9   Toland, *Christianity not Mysterious*, pp. 36–7 (italics in the original).

10   *The Westminster Confession of Faith* (1646), I. IV. In: Presbyterian Church (USA), 1999, Book of Confessions: Study edition, Louisville, Ky.: Geneva Press, p. 122. Also available from: http://www.reformed.org/documents/westminster_conf_of_faith.html.

11   Gower, *Scientific Method*, p. 33.

12   Scholder, *The Birth of Modern Critical Theology*, pp. 122–9.

13   In this section, I am largely following the argument of George Marsden, as set out in George M. Marsden, 1991, *Understanding Fundamentalism and Evangelicalism*, Grand Rapids, Mich.: W. B. Eerdmans; George M. Marsden, 2006, *Fundamentalism and American Culture*, 2nd edn, New York: Oxford University Press. I recommend these books to those interested in this field for further study.

14   Gideon Yaffe, 2005, 'Thomas Reid', in: *The Stanford Encyclopedia of Philosophy* (website, Winter 2005), edited by Edward N. Zalta. Available from http://plato.stanford.edu/archives/win2005/entries/reid.

15   Marsden, *Fundamentalism and American Culture*, pp. 110–11.

16   Marsden, *Fundamentalism and American Culture*, pp. 55–62 and 109–18.

17   Quoted by Marsden, *Fundamentalism and American Culture*, p. 112.

18   Quoted by Marsden, *Fundamentalism and American Culture*, p. 111.

19   Marsden, *Fundamentalism and American Culture*, p. 111.

20   Marsden, *Fundamentalism and American Culture*, p. 116.

21   John Maynard Keynes, *The General Theory of Employment, Interest and Money*, London: Macmillan, p. 383.

22   Jean Grondin, *Introduction to Philosophical Hermeneutics*, New Haven: Yale University Press, p. 60, referring to August Hermann Francke, 1723, *Praelectiones hermeneuticae ad viam dextre indagandi et exponendi sensum Scripturae: theologiae studiosis ostendendam, in Academia Hallensi, aliquot abhinc annis, publice habitae: Adiecta est in fine Brevis et luculenta Scripturam S. cum fructu legendi institutio, pro rudioribus scripta, et antea seorsim edita*, Halae Magdeburgicae: Litteris et impensis Orphanotrophei, p. 196.

23   Johann Jacob Rambach, 1725, *Institutiones hermeneuticae sacrae: variis observationibus copiossimisque exemplis Biblicis*, 2nd edn, Ienae: Ex officina Hartungiana, quoted from Grondin, *Introduction to Philosophical Hermeneutics*, p. 61.

6

Friedrich Schleiermacher: Hermeneutics as the Art of Understanding

Introduction and biography

Friedrich Daniel Ernst Schleiermacher (1768–1834) was arguably the most important theologian of the nineteenth century; his work has influenced all subsequent theology, either in being embraced or rejected. His main work, *The Christian Faith*, is one of the greatest theological works, together with Thomas Aquinas' *Summa Theologiae*, John Calvin's *Institutes of the Christian Religion* and possibly Karl Barth's *Church Dogmatics* – I write 'possibly', as the *Church Dogmatics* is not yet old enough to be regarded an enduring classic, although it is most likely to pass the test of time.

Schleiermacher was not only a theologian. He was at the centre of the early Romantic Movement which overcame the Enlightenment in broader cultural terms. He was an eminent classicist and philosopher, and his translation of Plato's dialogues into German is still the standard. In addition, Schleiermacher was deeply involved in reforming the German university system and bringing about the Prussian Union of Calvinist and Lutheran Churches.

Schleiermacher was born in 1768 as son of a Reformed military chaplain, who had sympathies with the Moravian Brethren (Herrnhuter Brüdergemeinde). He was educated in Moravian institutions, where he was formed in the pietistic traditions of this group. Due to his growing scepticism of the doctrines taught there, he moved to the University of Halle, where he was exposed to Enlightenment thought, especially Immanuel Kant's philosophy. After graduating, he worked as a private tutor and then as a country clergyman. In 1796 he moved to Berlin as chaplain to the Charité, an eminent hospital. During this time, he became involved in the romantic circle, which was at the centre of intellectual life in the Prussian capital at the time. While in Berlin Schleiermacher wrote and published his famous speeches *On Religion* (1799).

Schleiermacher left Berlin and, after some time as pastor in a country town, became professor at the University of Halle, where he developed a course of lectures on hermeneutics, which he taught repeatedly, both in Halle and later in Berlin, until his death.

During the Napoleonic Wars, after the French army had occupied Halle, Schleiermacher returned to Berlin, where he was involved in planning the new university. He became founding dean of the theological faculty in 1810. The following year, Schleiermacher was invited to join the Prussian Academy, in which he became an important figure. Among his addresses given to the Academy are two important lectures on hermeneutics.

Schleiermacher remained in Berlin until his death in 1834.

Sources

Schleiermacher's thoughts on hermeneutics are contained in his lectures, which were edited after his death by his friend Friedrich Lücke on the basis of Schleiermacher's handwritten manuscripts.[1] The manuscripts are also published in a critical edition.[2] Another source is the addresses to the Berlin academy of 1829.[3] Furthermore, in order to understand Schleiermacher's hermeneutics in the context of his thought, his speeches *On Religion*[4] of 1799 and his dogmatic work *The Christian Faith*[5] (first edition 1821/22, second, significantly revised edition 1830/31) are of importance.

Feeling and language

Due to his education and personal development, Schleiermacher combined two traditions within himself, namely the pietist tradition, which based its hermeneutics on the 'affect', and the Enlightenment tradition, including the critique of rationalism by Immanuel Kant (1724–1804) (see p. 86). His great achievement lies in the creative combination of these two traditions into a theology and, for our purposes more important, a hermeneutical theory that would be able to overcome the Enlightenment, both in its rationalist as well as in its naïve realist common-sense approach.

At the heart of Schleiermacher's theology lies the notion of feeling. For him, religion is not based on knowledge (metaphysics) or doing (ethics), but on feeling. The young Schleiermacher develops this theme in the *Speeches* using the terms 'intuition and feeling',[6] or 'sensibility and taste for the universe'.[7] In his later theology, he expresses this in terms of 'immediate [i.e. unmediated] feeling of absolute dependence'.[8]

When the young Schleiermacher speaks of 'intuition and feeling', he refers to romanticist epistemology. When encountering and perceiving something, there is first an immediate (unmediated) impression, which is not conceptual and therefore not yet understood. One type of this immediate experience is the experience of the universe, of the totality of being. This type of experience constitutes the religious experience. The immediate experience is consequently understood and conceptualized through the parallel processes of intuition and feeling. While one is 'intuiting' the universe (or a more mundane perception), a feeling is formed, in other words something changes in the beholder.[9] Religious language tries to communicate this feeling and the underlying immediate experience. We will come back to these concepts later in this chapter.

In his later life, Schleiermacher refers to the 'immediate feeling of absolute dependence' as the basis of religion. Every human being has an inborn feeling that we are not the origin of our own existence, but that we are dependent on something above us. (Note that 'feeling' [*Gefühl*] does not mean 'emotion' in this context, but a non-verbal form of self-consciousness.)[10] Some people have this feeling more strongly than others, and may express it in different ways. To communicate this feeling to others is the purpose of religious language.[11]

In both cases one has to communicate one's religious feeling in order to communicate religion. This takes place mainly, but not exclusively, through teaching and preaching.[12] The preacher communicates his or her feeling through language. This fundamental theological concern is the basis for Schleiermacher's hermeneutical thinking.

Schleiermacher uses the ancient distinction between the *verbum interius* and the *verbum externum*, the inner and the external word, which we encountered in Augustine's hermeneutical thinking (see p. 44). 'Thought is prepared by inner discourse, and to this extent discourse is only thought itself which has come into existence.'[14] (Note that Schleiermacher also draws on Plato's concept of thought as inner dialogue.) This short remark can be expanded by the notes taken by Schleiermacher's students:

This leads to the unity of speech and thought; language is the manner in which thought is real. For there are no thoughts without speech. The speaking of the words relates solely to the presence of another person, and to this extent is contingent. But no one can think without words. Without words the thought is not yet completed and clear.[15]

Schleiermacher does not, however, discuss the fundamental difficulties of the transition of pre-verbal thought to language that Augustine recognized and described, although there are clues elsewhere in his work that he is aware of this. Nevertheless, Schleiermacher recognizes a number of areas in which understanding is problematic.

The art of understanding

First of all, Schleiermacher asserts that in the realm of understanding, misunderstanding is the norm and understanding the exception. In this he goes beyond the hermeneutical tradition which assumed that understanding is the norm and misunderstanding the avoidable exception. If misunderstanding is the norm, then understanding must be a conscious act, guided by certain rules, which will enable successful understanding.[16] This may be different for trivial conversations and business communications, but for more complex and deeper utterances, such as letters, poems, novels, treatises and the like, understanding must be actively sought.

Schleiermacher suggests certain rules of interpretation that will enable the interpreter to understand an utterance properly. However, these rules are not to be followed slavishly – they are more like the rules of a game. Footballers, for example, know the rules of the game and possess a set of necessary skills. When a player gains possession of the ball, he or she will have to make an intuitive decision as to what to do next within the framework of the rules. The rules do not prescribe what the player is to do with the ball. This is the same with the interpreter, because in a given situation no one can tell the interpreter which rule to apply and how. Interpretation is both a rule-guided and an intuitive act, and thus Schleiermacher calls understanding a technique or an art.[17]

The aim of interpretation is, for Schleiermacher, the understanding of the thought content that is contained in an utterance.[18] The ideal to which interpreters aspire is that they may understand 'the utterance at first just as well and then better than its author'.[19] This may sound like an unrealistic expectation, and Schleiermacher is aware that this is an infinite task. It is an ideal towards which interpreters work. It also contains the recognition that an author is not always aware of all the influences on his or her writing; he or she may not be conscious of all the linguistic influences that shape the composition of the text, and of the psychological and external influences that shape his or her creativity at a particular time. In bringing these things to light, the interpreter will be aware of more factors that shaped the utterance than the author, and thus interpreters can potentially understand a work better than its author.

Grammatical and psychological interpretation

In his hermeneutical theory, Schleiermacher distinguishes between grammatical and psychological interpretation. Both are equally important, and none can be exercised before the other. Grammatical interpretation is concerned with the place of the text in the development of a language in general, while psychological interpretation, which Schleiermacher can misleadingly call technical interpretation, is concerned with the place of the text in the development of the author, both in his or her external life and inner development.

Grammatical interpretation

Grammatical interpretation relates to the relation between a text and the language in which it is written. It consists of two elements. First, it is concerned with the way in which the language in which the text is written influenced its composition, and second, with the influence of the particular text on the development of the language.

The first point contains a number of important insights. To begin with, language forms our thinking. We saw above that Schleiermacher thought that 'language is the manner in which thought is real'. Thought, as soon as it becomes conscious, is always constituted in language. Consequently, the language in which we think will always exercise a great deal of influence on our thought. There are certain connections and associations that can be made in English but not in German, and the difference will be even bigger when one compares Indo-European with non-Indo-European languages. Thoughts can be thought in certain ways in one language but not in another. Thus language determines what we can think.

An illustration of this can be found in George Orwell's famous novel *Nineteen Eighty-Four*. Orwell describes a totalitarian government that is determined to introduce a new language, known as Newspeak, in order to prevent people even from thinking seditious thoughts. An explanation of this is given by a character named Symes, who works on the revision of the new dictionary:

'It's a beautiful thing, the destruction of words. Of course the great wastage is in the verbs and adjectives, but there are hundreds of nouns that can be got rid of as well. It isn't only the synonyms; there are also the antonyms. . . .

'Don't you see that the whole aim of Newspeak is to narrow the range of thought? In the end we shall make thoughtcrime literally im-

94

possible, because there will be no words in which to express it. Every concept that can ever be needed will be expressed by exactly one word, with its meaning rigidly defined and all its subsidiary meanings rubbed out and forgotten.[20]

According to his students' notes, Schleiermacher makes the same point, although with a descriptive rather than prescriptive intention, when he says that the 'individual is determined in his thought by the (common) language and can think only the thoughts which already have their designation in language'.[21] Thus speech or writing can only be thought of as a modification of existing language, while language forms itself in the act of thinking, speaking or writing.

It is the task of grammatical interpretation to identify the way in which the language forms itself in the utterance. Thus interpreters need to be thoroughly familiar with the language of the utterance, be it a foreign language or their own language as it was used in another period. Then they will understand the individual utterance as an expression of the general language.[22]

At the same time, the utterance will change the language. This is obvious with the great works of literature, which make new connections by inventing metaphors and allusions. Think only of the contribution Shakespeare made to the development of the English language. However, not only the great classics, but also minor works (possibly even including this book) contribute to the growth of language by introducing minor innovations or promoting other recent developments. In this respect, the text under interpretation can be seen as a 'point of development for the language'.[23] Schleiermacher understands that this is something that cannot be found out by mere analysis – he says that the interpreter 'conjectures' how a given utterance influences the further development of the language.

Thus the grammatical interpretation seeks to understand the place of a given text within the context of the whole language in which it is written, how this language influenced the composition of the utterance, and how the utterance, in turn, influenced the development of the language. Schleiermacher gives a number of rules that will help interpreters to achieve this. These begin with profound knowledge of the language in question, to the extent that the interpreter should be independent of dictionaries, and thorough knowledge of its literature.[24] Further advice contains technical instruction (technical in our sense, not Schleiermacher's), which is not relevant in our context. Although Schleiermacher's grammatical interpretation may look formalistic, it is a necessary prerequisite for the psychological interpretation. It also serves as a reminder that interpretation of a text from a translation or with rudimentary knowledge of the language will always be superficial.[25]

Psychological interpretation

Psychological interpretation is concerned with the creative act of the individual. It seeks to establish how the utterance relates to previous utterance of the person, and how the person developed from the point when he or she made the utterance. Thus the aim of psychological interpretation is to establish how this particular utterance relates to the totality of the personal development of the author.[26]

It is a necessary prerequisite for psychological interpretation to establish the way in which the author was influenced by the literature of his or her time, by the development of literary genres and styles, and the conventions of his or her day. Also the author's general style (Schleiermacher uses the term 'manner') needs to be understood. This will enable the interpreter to read the utterance within the context of the possibilities of expression that were available to the author.[27] Only then can the interpreter begin to investigate 'that by which the author is moved to the utterance'.[28]

The interpreter employs two methods in order to achieve this, the divinatory and the comparative method. The comparative method consists in the comparison of the author and his or her utterance with other people and writings. Thus the individual contribution of the author can be recognized against the foil of the 'universal', of the characters and writings of his or her day.[29]

The divinatory method, in Schleiermacher's own words, 'is the one in which one, so to speak, transforms oneself into the other person and tries to understand the individual element directly'.[30] In other words, it consists of making an informed guess, based on the common humanity of author and interpreter, as to what thought the author tried to express.

Both methods, the divinatory and the comparative, are related to each other. In order to be able to make an *informed* guess, the interpreter needs sufficient background information, which is obtained by comparison, while comparison alone will never lead to the author's thought, so that at some point the interpreter has to leap, so to speak, and make the guess. The guess then is validated or falsified and corrected by comparison, and a new, refined guess is made. Thus the interpreter understands the author better and better, ideally to the point when the interpreter understands 'the utterance first as well and then better than its author'.[31] It must be emphasized again that Schleiermacher sees this as the ideal, which is an infinite task, which can only be achieved by approximation.[32]

Grammatical and psychological

Consequently, grammatical and psychological interpretation are inter-related. In order to understand the author's thought, the interpreter must know the ways in which the author was able to express himself or herself. Thus the language in which the author wrote must be fully known. At the same time, only to understand the language will never allow access to the author's thought and individuality. So the author must also be under-stood as an individual expressing a particular thought. This, in turn, is impossible without understanding the language.

In short, Schleiermacher's hermeneutics are an acknowledgement of the intimate connection between individuality, thought and language. One can only think using existing language, and at the same time lan-guage only exists as concrete thought or utterance. One's individuality is constituted in one's thoughts, and thus in language. So Schleiermacher can describe the individual as the 'location in which a given language forms itself in an individual manner'.[33] Thus the individual is constituted in language, but at the same time remains an individual. Schleiermacher is raising a number of questions here that were to be taken up and dis-cussed widely in the twentieth century.

Historical criticism

The emphasis on the need to read a text within the context of its time and culture raises the need for historical criticism. Both grammatical and psychological interpretation set the author within his or her context, and analyse which ways of thinking and expressing thought were available to the author. We recall the hermeneutics of the Enlightenment, both the rationalist approach, which would only accept as true what conforms to human reason, and the common-sense realist approach, which focused on the text as repository of plain facts. In this context, Schleiermacher's hermeneutics show an important way forward; it is not only the reliable transmission of facts that makes a text relevant, but the thought that the author wants to communicate. Thus Schleiermacher can assume the his-torical unreliability of much of the Bible, and at the same time affirm its authority. This authority is based on the thought that the authors want to communicate, and this is their faith which they found in the encounter with Jesus Christ or with those who communicated this faith to them.[34]

Thus Schleiermacher views the New Testament as a selection of texts that were written to communicate faith, which is the religious feeling or consciousness brought about by the encounter with Jesus or the testimony to him. Historical inaccuracies do not impede this function of Scripture. This gives Schleiermacher and those who follow him a great deal of flexibility in their approach to Scripture, as historical finding will not be able to destroy the foundation of the authority of Scripture, which is the communal faith of the Church in the religion the Bible communicates.

The hermeneutic circle

Understanding is, for Schleiermacher, an indefinite, a never-ending task. It will have become apparent in the earlier discussion that Schleiermacher sees understanding as essentially circular in so far as it is concerned with understanding something particular, such as a passage of a text, or a particular text, or a particular author, while the particular can only be understood if one has understood the whole – the whole text, if one is interpreting a passage, the whole of an author's work and related literature for the interpretation of a text, and humankind in order to understand an individual. However, the whole is always the sum of its parts, so it cannot be understood without understanding of the parts. For Schleiermacher, the circularity of understanding is a universal principle, underpinning all interpretation.

The basic form of the circle is that a text can only be understood from its parts, and the parts only from the whole.[35] Schleiermacher goes beyond this and posits that the 'vocabulary and the history of the era relate the whole from which his writings must be understood as the part, and the whole must, in turn, be understood from the part'.[36] By extension, an individual work can only be understood within the context of the complete life and work of the author, the author's work only within the context of all the literature written in this language, and so forth *ad infinitum*. The question is how to get into the circle. This is where Schleiermacher's divination and comparison come into play again and assume a universal role. One enters the circle by making an informed guess, but this guess then needs to be controlled and corrected by the emerging understanding of the whole. The corrected guess, which will hopefully be better than the initial one, is then controlled by an even better informed comparison and so forth. Thus the hermeneutic circle is not really a circle, but an upward spiral of ever-better understanding. This task is never finished, because there is always something more to understand – there is always something else that needs to be added to the universal against which the individual is understood. One work needs to be understood against the whole work of the author; the whole work of the author in the context of all the literature in that language; this, in turn, in the context of literature of different languages that may have influenced or have been influenced either by this work or by the development of literature in this particular language. Then there is the language, which can only be understood by knowledge of literature, and by comparison with other languages and so forth *ad infinitum*.

For example, Augustine's *Confessions* can only be understood in the context of Augustine's whole work, which can only be understood as part of Latin theological and devotional literature, which can only be understood as part of early Christian literature in both Greek and Latin, and neo-Platonic thought, which can only be understood in the context of Greek philosophical writings. This list could be extended indefinitely.

Consequently, the task of understanding will never be fully accomplished. For practical reasons, the interpreter will have to call this to a halt and interpret another book when he or she has understood it sufficiently for the present purpose. However, the process of understanding still never stops, as one learns more and more about literature, language and life. Everyone will be familiar with the much better understanding of a book which one re-reads after some time has passed since the first reading.

The problem of hermeneutics for Schleiermacher is that there is always something else to be understood in order to gain an even better understanding of the given utterance. Interestingly, he does not discuss the problem Augustine posed when he recognized that something is lost in the translation from the pre-verbal thought, the *verbum interius*, into the conceptual thought or utterance, the *verbum externum*, and the resulting fundamental inability to understand fully and completely, even if the interpreter had all possible information at hand (see pp. 45–7). Schleiermacher also does not discuss the role of the interpreter's subjectivity in the process of understanding. As we will see, the combination of these issues will occupy much of twentieth-century hermeneutical thinking.

Outlook: Perception, feeling and language

At one point in Schleiermacher's early work, namely in the *Speeches* of 1799, he introduces a train of thought that will be the starting point for

interesting later developments in hermeneutical thinking. It is his understanding of the pre-lingual and pre-conceptual perception of the world,
which he describes in one of the key passages of the *Speeches*:

> That first mysterious moment that occurs in every sensory perception,
> before intuition and feeling are separated, where sense and its objects
> have, as it were, flowed into one another and become one, before both
> turn back to their original position – I know how indescribable it is
> and how quickly it passes away. But I wish that you were able to hold
> on to it and also to recognize it again in the higher and divine religious
> activity of the mind. Would that I could and might express it, at least
> indicate it, without having to desecrate it! It is as fleeting and transpar-
> ent as the first scent with which the dew gently caresses the waking
> flowers, as modest and delicate as a maiden's kiss, as holy and fruitful
> as a nuptial embrace; indeed, not *like* these, but it is itself all of these. A
> manifestation, an event develops quickly and magically into an image
> of the universe.[37]

In this flowery language, which is typical of the *Speeches*, Schleiermacher
expresses a profound insight. We remember that for Augustine, the content of the mind, of the memory, was always complete, put there by God
(see pp. 41–2). From this repository of memories thought would enter
consciousness and there be translated into language. This neo-Platonic
understanding of knowledge was not tenable any more in Schleiermacher's time. Following authors like John Locke people understood
that the mind is initially an empty slate, which is gradually filled by sensory impressions. This attitude, however, neglected the problem of the
verbum interius and the *verbum externum*. In this context it is interesting to observe that Schleiermacher sees knowledge entering the mind in
an event, when the universe discloses itself to the beholder in a direct and
immediate impression, an impression that is pre-verbal, not conceptual.
Schleiermacher does not draw out the conclusions from this in the context of his Augustinian hermeneutics. It will be left to the existentialist
hermeneutics of the twentieth century to investigate this problem further
(see pp. 137–8). However, in raising the problem of pre-verbal manifestation of reality, Schleiermacher prepared the ground for a discussion on a
scope which he himself would have been unable to imagine.

While the young Schleiermacher sees language as referring to the pre-
verbal experience of the immediate encounter with the universe, that is,
the totality of being, the mature Schleiermacher will see religious language
primarily referring to the immediate feeling of absolute dependence, or,

in other words, the religious self-consciousness. In *The Christian Faith*, Schleiermacher argues that all theological propositions can point back to the immediate feeling of absolute dependence.

> Since the feeling of absolute dependence, even in the realm of redemption, only puts in an appearance, i.e. becomes real self-consciousness in time, in so far as it is aroused by another determination of the self consciousness and unites itself therewith, every formula for that feeling is a formula for a definite state of mind; and consequently all propositions of Dogmatics must be capable of being set up as such formulæ.[38]

In other words, the fundamental form of theological language is that which refers to human states of mind, that is, to the immediate feeling of absolute dependence. Other theological language, in order to be proper theological language, must be derived from this fundamental form. Schleiermacher defines two other forms of theological language, which are 'conceptions of divine attributes and modes of action', on the one hand, and 'utterances regarding the constitution of the world', on the other.[39] Thus all theological language regarding God and God's action as well as about the world, including human society, are derived from the fundamental form, namely that referring to the religious self-consciousness.

Consequently, Schleiermacher organizes his dogmatic work *The Christian Faith* according to these forms of theological language. He discusses the development of religious self-consciousness and the dialectic between sin and redemption according to the three forms first in relation to the religious self-consciousness, and then in relation to the divine and to the world.

Again, as we will see below, Schleiermacher's insight that the basic form of theological language is the religious self-consciousness, and all other theological language is derived from it, have significant implications for the hermeneutical debate in the twentieth and twenty-first centuries.

Conclusion

Friedrich Schleiermacher has been called the father of modern hermeneutics, and justifiably so.[40] Earlier, we suggested that Augustine might then be the grandfather of modern hermeneutics. This is because Schleiermacher's achievement consists in introducing Augustinian hermeneutical thinking into the modern debate. He combines the distinction between the inner and the external word with a modern theory of mind. And although he views hermeneutics as the art of understanding, that is, as the theory and practice of textual interpretation, he widens the field significantly in two ways. First, Schleiermacher posits that misunderstanding is the norm in the interpretation of human utterances. This widens the significance of hermeneutics, because it is now not only a tool to be employed if we encounter difficulties in understanding an utterance, but one that must be employed in every act of interpretation in order to avoid the otherwise inevitable misunderstanding. Thus hermeneutics becomes universally applicable.

Second, Schleiermacher raises the question of the role of hermeneutics in our understanding not only of texts, but also the self when he suggests that in the 'event' reality manifests itself immediately and pre-lingually. So what happens if this pre-lingual presence is translated into conscious and conceptual thought, into language? Schleiermacher did not develop this question any further, but as we will see, it would become the foundation of an important tradition of hermeneutical thinking in the twentieth and twenty-first century (see pp. 137, 212–13).

In sum, Schleiermacher stands at the threshold between pre-modern and modern hermeneutics. He formulates new questions and raises problems that are typical of modern hermeneutics in the twentieth and twenty-first centuries, combining them with the insights of classical ancient hermeneutics, especially that of Augustine of Hippo. In this he is a giant on whose shoulders twentieth-century hermeneutical thinkers and interpreters of texts stand.

Further reading

Clements, K. W., 1987, *Friedrich Schleiermacher: Pioneer of Modern Theology, The Making of Modern Theology*, London and San Francisco: Collins.

Crouter, Richard, 2005, *Friedrich Schleiermacher: Between Enlightenment and Romanticism*, Cambridge and New York: Cambridge University Press.

Gerrish, B. A., 1984, *A Prince of the Church: Schleiermacher and the Beginnings of Modern Theology*, Philadelphia: Fortress Press.

Lawler, Edwina G., Jeffrey Kinlaw and Ruth D. Richardson (eds), 2006, *The State of Schleiermacher Scholarship today: Selected Essays*, Lewiston, NY: Edwin Mellen Press.

Mariña, Jacqueline, 2005, *The Cambridge Companion to Friedrich Schleiermacher, Cambridge Companions to Religion*, Cambridge and Melbourne: Cambridge University Press.

Orwell, George, 1990, *Nineteen Eighty-Four*, Harmondsworth: Penguin.

Palmer, Richard E., 1969, *Hermeneutics: Interpretation Theory in Schleiermacher, Dilthey, Heidegger, and Gadamer, Northwestern University Studies in Phenomenology & Existential Philosophy*, Evanston: Northwestern University Press.

Redeker, Martin, 1973, *Schleiermacher: Life and Thought*, Philadelphia: Fortress Press.

Schleiermacher, Friedrich, 1977, *Hermeneutics: The Handwritten Manuscripts*, edited by Heinz Kimmerle, Missoula, Mont.: Scholars Press.

Schleiermacher, Friedrich, 1996, *On Religion: Speeches to its Cultured Despisers*, edited by Richard Crouter, *Cambridge Texts in the History of Philosophy*, Cambridge and New York: Cambridge University Press.

Schleiermacher, Friedrich, 1998, *Hermeneutics and Criticism and other Writings*, translated by Andrew Bowie, *Cambridge Texts in the History of Philosophy*, Cambridge and New York: Cambridge University Press.

Schleiermacher, Friedrich, 1999, *The Christian Faith*, translated by James S. Stewart and H. R. Mackintosh, Edinburgh: T & T Clark.

Sorrentino, Sergio, 1992, *Schleiermacher's Philosophy and the Philosophical Tradition*, *Schleiermacher Studies and Translations*, vol. 11, Lewiston, NY: E. Mellen Press.

Sykes, S. W., 1971, *Friedrich Schleiermacher, Makers of Contemporary Theology*, London Lutterworth Press.

Notes

1 Lücke's edition is published, together with other writings on hermeneutics, in Friedrich Schleiermacher, 1998, *Hermeneutics and Criticism and other Writings*, translated by Andrew Bowie, *Cambridge Texts in the History of Philosophy*, Cambridge; New York: Cambridge University Press. An abridged version is also contained in Kurt Mueller-Vollmer (ed.), 1989, *The Hermeneutics Reader: Texts of the German Tradition from the Enlightenment to the Present*, New York: Continuum, pp. 73–96.

2 Friedrich Schleiermacher, 1977, *Hermeneutics: The Handwritten Manuscripts*, edited by Heinz Kimmerle, Missoula, Mont.: Scholars Press.

3 Schleiermacher, *Hermeneutics: The Handwritten Manuscripts*, pp. 175–214, also contained in: David E. Klemm (ed.), 1986, *Hermeneutical Inquiry: Volume 1: The Interpretation of Texts, AAR Studies in Religion*, vol. 43, Atlanta: Scholars Press, pp. 61–88.

4 Friedrich Schleiermacher, 1996, *On Religion: Speeches to its Cultured Despisers*, edited by Richard Crouter, *Cambridge Texts in the History of Philosophy*, Cambridge and New York: Cambridge University Press.

5 Friedrich Schleiermacher, 1999, *The Christian Faith*, translated by James S. Stewart and H. R. Mackintosh, Edinburgh: T & T Clark.

6 Schleiermacher, *On Religion*, p. 22.

7 Schleiermacher, *On Religion*, p. 23.

8 Schleiermacher, *The Christian Faith*, §32, p. 131.

9 Schleiermacher, *On Religion*, p. 29.

10 Schleiermacher, *The Christian Faith*, §3.2, pp. 6–7.

11 Schleiermacher, *The Christian Faith*, §133, pp. 611–13.

12 Schleiermacher, *The Christian Faith*, §133, pp. 611–13.

13 Schleiermacher, *Hermeneutics and Criticism*, pp. 7–8.

14   Schleiermacher, *Hermeneutics and Criticism*, p. 7.

15   Schleiermacher, *Hermeneutics and Criticism*, p. 8.

16   Schleiermacher, *Hermeneutics and Criticism*, pp. 21–2

17   The term *Kunstlehre*, which Schleiermacher uses in the original German, bears resonances of the Greek word *technē*, which means craft or technique.

18   Schleiermacher, *Hermeneutics and Criticism*, p. 8

19   Schleiermacher, *Hermeneutics and Criticism*, p. 23.

20   George Orwell, 1990, *Nineteen Eighty-Four*, Harmondsworth: Penguin, pp. 44–5.

21   Schleiermacher, *Hermeneutics and Criticism*, p. 9.

22   It may be worthwhile pointing out here that these insights foreshadow Ferdinand de Saussure's distinction between *la langue* (the totality of a language as system) and *parole* (the utterance as a manifestation of *la langue*). (See pp. 162–3.)

23   Schleiermacher, *Hermeneutics and Criticism*, p. 23.

24   Schleiermacher, *Hermeneutics and Criticism*, pp. 24f, 38f.

25   This should raise questions about the neglect of classical scholarship in schools and universities in our time.

26   Schleiermacher, *Hermeneutics and Criticism*, p. 23, 107.

27   Schleiermacher, *Hermeneutics and Criticism*, p. 92.

28   Schleiermacher, *Hermeneutics and Criticism*, p. 90.

29   Schleiermacher, *Hermeneutics and Criticism*, p. 92.

30   Schleiermacher, *Hermeneutics and Criticism*, p. 92.

31   Schleiermacher, *Hermeneutics and Criticism*, p. 23.

32   Schleiermacher, *Hermeneutics and Criticism*, pp. 23, 91–2.

33   Schleiermacher, *Hermeneutics and Criticism*, p. 8.

34   See the sections on Holy Scripture in Schleiermacher, *The Christian Faith*, pp. 591–611.

35   Schleiermacher, *Hermeneutics and Criticism*, p. 27.

36   Schleiermacher, *Hermeneutics and Criticism*, p. 25.

37   Schleiermacher, *On Religion*, pp. 31–2 (italics in the original).

38   Schleiermacher, *The Christian Faith*, §30, p. 125.

39   Schleiermacher, *The Christian Faith*, §30, p. 125.

40   Werner G. Jeanrond, 1994, *Theological Hermeneutics: Development and Significance*, London: SCM Press, p. 44.

7

Historicism

One important element in Schleiermacher's hermeneutical theory was that a text needs to be understood in its own context. This may sound obvious to an early twenty-first century interpreter, but it was an innovation of the early nineteenth century. We recall that the Enlightenment believed in the absolute sovereignty of human reason. There was only one rational truth, and every properly trained and unbiased person could attain this truth by the use of his or her reason. The task of interpretation was merely to judge if the content of a text was true, that is, if it conformed to reason. Such an approach does not allow for different cultural and intellectual contexts. It is essentially a-historical, as it is concerned with the discernment of eternal truths.

From the late eighteenth century onwards, an awareness of the historical condition of humankind began to grow. People came to realize that texts and other utterances have to be understood within their own historical context, within their intellectual environment and within their culture. They are not to be measured against a universal law or truths of reason, but on their own terms. We have seen such an approach at work in Schleiermacher's hermeneutics. Schleiermacher was concerned to understand a text as the creative product of a human individual in a particular place and at a particular time. Thus he endeavoured to understand authors on their own terms. This attitude – to understand texts as well as other utterances and artefacts within their historical contexts and not judging them against universal and timeless laws and truths – is called historicism. It became an influential school of thought in the nineteenth century, and is connected with names like Leopold von Ranke (1795–1886), Johann Gustav Droysen (1808–84), Wilhelm Dilthey (1833–1911) and R. G. Collingwood (1889–1943).

For the purposes of our discussion of the development of hermeneutical theory, we will focus on Wilhelm Dilthey, who was highly influential on the development of hermeneutics, and whose writings display both the strengths and weaknesses of the historicist approach. The discussion of Dilthey's hermeneutics will be followed by a short overview of the so-called history of religion school, which applied historicist hermeneutics to biblical and theological texts.

The nineteenth century also gave birth to another historicist approach, driven by rather different agendas. This approach, which is exemplified by Karl Marx (1818–83), Friedrich Nietzsche (1844–1900) and Sigmund Freud (1856–1939), treats texts and other utterances and artefacts with great suspicion, because their real meaning is way beyond what the author intended to say. For Marx, texts refer to the means of production and class structure of their time. For Nietzsche, texts refer to the universal will to power, or to the slave morality of those who cannot obtain the desired power. Finally, for Freud, texts refer to the authors' psychological condition. All three will be highly influential, especially in the second part of the twentieth century – so much so that they earned the epithet 'masters of suspicion'.[1] We will look at these more in detail later in this section.

The text as source for the study of history: Dilthey and the history of religion school

Wilhelm Dilthey: hermeneutics as the foundation of the human sciences

At the end of the eighteenth century, Immanuel Kant gave the sciences a new philosophical foundation in his *Critique of Pure Reason* and *Metaphysical Foundations of Natural Science* in which he develops the criteria for what may count as pure science.[2] We cannot go into details here, so it will suffice to say that Kant's philosophical foundation gave the natural sciences renewed self-confidence and laid the foundation for the scientific advances of the nineteenth and twentieth centuries. In his *Critique of Practical Reason* and *The Groundwork of the Metaphysics of Morals*, Kant laid the foundation for ethical thinking,[3] and in the *Critique of Judgement* for aesthetic judgement.[4] So science, ethics and art were provided with a solid and generally accepted basis on which to build their methodologies. Most of the great achievements of the nineteenth century and early twentieth century were built on this.

What is noticeably absent in this foundation of the sciences and arts are the humanities, those fields of study that are concerned with history and the interpretation of texts and artefacts. Thus a need was perceived to provide such a foundation, which would be a *Critique of Historical Reason*.

Dilthey saw it as his life's work to provide the long desired *Critique of Historical Reason*, and his *Introduction to the Human Sciences*[5] was meant to be the first volume of this. In this book, Dilthey attempted to use descriptive psychology as the methodological foundation for the humanities. After the first volume, however, he found that he could not bring this project to a satisfactory conclusion and never published the second volume. In the papers and essays he wrote from 1900, Dilthey then turned to hermeneutics, and especially to Schleiermacher's hermeneutics, as a basis for the human sciences. In fact, Schleiermacher's hermeneutics had been largely forgotten throughout the nineteenth century, and so Dilthey's endeavours brought Schleiermacher's thoughts to the attention of philosophers and theologians again – although it was Schleiermacher as interpreted by Dilthey.

Dilthey agreed with Schleiermacher that the aim of interpretation is to understand the text by reliving the creative moment in which it was written. He, too, assumed that we need to understand the text first as well as, and then better than the author her- or himself.

Yet he differed from Schleiermacher in what he saw as the aim of interpretation. We recall that the aim of Schleiermacher's interpretation was the understanding of a text. For Dilthey, understanding a text was only a step in a much larger project, which was the understanding of 'universal history', that is, the historical development of humankind, and in the end human life in itself. Thus understanding an author was a means to the understanding of history. The text itself became merely a source for the interpreter's understanding of history, and had no significance in itself.[6]

Furthermore, Dilthey went beyond Schleiermacher by insisting that the interpretation of texts is objective. 'How then, can an individually structured consciousness reconstruct – and thereby know objectively – the distinct individuality of another?'[7] Such objectivity is important if the humanities are to be remodelled as exact sciences. It requires that interpretation is systematic and governed by methods. Hermeneutics is the 'methodology of the interpretation of written records'.[8] Hermeneutics 'is to counteract the constant irruption of romantic whim and sceptical subjectivity into the realm of history by laying the historical foundations of valid interpretation on which all certainty in history rests'.[9]

This insistence on methodology and objectivity was an important part of Dilthey's enterprise, because these are required if one wants to make history one of the exact sciences. It is through methodical interpretation that we arrive at an objective interpretation. And this is where Dilthey and Schleiermacher differ – Dilthey wanted to use hermeneutics as the methodological foundation for the human sciences, while Schleiermacher was interested in intersubjective understanding. Consequently, the subjectivity of the human individual was in the foreground of Schleiermacher's thoughts, while Dilthey endeavoured to find an objective and method-based approach to the human science. However, as we will see in the following chapters, such objectivity in interpretation is questionable in principle, and possibly not even desirable.

History of religion school

We turn now to the so-called history of religion school. This school of thought developed within a circle of like-minded theologians at the University of Göttingen, including Ernst Troeltsch, Herman Gunkel, Wilhelm Wrede, Wilhelm Bousset and others. This group endeavoured to apply historicism consistently to the study of Christianity. Their agenda is put concisely in an article by Herman Gunkel in 1903, which can be read as the manifesto of the history of religion school:

> The study of the history of religion endeavours to take seriously the insight that religion, including the religion of the Bible, has its own history just as everything human. Human life is history, i.e. it is an enormous organism, a great whole, a gigantic connection in which all is fruit and all is seed. Religion belongs straight into the centre of this entwined chain of cause and effect. It can be understood only within this context. Thus the history of religion approach . . . consists of continuous attention to the historical context of each religious phenomenon. We ask over and over again: why did it [i.e. the religious phenomenon] appear at this point in history and not at another? What had to happen before so that it could develop as it is? How do religious phenomena evolve in general?[10]

Already from this short excerpt it should be clear that for the history of religion school the text, the expression of a religious phenomenon, is merely a source that is used in order to reconstruct the history of religion. Just as Dilthey subordinated each individual utterance to the study of universal history, the history of religion school subordinated it to the study of the history of religion. Consequently, the aim of the study is not to understand what thought an author wanted to express with a particular utterance, but to learn how this utterance fits into the development of religion in general.

The great achievement of the history of religion school was to discover the organic development of religion, and the essential interconnectedness of biblical religion – Judaism and Christianity – with other religions of the ancient Middle East and Roman Empire. This opened new horizons for a better understanding of Judaism and Christianity. But this was achieved at the price of giving up the notion that the text might have something new to say. The inner word contained within the text had lost its relevance.

It will be the task of later developments in hermeneutical thinking to combine the two notions, that of the historical nature of religion with that of the relevance of the inner word. This will be at the very heart of the existentialist interpretation of the Bible, which we will encounter in the next chapter.

Hermeneutics of suspicion: Marx, Nietzsche and Freud

Before we can turn to the existentialist interpretation, however, we need to explore another related development that will become significant for the development of hermeneutical thinking in the twentieth century. These are the critical approaches to utterances, texts or other, introduced by three thinkers whom Paul Ricoeur called the 'masters of suspicion' – Karl Marx, Friedrich Nietzsche and Sigmund Freud.[11] In short, all three of these thinkers introduced an element of suspicion into the interpretation of utterances. As Ricoeur pointed out, philosophy since the Enlightenment assumed an autonomous self, which makes rational decisions and is fully aware of what it is doing. This very notion of the self is called into question by the three masters of suspicion. Are there factors that influence utterances that the self does not consciously control?

Karl Marx

Karl Marx was a materialist and atheist thinker. For him, there was nothing beyond the material world, which is governed by its own laws. Even human history, for Marx, follows discernible laws. The most important of the laws of human society is that a society with all its institutions, culture and religion is determined by its means of production. For the Marxist, the modes of production are the foundation of a society, and the society's ideology, its legal system, political system and its religions are a superstructure, which is usually imposed by the ruling class and reflects its interests. The superstructure is there to reinforce the rule of the ruling class. As Marx puts it in his 'Preface' to *A Contribution to the Critique of Political Economy*:

> In the social production of their life, men enter into definite relations that are indispensable and independent of their will, relations of production which correspond to a definite stage of development of their

material productive forces. The sum total of these relations of production constitutes the economic structure of society, the real foundation, on which rises a legal and political superstructure and to which correspond definite forms of social consciousness.

The mode of production of material life conditions the social, political and intellectual life process in general. It is not the consciousness of men that determines their being, but, on the contrary, their social being that determines their consciousness.[12]

Consequently, if consciousness is determined by social being, then the self is not autonomous but determined by external forces. This will, obviously, affect the interpretation of texts. We have seen that Schleiermacher and Dilthey (although Dilthey wrote after Marx) saw the reproduction of the creative act in the consciousness of the author as the aim of interpretation. For Marx and his followers, this act is determined by the modes of production of the author's society. So the latter is the proper meaning of the text that the interpreter aims to discover.

Using such a framework, works of literature would have to be read as a reflection of the social conditions, which, in turn, are determined by the modes of production. For example, Jane Austen's novels take for granted a particular economic order, which is in transition from agrarian to early industrial society, and the resulting class structure. Austen was probably not aware that she had these presuppositions, but for the Marxist interpreter they are the main point of interest. Conversely, religious texts are the expression of the religious and ideological part of a society's superstructure. So one can understand the Reformation and its religious literature as an expression of changing modes of production leading to a shift from medieval feudal society to early capitalism. The religion conveyed by these texts is only a reinforcement of the new social structures by creating a false, that is, religious, consciousness in people's minds, so that they will be useful subjects of the new order. The same applies to biblical and all other religious texts.

Friedrich Nietzsche

Friedrich Nietzsche's philosophy is based on the assumption that human beings are exclusively driven by the will to power. People want to dominate other people. Everything they do is, ultimately, in pursuit of this desire. However, there are also those who are too weak to dominate, and who will therefore be dominated by the strong. Domination and servitude are, for Nietzsche, natural and morally neutral – for one's morality is determined by one's perspective. The strong will have an ideology or religion that affirms their strength, while the weak construct a slave morality, which affirms their weakness as morally superior. So the weak consider as evil all those things that they cannot achieve, such as beauty, power, strength and wealth. Moreover, the exaltation of the virtues of poverty and charity are also an expression of weakness – one only has to exalt such inferior values if one cannot attain power over other people. Christianity (as Nietzsche perceived it) is, obviously, a prime example of slave morality:

> There are recipes for the feeling of power, firstly for those who can control themselves and who are thereby accustomed to a feeling of power; then for those in whom precisely this is lacking. Brahmanism has catered for men of the former sort, Christianity for men of the latter.[13]

Nietzsche developed this idea in his 'genealogy of morals'. All morality is contingent and determined by the perspective of those formulating it, that is, their power or lack of it. Consequently, morals do not bear any value in themselves, but they can be comprehensively explained from the perspective of the person or group putting them forward. In the end, all morals are merely the legitimation for one's position, either in power or without it.

Applied to the interpretation of texts or other utterances, the morals or ideology a text conveys is actually not what the text is really about, because they are merely the product of the perspective of the author, either as powerful over against other people, or as powerless and subject to domination.

Consequently, all religious texts are either the expression of master morality, if they express the self-understanding of those in power, or they are the expression of slave morality, if they try to make up for the lack of power of the powerless. Nietzsche believed that Christian texts belonged to the second category. 'Blessed are the poor' is something which only the poor would say in order to console themselves in their poverty. In short, there is no intrinsic value or truth in texts, only the perspective of those who wrote them.

Sigmund Freud

In his discussion of Sigmund Freud's work, Ricoeur attributes to him not only significance as the founder of psychoanalysis, but also as a hermeneutical thinker, as the founder of a hermeneutic of suspicion. For Freud, the human self is not entirely in control of itself, because the processes of the unconscious make people do and believe things which are not entirely rational, but the product of suppressed memory or emotion. In consequence, utterances must be seen not only within their historical context, but possibly also as expressions of a distorted ego.

According to Freud, many, if not all of our actions are controlled by our unconscious, and the real reasons for our behaviour are anything but rational. However, we will always try to rationalize what we are doing. For example, if someone, as a result of a neurosis, is driven by a compulsive need to wash his or her hands, he or she would have a perfectly rational explanation for this behaviour. The rational explanation, however, does not have anything to do with the real reason for this compulsive behaviour.

The same applies to texts. What an author writes in a text, for example, is not necessarily to be read at face value, but it may point to a deeper, unconscious and irrational motivation for this rationalized argument or narrative. For example, could the erotic description of the love for Jesus in some of the mystic writers be, on another level, an expression of suppressed sexuality? Or could certain patriarchal images of God be the product of the author's relation with his or her father? An interpreter taking seriously Freud's insights would have to take this possibility into account and read the text with a certain suspicion that something else may be the driving force behind the text than the stated reasons.

In sum, all three masters of suspicion do not take utterances at face-value, but suspect that another motivation lies behind them. Thus they add another dimension to historicism. While the historicism of Dilthey and others assumed that utterances could be understood within their historical context and allow the interpreter to gain new insights into universal history or the history of religion, Marx, Nietzsche and Freud add the critical notion that the utterance may not at all tell the interpreter about history, but about the ideology, the will to power or the unconscious of the author. Consequently, the utterance is not the product of an autonomous self, but of a distorted self, which is not in control of its own thoughts, word and deeds, and which is not even aware of this distortion. Any critical hermeneutical theory must take into account this possibility. However, as we will see later, it must also be possible to take seriously the author's utterance as a genuine expression of a human self (as distorted as it may be), and to recover the inner word, the meaning of the utterance.

Further reading

Bambach, Charles R., 1995, *Heidegger, Dilthey, and the Crisis of Historicism*, Ithaca: Cornell University Press.

De Mul, Jos, 2004, *The Tragedy of Finitude: Dilthey's Hermeneutics of Life, Yale Studies in Hermeneutics*, New Haven, Conn.; and London: Yale University Press.

Dilthey, Wilhelm, 1986, 'The Development of Hermeneutics', in: David E. Klemm (ed.), *Hermeneutical Inquiry*, vol. 1, Atlanta: Scholars Press, pp. 93–105.

Dilthey, Wilhelm, 1989, *Introduction to the Human Sciences*, edited by Frithjof Rodi and Rudolf A. Makkreel, Princeton: Princeton University Press.

Ermarth, Michael, 1978, *Wilhelm Dilthey: The Critique of Historical Reason*, Chicago: University of Chicago Press.

Gunkel, Hermann, 1904, 'Rezension von Max Reischle: Theologie und Religionsgeschichte', *DDeutsche Leteraturzeitung* 25, pp. 1100–10.

Hamilton, Paul, 2003, *Historicism, The New Critical Idiom*, 2nd edn, New York: Routledge.

Hodges, H. A., 1998, *Wilhelm Dilthey: An Introduction*, London: Routledge.

Makkreel, Rudolf A., 1975, *Dilthey: Philosopher of the Human Studies*, Princeton, NJ: Princeton University Press.

Marx, Karl, 1859, 'Economic Manuscripts: Preface to A Contribution to the Critique of Political Economy', in: *Marx & Engels Internet Archive* (website, accessed 14 September 2006). Available from http://www.marxists.org/archive/marx/works/1859/critique-pol-economy/preface.htm.

Marx, Karl, 1977, *A Contribution to the Critique of Political Economy*, Moscow: Progress Publishers.

Nietzsche, Friedrich Wilhelm and R. J. Hollingdale, 1977, *A Nietzsche Reader*, Harmondsworth: Penguin.

Özen, Alf, 1996, 'Der "religionsgeschichtliche Ansatz" oder: das "Programm" der "Religionsgeschichtlichen Schule"', in: *Die 'Religionsgeschichtliche Schule'* (website, accessed 19 December 2005). Available from http://wwwuser.gwdg.de/~aoezen/Archiv_RGS/index.htm.

Palmer, Richard E., 1969, *Hermeneutics: Interpretation Theory in Schleiermacher, Dilthey, Heidegger, and Gadamer, Northwestern University Studies in Phenomenology & Existential Philosophy*, Evanston: Northwestern University Press.

Philp, H. L., 1975, *Freud and Religious Belief*, Westport: Greenwood Press.

Plantinga, Theodore, 1980, *Historical Understanding in the Thought of Wilhelm Dilthey*, Toronto; Buffalo: University of Toronto Press.

Rickman, Hans Peter, 1979, *Wilhelm Dilthey: Pioneer of the Human Studies*, London: Elek.

Notes

1 Paul Ricoeur, 1970, *Freud and Philosophy: An Essay on Interpretation*, translated by Denis Savage, *Terry Lectures*, New Haven; London: Yale University Press, p. 32.

2 Eric Watkins, 2003, 'Kant's Philosophy of Science', in: *The Stanford Encyclopedia of Philosophy* (website, Winter 2003), edited by Edward N. Zalta. Available from http://plato.stanford.edu/archives/win2003/entries/kant-science/.

3 Robert Johnson, 2004, 'Kant's Moral Philosophy', in: *The Stanford Encyclopedia of Philosophy* (website, Spring 2004), edited by Edward N. Zalta. Available from http://plato.stanford.edu/archives/spr2004/entries/kant-moral/.

4 Hannah Ginsborg, 2005, 'Kant's Aesthetics and Teleology', in: *The Stanford Encyclopedia of Philosophy* (website, Fall 2005), edited by Edward N. Zalta. Available from http://plato.stanford.edu/archives/fall2005/entries/kant-aesthetics/.

5 Wilhelm Dilthey, 1989, *Introduction to the Human Sciences*, edited by Frithjof Rodi and Rudolf A. Makkreel, Princeton: Princeton University Press.

6 Cf Rudolf Bultmann, 1955, 'The Problem of Hermeneutics', in: *Essays, Philosophical and Theological, Library of Philosophy and Theology*, London: SCM Press, p. 247.

7 Wilhelm Dilthey, 1986, 'The Development of Hermeneutics', in: David E. Klemm (ed.), *Hermeneutical Inquiry*, vol. 1, Atlanta: Scholars Press, p. 94 (italics not in the original).

8 Dilthey, 'The Development of Hermeneutics', p. 95.

9 Dilthey, 'The Development of Hermeneutics', p. 105.

10 Hermann Gunkel, 1904, 'Rezension von Max Reischle: Theologie und Religionsgeschichte', *Deutsche Literaturzeitung* 25, cols 1109–10, quoted in: Alf Özen, 1996, 'Der "religionsgeschichtliche Ansatz" oder: das "Programm" der "Religionsgeschichtlichen Schule"', in: *Die 'Religionsgeschichtliche Schule'*. Available from http://wwwuser.gwdg.de/~aoezen/Archiv_RGS/index.htm (accessed 19 December 2005) – my translation.

11 Paul Ricoeur, 1970, *Freud and Philosophy: An Essay on Interpretation*, New Haven: Yale University Press, p. 32.

12 Karl Marx, 1977, *A Contribution to the Critique of Political Economy*, Moscow: Progress Publishers, quoted from: Karl Marx, 1859, 'Economic Manuscripts: Preface to A Contribution to the Critique of Political Economy', in: *Marx & Engels Internet Archive*. Available from http://www.marxists.org/archive/marx/works/1859/critique-pol-economy/preface.htm (accessed 14 September 2006).

13 *Daybreak*, quoted from Friedrich Wilhelm Nietzsche and R. J. Hollingdale, 1977, *A Nietzsche Reader*, Harmondsworth: Penguin, p. 217.

8

Existentialism I: Martin Heidegger and Rudolf Bultmann

Introduction

After the First World War, a new orientation took place in theology, which sought to overcome the liberal theology and historicism of the late nineteenth century. At the heart of this new perspective was the so-called dialectical theology movement. It proclaimed the infinite, qualitative difference between God and the world, that is, God's transcendence, God's otherness. Theology was not to be concerned with human faith or religious consciousness any more, but with the transcendent God and God's fundamental difference from humankind and the world.

This new approach brought with it a number of hermeneutical questions. If we take God's transcendence, God's complete otherness from the world, seriously, how can we know God? And, if God is beyond this world and thus beyond human comprehension, how can we speak of God? These questions moved a group of theologians, known as the dialectical theology movement, during the 1920s. Moreover, in different guises these questions would come to dominate the theological debate for much of the twentieth century.

The key proponents of the dialectical theology movement were Karl Barth (1886–1968) and Rudolf Bultmann (1884–1976). For the larger part of the 1920s, these two theologians collaborated closely in the formulation of dialectical theology. In his early work, *The Epistle to the Romans*, Karl Barth showed the direction this new movement was to take. 'God is in heaven, and thou art on earth'[1] was the battle cry of the dialectical theologians. God is absolutely inaccessible, and all human activity can at best be 'no more than a crater formed by the explosion of a shell', in other words, the trace that revelation has taken place, that the word of God has occurred. All activity of the Church, its teaching, ethics and worship, can therefore seek 'to be no more than a void in which the Gospel reveals itself'.[2] Thus human activity, including the use of human language, can never be directly related to the word of God itself. Barth insisted that the word of God would always come 'straight from above',[3] that is, without any worldly mediation. This was a strong rejection of all that nineteenth-century liberal theology had stood for, and marked a new departure for theology.

Throughout the first half of the 1920s, the dialectical theologians restricted themselves to attacking liberal theology and defending their new approach. In the mid-1920s, however, in response to perceptive criticism by the theologian Erik Peterson (1890–1960), Barth and Bultmann were forced to develop constructive ways in which to speak of God legitimately. Peterson had attacked the dialectical theology of Barth and Bultmann by pointing out that a theology that claims that it cannot speak of God is no theology at all. Furthermore, such a theology could not develop an adequate notion of revelation, faith and obedience.[4] Also, Peterson had pointed out that, if we hold on to the notion that the eternal *logos* is incarnate and reveals God, we must be able (with due reservations) to speak of God, and to develop positive theological doctrine.[5]

Although they were reluctant to admit it, Peterson's perceptive criticism forced Barth and Bultmann to develop a hermeneutical theory that would allow them to speak of the transcendent God. In this, Barth and Bultmann took very different approaches, at least partially due to their different denominational backgrounds; Barth was Swiss Reformed and Bultmann Lutheran. Consequently their ways parted and the dialectical theology movement disintegrated. The result of this was a lasting debate about the nature of theology, and about what turned out to be the main hermeneutical theological issue: how can we speak of God? Further questions of biblical hermeneutics would follow from their respective approaches to this main question.

The controversy on hermeneutical issues resulting from the break-up of the dialectical theology movement came to dominate the theological debate of the largest part of the twentieth century. We will come back to the debate between Karl Barth and Rudolf Bultmann in a later chapter. For now, we will look at the way in which Rudolf Bultmann solved the hermeneutical problem, and at his interaction with the German philosopher Martin Heidegger (1889–1976). In the next chapter, we will follow the development of hermeneutical thought in the existentialist tradition. This will be followed by a chapter on 'open sign systems', in which we will discuss structuralism, post-structuralism and deconstruction. Only then will we focus on Karl Barth's hermeneutical principles and their reception in more recent theology in contrast with the insights gained in our discussion of existentialist hermeneutics.

Bultmann and Heidegger: Sources

Martin Heidegger and Rudolf Bultmann are the founders of the existentialist school in philosophy and theology respectively. Although it has been said that Bultmann took over Heidegger's philosophical existentialism, the relation between the two thinkers is much more complex. While Bultmann and Heidegger were colleagues at the University of Marburg between 1923 and 1927, they developed their existentialist thought together. Heidegger's main work *Sein und Zeit* (*Being and Time*) appeared in 1927, based on thinking he developed throughout the previous years. Bultmann laid out the foundations of his thinking in the essay 'What does it mean to speak of God?'[6] (1925). This essay is already an important step towards the existentialist approach. Therefore, it would be oversimplifying to say that Bultmann simply took over Heidegger's thought and adapted it for use in theology. It is much more accurate to assume that the two worked together in developing existentialism and its hermeneutics.

Martin Heidegger began his academic career with a strong interest in hermeneutics. Although Heidegger published his hermeneutical thinking only in sections 31–4 of *Being and Time*,[7] unpublished works which were edited and published after Heidegger's death show how his thought developed from the incidental writing 'Phenomenological Interpretations with Respect to Aristotle: Indication of the Hermeneutical Situation',[8] which Heidegger composed in order to support his application for positions in Göttingen and Marburg in 1922. This text constitutes an important source for Heidegger's early hermeneutical thinking. This is followed by a lecture course given in 1923 called *Ontology: The Hermeneutics of Facticity*.[9] These texts show the development of Heidegger's hermeneutical thinking up to the publication of *Being and Time*.

After *Being and Time*, Heidegger seems to have lost interest in hermeneutical questions until his so-called 'turn to language', which led him to a renewed interest in the issues of language, being and meaning after the Second World War.[10] This period of Heidegger's work, however, is not of interest in our discussion of this period. We will return to it at a later stage, when I will also give an overview of the relevant literature (see p. 135).

The development of Rudolf Bultmann's thought is much more consistent than that of Heidegger's, as he did not follow the latter's 'turn to language'. This, however, leaves Bultmann's hermeneutical theory open to some substantial criticism (see p. 129). Bultmann's interest in hermeneutical issues surfaces in the essay 'What does it mean to speak of God?' From then on, his concern with hermeneutics is apparent in all his writings. It culminates in the essay 'New Testament and Mythology' (German: 'Neues Testament und Mythologie'),[11] which was first given as a lecture to a theological conference of the Confessing Church in Germany in 1941, at the height of the Second World War. This essay, which proposed the so-called demythologization programme, was meant to be the consistent application of the existentialist interpretation to the New Testament. It led to a vigorous theological debate which is well documented in the volumes of *Kerygma and Myth*, which contain the most significant contributions to the debate.[12] Later in his life, Bultmann summarized his hermeneutical thinking in the essay 'The Problem of Hermeneutics' (1950).[13] Finally, Bultmann's existentialist interpretation can be seen applied in, besides some smaller writings, his commentary on John's Gospel[14] and in his *Theology of the New Testament*.[15] A good detailed study of the hermeneutics of Heidegger, Bultmann and Gadamer can be found in Antony Thiselton's book *The Two Horizons*.[16]

Existentialism

As I pointed out above, it is difficult to say who influenced whom in the development of existentialist hermeneutics. So when I begin with discussing Martin Heidegger's hermeneutical approach, this does not imply that he developed it first and Bultmann took it over afterwards. The reason for this arrangement is that Heidegger presents a clear and systematic explanation of this approach in the hermeneutical sections of *Being and Time*, that is, sections 31–4.[17] With the understanding gained in the discussion of these passages and some related writings, we will be able to identify Bultmann's hermeneutics.

The following discussion of Heidegger's hermeneutics will be centred on the key terms which he introduces in sections 31–4, namely, 'understanding', 'state-of-mind', 'interpretation', 'language' and 'discourse'. This will clarify Heidegger's sometimes idiosyncratic terminology, and lead to the centre of his hermeneutical thinking.

Heidegger

Understanding

In traditional hermeneutics, understanding used to be the aim of the interpretative endeavour. A text or any kind of utterance was interpreted in order to gain understanding of its subject matter. However, understanding would never be complete, and so the interpreter would never be able to leave the hermeneutic circle. Understanding the utterance better and better was the objective of interpretation, and hermeneutics was understood to be the theory of this endeavour. Heidegger revolutionized the concept of understanding by moving it from the end to the very beginning of the process: we do not achieve understanding as a result of interpretation, but we already understand even before we interpret. The task of interpretation is to bring to light the interpreter's previous understanding.[18]

In Heidegger's own language, in 'the "for-the-sake-of-which," existing Being-in-the-world is disclosed as such, and this disclosedness we have called "understanding."'[19] In plain words, whenever we encounter an object in the world, we already have an understanding of its purpose for us. If I see a knife, for example, I immediately give it meaning. It may be that I see the knife as irrelevant at the moment and ignore it. Or I am hungry and use it to cut bread and butter it. Or I feel threatened by an intruder in the house and take the knife to defend myself. Or I am afraid that a child might be hurt using the knife, and so I put it into the drawer. In each of these situations, I have found meaning in the knife, I have understood what it is for. This is what Heidegger calls the 'for-the-sake-of-which'. Thus we only encounter things in the world by understanding them. Meaningful relations of being, which Heidegger calls 'signifying', disclose them.[20] The 'act of understanding holds them [i.e. the meaningful relations] in this disclosedness'.[21] Thus Being is disclosed, made comprehensible for the *Dasein* (which, in short, stands for the human self) by being meaningful, by relating to the *Dasein* and to other beings. Meaning means, for Heidegger, that something is there for something, that it is comprehended in its 'that for which', in its purpose in the great (or small) scheme of things.

This does not only apply to a single object, such as a knife, but to the whole world as we encounter it. In fact, world, as Heidegger understands it, is the world in which we understand ourselves, it is the totality of meaningful relationships, which he calls 'significance'.[22] It is a web of meaning, with the *Dasein*, which is the subject that seeks understanding, in the centre.

These relationships are bound up with one another as a primordial totality; they are what they are as this signifying in which *Dasein* gives itself beforehand its Being-in-the-world as something to be understood. The relational totality of this signifying we call 'significance'. This is what makes up the structure of the world – the structure of that wherein *Dasein* already is.[23]

In other words, we find ourselves in the world, and we already have an understanding of the world in which we live as a meaningful web of relationships of all we know. Understanding is, therefore, not a theoretical exercise, but something eminently practical. Heidegger likens understanding (*verstehen*) to *sich auf etwas verstehen*, which means 'being able to manage something' or 'being competent to do something'. In its most basic sense, understanding means to be able to find one's way around in the world, being able to make sense of the world. This expresses itself in two ways, in the state-of-mind (*Befindlichkeit*) and in language.

State-of-mind

The state-of-mind is, in short, 'the most familiar and every day sort of thing; our mood, our Being-attuned'.[24] In this interesting move, Heidegger attributes to human moods philosophical, to be more precise, even ontological significance.

First of all, state-of-mind is significant in so far as it expresses the *Dasein*'s 'thrownness'.[25] Thrownness means, for Heidegger, that we find ourselves in the world, that we are 'delivered over' to the world in which we are. *Dasein*, being-there, is thrown into its there, that is, it is thrown into a given world which it has not chosen.[26] It is where it is. The reaction to being delivered over to the world is that we have a state-of-mind. So that fact that we have a state-of-mind, which is, as most people will experience, changeable, points at the fact that we are thrown into the world.

Second, state-of-mind is an expression of our interpretation of the world into which we are thrown. 'The mood has already disclosed, in every case, Being-in-the-world as a whole, and makes it possible first of all to direct oneself towards something.'[27] In other words, mood discloses how we understand ourselves in the world, how we make sense of it, and what purpose we find in it, which we may try to realize. For example, if someone understands his or her place in the world as insignificant, that one has no control over one's life, that one is merely subject to other agencies, then this will express itself in a particular mood, which could be melancholy resignation or defensive bad mood. Or, otherwise, if one understands the world as a generally benevolent place which provides sustenance and opportunity, this will result in a very different state-of-mind. Thus state-of-mind discloses how we understand the world. However, this disclosure of the understanding of the world is by no means reflected or conscious. It is implicit in our state-of-mind, and can be made conscious and reflected upon in interpretation.

Discourse and language

The other means by which our understanding of the world is disclosed is through language. Language, in Heidegger's terminology, is the means by which discourse is expressed, while 'discourse is the articulation of intelligibility'.[28] In other words, discourse means for Heidegger the inner speech, the inner discourse of the mind, while language is this inner discourse expressed in audible language. In discourse, we articulate our understanding of the world, the significance, that is, the totality of meaningful relationships. Heidegger does not envisage here someone explaining his or her understanding of the world in straightforward language – understanding of the world is only brought to consciousness in the act of interpretation – but it is in all discourse, whatever its superficial subject, that we find the understanding of the world expressed. For example, if someone talks or writes about his or her political attitude, the author's understanding of the world is always contained in what he or she writes.

Heidegger's pupil Hans Jonas presents an excellent example of this in his work on Gnosticism.[29] Jonas analysed the religious language, imagery and theology of ancient Gnosticism and highlighted the particular understanding of human existence that is implicitly expressed in the professed religion. Thus while the Gnostic writers were speaking about religious doctrine and the Gnostic myth of redemption, they really expressed something much more profound, which are the fundamental questions of human existence: *who we are* (as human beings), *where we have come from*, and *where we are heading*, historically and spiritually.[30] A much shorter example can be found in Rudolf Bultmann's essay 'New Testament and Mythology', which draws on Jonas' work.[31] Both show how the understanding of human existence, clad in mythological language, is really at the heart of the Gnostic authors' concern. This applies not only to political or religious language, but to all discourse and language. Whatever we think or say, it contains the significance that we find in the world, our particular understanding of human existence. Thus 'in talking, *Dasein* expresses itself'.[32] In this, Heidegger and Bultmann take up a key insight, which we have already discovered in Schleiermacher's hermeneutics; theological language always refers back to the speaker, to the religious self-consciousness or to the self-understanding (see pp. 99–101).

We recall that Heidegger sees the state-of-mind as the inarticulate disclosure of our understanding of the world. Now, in discourse and language, the understanding of the world is put into words, but not necessarily consciously.

Interpretation

By interpretation, *Dasein's* understanding of the world is made conscious and can be contemplated. Or, in Heidegger's words,

> As understanding, *Dasein* projects its Being upon possibilities. . . . This projecting of the understanding has its own possibility – that of developing itself. This development of understanding we call 'interpretation'. In it, the understanding appropriates understandingly that which is understood by it. In interpretation, understanding does not become something different. It becomes itself.[33]

Understanding always contains the notion of possibilities. What possibilities do I have in a given situation into which I am thrown? How can I develop myself here, how can I make use of it in order to become what I want to be? This does not need to include a great plan for one's life, but it may be concerned with more immediate possibilities. To return to the example of the knife, when I am hungry and see a knife in the kitchen, I realize (consciously or unconsciously) that there is the possibility of getting something to eat. Or if I am afraid, I see the possibility of making myself safer by taking the knife as a weapon for my defence. Thus I project myself upon certain possibilities.

Such understanding or interpretation of my existence in a given situation may often take place unconsciously. However, I can also make it conscious by analysing it. Thus I develop my understanding, deepen it, reflect on it, so that I can project my being upon other possibilities, based on a deeper understanding of my existence. In short, in interpretation I analyse my existence and the possibilities that are open to me.

This implies that everything that the *Dasein* perceives is already interpreted, because we always recognize something as something. I perceive the object on the table as a knife, and know what I could do with it. Even if I come upon something unfamiliar, for example a strange plant, then I already recognize it as a plant, even if I do not know if it is edible or poisonous. However, even the fact that I identify this new thing as a plant and ask myself if it may be edible or poisonous shows that I have already interpreted the object and am wondering about the possibilities that might be connected with it. Thus the whole world, the totality of significance, is always already interpreted.

In assuming that everything the *Dasein* encounters is already interpreted, Heidegger gives the hermeneutic circle a new form. Interpretation begins with the interpreter's previous understanding of the subject matter, which is then interpreted anew, which leads to a better understanding, which in turn becomes the basis for further interpretation. Heidegger welcomes the circularity of interpretation: 'What is decisive is not to get out of the circle but to come into it in the right way.'[34]

In this context Heidegger makes an interesting observation concerning textual interpretation. If an interpreter ignores his or her previous understanding of a subject matter, he or she will inevitably find in the text what he or she already knows about the subject matter:

> If, when one is engaged in a particular concrete kind of interpretation, in the sense of exact textual interpretation, one likes to appeal to what 'stands there', then one finds that what 'stands there' in the first instance is nothing other than the obvious undiscussed assumption of the person who does the interpreting.[35]

Finally, Heidegger assumes that interpretation, the making sense of something within one's world, is the fundamental mode of language. One always understands something as something, the knife as a tool for making food, for example. For Heidegger, to describe something as something is the primary mode of language. Apophantic statements or assertions, such as 'The hammer is heavy', are derived from interpretation. This means that 'The hammer is heavy', in order to be a meaningful statement, must say something about the speaker's interpretation of the object. So it could mean 'The hammer is too heavy for this job', and be followed by the speaker putting this hammer aside and taking another one.[36]

Thus, in saying 'The hammer is heavy', the speaker does not make an objective statement about the hammer, but expresses his or her interpretation of the object. So even language that is seemingly objective contains always the speaker's interpretation. Heidegger dedicates a whole section of *Being and Time* to the derivative nature of 'assertions' or apophantic statements, which indicates the significance of this aspect of this hermeneutical thinking.

We will see later that both Paul Ricoeur and Hans-Georg Gadamer take up the notion of language referring to the author's interpretation of the world. In fact, it can be argued that it is one of the most fundamental assumptions for existentialist hermeneutics. We have seen above that many people would instinctively follow the approach of Thomas Reid and the Scottish common-sense philosophy, that is, they would assume that utterances directly refer to simple facts or states of affair. However, if we take seriously Heidegger's insights, language does not refer to naked 'facts', not even to interpreted facts, but to the interpretation of fact. Even so-called statements of fact do not primarily refer to 'facts', but to the speaker's or writer's interpretation of the world.

Interestingly, after *Being and Time*, Heidegger did not develop his hermeneutical thought any further for nearly a quarter of a century. Only in the 1950s, when his philosophy took the 'turn to language', did Heidegger become interested in hermeneutical questions again. We will discuss this renewed interest and the direction in which Heidegger took his hermeneutical investigations in the following chapter.

Bultmann

Rudolf Bultmann can be credited with developing an existentialist hermeneutical approach to theology. As I said above, it is most likely that Bultmann did not merely take over existentialism from Martin Heidegger, but that the two developed this way of thinking during their time in Marburg together. We can see the beginnings of Bultmann's hermeneutical interest in his essay 'What does it mean to speak of God?' In this essay, which was a response to Erik Peterson's attack on the dialectical theology movement, Bultmann developed the main features of what would later be known as his existentialist interpretation (see p. 116).

First of all, Bultmann acknowledges the difficulty, if not impossibility, of speaking about God, given that God is the wholly other, that is absolutely transcendent.

> If 'speaking of God' is understood as *'speaking about God'*, then such speaking has no meaning whatsoever, for its subject, God, is lost in the very moment it takes place. Whenever the idea, God, comes into mind, it connotes that God is the Almighty; in other words, God is the reality determining all else. But this idea is not recognized at all when I speak *about* God, i.e. when I regard God as an object of thought, about which I can inform myself if I take a standpoint where I can be neutral on the question of God and can formulate propositions dealing with the reality and nature of God, which I can reject or, if they are enlightening, accept.[37]

So taking the notion of God as almighty seriously, or, as he will say later in the essay, as the 'wholly other', as the one who determines our human existence, Bultmann concludes that, if we attempt to speak of God, then the speaking self is always included in the speech.[38] Or, as Bultmann puts it, 'it is therefore clear that if a man will speak of God, he must evidently speak of himself'.[39] Thus speaking of God means speaking of human existence. When one speaks of God, then he or she refers to God in terms of what God does to the speaker – Bultmann quotes Wilhelm Herrmann here, who once wrote that 'of God we can only tell what he does to us'.[40] This is in line with a long tradition of Lutheran theological thought, beginning with Philipp Melanchthon's famous statement that 'to know Christ means to know his benefits'.[41]

Therefore, if we want to speak of God, we must speak of the works of God in relation to human existence. Bultmann does not think of pietistic conversion stories or accounts of how blessed one was by God, but of what the word of God does to the human self. 'Wholly fortuitously, wholly contingently, wholly as specific event, the Word enters our world. No guarantee comes with it by virtue of which it is to be believed. . . . Faith is continually a fresh act, as new obedience.'[42] Thus the word of God is the prime agent, which we encounter in the world (Bultmann refers to the word of the Bible and the words of the Church's proclamation here), and which calls the hearer to faith. This call to faith, which is the essence of Christian proclamation, Bultmann calls the *kerygma* (from the Greek for 'proclamation').

In this short essay by Bultmann, we thus have all the key elements of his later work; first, the insight that we cannot speak of God as apart from our own existence – on the contrary, all authentic speaking of God is speaking of one's own existence. Second, defining the way in which we speak of human existence as speaking of the benefits of God and how they affect human existence. Third and finally, the assumption that the word of God is active in the world, that we encounter it in specific situations. Although all three points will need greater precision and elaboration, they form the foundation for Bultmann's further thinking.

Human existence

As we have seen above in our discussion of Heidegger's thought, to speak of human existence does not mean that we do so explicitly (see p. 121). At the heart of all language is the human self-understanding, one's interpretation of one's own existence. Thus it is not necessary to speak about oneself in order to speak of one's understanding of human existence, as all language, properly understood, refers to human self-understanding. All factual statements, all assertions are essentially derived from interpretation of being, as we have seen above. A text, therefore, which superficially seems to be about religious myth or doctrine, is essentially about the interpretation of human existence. Bultmann applies this insight to biblical texts in some of his major writings. In his *Theology of the New Testament*, Bultmann applies it to the theology of the various writers of the books of the Bible. Most remarkable is, in this context, his treatment of the theologies of Paul and of John.[43] In the famous essay 'New Testament and Mythology', which provides a comparatively concise summary of Bultmann's theology, he applies it to some key concepts of Christian faith, such as 'Human Existence apart from Faith', 'The Life in Faith', The Event of Redemption', 'The Cross' and 'The Resurrection'.[44] For example, Bultmann describes Paul's understanding of the concept of 'flesh' thus:

> But what does he [Paul] mean by 'flesh'? Not the bodily or physical side of human nature, but the sphere of the visible, concrete, tangible, and measurable reality, which as such is also the sphere of corruption and death. When a man chooses to live entirely in and for this sphere, or, as St Paul puts it, when he 'lives after the flesh', it assumes the shape of a 'power'. There are indeed many different ways of living after the flesh. There is the crude life of sensual pleasure and there is the refined way of basing one's life on the pride of achievement, on the 'works of the law' as St Paul would say. These distinctions are ultimately immaterial. For 'flesh' embraces not only the material things of life, but all human creation and achievement pursued for the sake of some tangible reward, such as for example the fulfilling of the law (Gal. 3.3). It includes every passive quality, and every advantage a man can have, in the sphere of visible, tangible reality (Phil. 3.4ff.).[45]

Life in faith, then, means for Bultmann 'the deliverance from all worldly, tangible objects, leading to complete detachment from the world and thus to freedom'.[46] In consequence, 'now that he is delivered from anxiety and from the frustration which comes from clinging to the tangible realities of the visible world, man is free to enjoy fellowship with others. Hence faith is described as "working through love" (Gal. 5.6). And this means being a new creature (cf. Gal. 5.6 with 6.15).'[47]

Thus Bultmann describes human existence apart from faith on the one hand, and life in faith on the other. The transition between the two, and Bultmann is adamant on this, is not possible apart from God's work. And, in line with the Lutheran tradition, Bultmann sees God at work though God's word.

The word of God

So, 'are there still any surviving traces of mythology? There certainly are for those who regard all language about an act of God or of a decisive, eschatological event as mythological.'[48] The decisive eschatological event is for Bultmann the encounter with the word of God, which calls the hearer to abandon reliance on the 'the tangible realities of the visible world'[49] and into freedom. The word of God became incarnate, which, for Bultmann, is not 'a miracle that happened about 1950 years ago, but . . . an eschatological happening, which, beginning with Jesus, is always present in the words of man proclaiming it to be a human experience'.[50] Thus the word of God was incarnate in Jesus of Nazareth, and is again incarnate wherever he is proclaimed.

> Thus the revelation has to be an event, which occurs whenever and wherever the word of grace is spoken to a man. The 'demythologized' sense of the Christian doctrine of incarnation, of the word that 'was made flesh' is precisely this, that God manifests himself not merely as the idea of God – however true this idea may be – but as 'my' God, who speaks to me here and now, through a human mouth.[51]

Thus Bultmann, himself a theologian within the Lutheran tradition, takes up Luther's notion that the word of God is incarnate in the human word, through which Christ comes to the hearer or reader (see p. 70). For both Luther and Bultmann, the word of God, the *kerygma*, is contained in the human words of the proclamation. Both agree that human language is able to contain the word of God. So again, in the work of the twentieth-century theologian whose reputation is that of extreme criticism, we find Augustine's doctrine of the incarnation of the incarnation of the inner word in the spoken word at work (see pp. 45–7). This train of thought is, in my opinion, of the greatest importance for our understanding of existentialist theology, but it is also the most neglected.

Bultmann has entered an area of hermeneutical thinking here which is beyond the scope of Heidegger's hermeneutical thought, although it does not contradict it. However, as we will see later, after Heidegger's 'turn to language', he will take up Augustine's teaching of the inner word (see pp. 137–8).

For Bultmann, speaking of God means to speak of God working through the word of God within the human experience. Thus, the aim of the demythologization programme is to understand Christian religious texts as the proclamation of the fundamental change in human self-understanding as a result of the encounter with the word of God in the *kerygma*. And in the *kerygma* the word of God itself is incarnate. Thus Bultmann has solved the problem he posed himself in the essay 'What does it mean to speak of God?' Now he can speak of God by speaking the word of God as proclamation, and at the same time Bultmann has found an approach that allows the biblical texts to be read as an embodiment of that proclamation, expressed within the frame of mind of a particular time. Thus Bultmann can interpret the biblical texts as authoritative while removing the obstacle to understanding which is posed to the modern mind by the mythological world-view of the biblical authors.

Conclusion

Rudolf Bultmann transformed the significance of hermeneutics in theology as Martin Heidegger did for philosophy. While hermeneutics used to be an ancillary field of study in the service of biblical interpretation, it has now become a foundational subject of all areas of theology (and philosophy). Theology that follows the thought of Bultmann has rightly been called hermeneutical theology.

As we will see in the next chapter, Martin Heidegger moved on in his hermeneutical thinking and, in his later work after the Second World War, developed a theory of the relation between spoken language, the inner word and being. Bultmann, on the other hand, did not move in this direction. Bultmann has been accused of many failings, among them that he has dissolved theology into anthropology. Karl Barth, for example, points out in his essay 'Rudolf Bultmann – An Attempt to Understand Him' that for Bultmann 'all understanding is concerned, in one way or the other, with man's understanding of himself, his self-understanding. . . . Thus the primary concern of the New Testament is with anthropology, an anthropology structured in this particular way [i.e. according to Heidegger's existentialism].'[52] After the discussion of Bultmann's hermeneutical approach above, we can say that this particular criticism does not take seriously the depth of the existentialist interpretation, and does not take into account the Lutheran foundation of the theology of the word of God that undergirds his hermeneutics. Karl Barth continues that Heidegger himself has left the 'anthropological straitjacket'[53] behind in his later philosophy, thus showing that Bultmann is wrong in maintaining it.

Although I do not think that Karl Barth interprets Bultmann's existentialist interpretation appropriately, he still points at an important weakness. Paul Ricoeur recognizes the same weakness with much greater appreciation and understanding of Bultmann's work. Ricoeur is concerned that Bultmann reduces the meaning of mythological language in the Bible to the call to the existentialist decision before God, which can be expressed in neutral or 'innocent' language. Thus he separates the meaning of the text from its actual language, and one can take the concepts contained in the text and interpret them existentially, understand and apply them directly.[54] As we will see in later chapters, there is no such thing as 'innocent' language, and so Ricoeur is right in saying that the meaning of the text is not available without the language of the text, which is the bearer of meaning.[55] If we follow Ricoeur in this respect, then 'there is no shorter path for joining a neutral existential anthropology, according to philosophy, with the existential decision before God, according to the Bible. But there is the long path of the question of being and of the belonging of saying to being.'[56] In the next chapter we will focus on the way in which the later Heidegger, Hans-Georg Gadamer, Paul Ricoeur and their theological counterparts, among them Gerhard Ebeling and Ernst Fuchs, follow this 'long path of the question of being and of the belonging of saying to being'.

Further reading

Bambach, Charles R., 1995, *Heidegger, Dilthey, and the Crisis of Historicism*, Ithaca: Cornell University Press.

Bartsch, Hans Werner (ed.), 1972, *Kerygma and Myth: A Theological Debate*, translated by Reginald Horace Fuller, London: SPCK.

Bartsch, Hans-Werner and Rudolf Karl Bultmann, 1953, *Kerygma and Myth: A Theological Debate*, London: SPCK.

Bartsch, Hans Werner and Rudolf Karl Bultmann, 1962, *Kerygma and Myth: A Theological Debate*, vols I and II combined, translated by Reginald Horace Fuller, vol. II, London: SPCK.

Bourgeois, Patrick L. and Frank Schalow, 1990, *Traces of Understanding: A Profile of Heidegger's and Ricoeur's Hermeneutics, Elementa; Schriften zur Philosophie und ihrer Problemgeschichte*, vol. 53, Würzburg: Könighausen & Neumann.

Bultmann, Rudolf, 1941, *Das Evangelium des Johannes*, 10th edn, Göttingen: Vandenhoeck & Ruprecht.

Bultmann, Rudolf, 1948, *Theologie des Neuen Testaments*, Tübingen: J. C. B. Mohr (Paul Siebeck).

Bultmann, Rudolf, 1952, *Theology of the New Testament*, translated by Kendrick Grobel, 2 vols, London: SCM Press.

Bultmann, Rudolf, 1955, 'The Problem of Hermeneutics', in: *Essays, Philosophical and Theological, Library of Philosophy and Theology*, London: SCM Press, pp. 234–61.

Bultmann, Rudolf, 1961, 'Welchen Sinn hat es, von Gott zu reden?', in: *Glauben und Verstehen*, vol. 1, Tübingen: J. C. B. Mohr (Paul Siebeck), pp. 26–37.

Bultmann, Rudolf, 1969, 'What does it mean to speak of God?', in: *Faith and Understanding*, vol. 1, London: SCM Press, pp. 53–65.

Bultmann, Rudolf, 1971, *The Gospel of John: A Commentary*, translated by G. R. Beasley-Murray, Oxford: Blackwell.

Bultmann, Rudolf, 1972, 'New Testament and Mythology', in: Hans Werner Bartsch (ed.), *Kerygma and Myth: A Theological Debate*, London: SPCK, pp. 1–44.

Bultmann, Rudolf, 1972, 'The Case for Demythologizing', in: Hans Werner Bartsch (ed.), *Kerygma and Myth: A Theological Debate*, vol. 2, London: SPCK, pp. 181–94.

Bultmann, Rudolf, 1985, *Neues Testament und Mythologie: Das Problem der Entmythologisierung der neutestamentlichen Verkündigung*, München: Chr. Kaiser.

Bultmann, Rudolf, 1985, *New Testament and Mythology: and other basic Writings*, translated by Schubert Miles Ogden, London: SCM Press.

Coltman, Rodney R., 1998, *The Language of Hermeneutics: Gadamer and Heidegger in Dialogue*, *SUNY Series in Contemporary Continental Philosophy*, Albany: State University of New York Press.

DiCenso, James, 1990, *Hermeneutics and the Disclosure of Truth: A Study in the Work of Heidegger, Gadamer and Ricoeur*, Charlottesville: University Press of Virginia.

Gadamer, Hans-Georg, 1994, *Heidegger's Ways*, translated by John W. Stanley, *SUNY Series in Contemporary Continental Philosophy*, Albany: State University of New York Press.

Guignon, Charles B., 1993, *The Cambridge Companion to Heidegger*, *Cambridge Companions to Philosophy*, Cambridge: Cambridge University Press.

Heidegger, Martin, 1959, 'Der Weg zur Sprache', in: *Unterwegs zur Sprache*, Pfullingen: Neske, pp. 239–68.

Heidegger, Martin, 1959, *Unterwegs zur Sprache*, Pfullingen: Neske.

Heidegger, Martin, 1962, *Being and Time*, translated by John Macquarrie and Edward Robinson, Oxford: Basil Blackwell.

Heidegger, Martin, 1971, 'Language', in: *Poetry, Language, Thought*, New York: Harper & Row, pp. 187–210.

Heidegger, Martin, 1971, 'The Origin of the Work of Art', in: *Poetry, Language, Thought*, New York: Harper & Row, pp. 15–86.

Heidegger, Martin, 1971, 'The Way to Language', in: *On the Way to Language*, New York: Harper & Row, pp. 109–36.

Heidegger, Martin, 1971, *On the Way to Language*, New York: Harper & Row.

Heidegger, Martin, 1986, 'Language', in: David E. Klemm (ed.), *Hermeneutical Inquiry*, vol. 1, Atlanta: Scholars Press, pp. 141–55.

Heidegger, Martin, 1988, *Ontologie (Hermeneutik der Faktizität)*, *Gesamtausgabe*, vol. 63, Frankfurt am Main: Vittorio Klostermann.

Heidegger, Martin, 1989, 'Phänomenologische Interpretation zu Aristoteles (Anzeige der Hermeneutischen Situation)', *Dilthey Jahrbuch für Geschichte und Geisteswissenschaften* 6, pp. 236–69.

Heidegger, Martin, 1992, 'Phenomenological Interpretations with Respect to Aristotle: Indication of the Hermeneutical Situation', *Man and World* 25, pp. 355–93.

Heidegger, Martin, 1993, *Sein und Zeit*, 17th edn, Frankfurt am Main: Vittorio Klostermann.

Heidegger, Martin, 1995, 'Augustinus und der Neuplatonismus', in: *Phänomenologie des religiösen Lebens, Gesamtausgabe*, vol. 60, Frankfurt am Main: Klostermann, pp. 157–299.

Heidegger, Martin, 1999, *Ontology: The Hermeneutics of Facticity*, Bloomington, Ind.: Indiana University Press.

Jaeger, Hans, 1971, *Heidegger und die Sprache*, Bern: Francke.

Jonas, Hans, 1934, *Gnosis und spätantiker Geist*, Göttingen: Vandenhoeck & Ruprecht.

Jonas, Hans, 1958, *The Gnostic Religion: The Message of the Alien God and the Beginnings of Christianity*, Boston: Beacon Press.

Kisiel, Theodore J. and John Van Buren (eds), 1994, *Reading Heidegger from the Start: Essays in his Earliest Thought SUNY Series in Contemporary Continental Philosophy*, Albany: State University of New York Press.

Kockelmans, Joseph J., 1972, *On Heidegger and Language, Northwestern University Studies in Phenomenology & Existential Philosophy*, Evanston, Ill.: Northwestern University Press.

Macquarrie, John, 1966, *The Scope of Demythologizing: Bultmann and his Critics, Harper Torchbooks. Cloister Library*, New York: Harper & Row.

Macquarrie, John, 1973, *An Existentialist Theology: A Comparison of Heidegger and Bultmann*, Harmondsworth: Penguin.

Ott, Hugo, 1993, *Martin Heidegger: A Political Life*, translated by Allan Blunden, London: HarperCollins.

Palmer, Richard E., 1969, *Hermeneutics: Interpretation Theory in Schleiermacher, Dilthey, Heidegger, and Gadamer, Northwestern University Studies in Phenomenology & Existential Philosophy*, Evanston: Northwestern University Press.

Peterson, Erik, 1971, 'Was ist Theologie?', in: Gerhard Sauter (ed.), *Theologie als Wissenschaft: Aufsätze und Thesen, Theologische Bücherei*, vol. 43, München: Kaiser, pp. 132–51.

Schmithals, Walter, 1968, *An Introduction to the Theology of Rudolf Bultmann*, London: SCM Press.

Scott, Charles E., 2001, *Companion to Heidegger's Contributions to Philosophy, Studies in Continental Thought*, Bloomington: Indiana University Press.

Thiselton, Anthony C., 1980, *The Two Horizons: New Testament Hermeneutics and Philosophical Description with special Reference to Heidegger, Bultmann, Gadamer, and Wittgenstein*, Exeter: Paternoster.

Notes

1 Karl Barth, 1933, *The Epistle to the Romans*, translated by Edwyn Clement Hoskyns, Oxford: Oxford University Press, p. 10.

2 Barth, *The Epistle to the Romans*, p. 36.

3 The first occurrence of the famous 'straight from above' is in Karl Barth, 1989, *Der Römerbrief*, 14th edn, Zürich: Theologischer Verlag, p. 6. The English translation translates it as 'vertically from above' (Barth, *The Epistle to the Romans*, p. 30).

4 Erik Peterson, 1971, 'Was ist Theologie?', in: Gerhard Sauter (ed.), *Theologie als Wissenschaft: Aufsätze und Thesen, Theologische Bücherei*, vol. 43, München: Kaiser, pp. 137–8.

5 Peterson, 'Was ist Theologie?', pp. 145–6.

6 Rudolf Bultmann, 1969, 'What does it mean to speak of God?', in: *Faith and Understanding*, vol. 1, London: SCM Press (German: Rudolf Bultmann, 1961, 'Welchen Sinn hat es, von Gott zu reden?', in: *Glauben und Verstehen*, vol. 1, Tübingen: J. C. B. Mohr (Paul Siebeck)).

7 Heidegger, 1962, *Being and Time*, translated by John Macquarrie and Edward Robinson, Oxford: Basil Blackwell, pp. 182–203 (German: Martin Heidegger, 1993, *Sein und Zeit*, 17th edn, Frankfurt am Main: Vittorio Klostermann, pp. 142–60).

8 Martin Heidegger, 'Phenomenological Interpretations with Respect to Aristotle: Indication of the Hermeneutical Situation', *Man and World* 25 (1992), pp. 355–93 (German: Martin Heidegger, 'Phänomenologische Interpretation zu Aristoteles (Anzeige der Hermeneutischen Situation)', *Dilthey Jahrbuch für Geschichte und Geisteswissenschaften* 6 (1989), pp. 236–69).

9 Martin Heidegger, 1999, *Ontology: The Hermeneutics of Facticity*, Bloomington, Ind.: Indiana University Press (German: Martin Heidegger, 1988, *Ontologie (Hermeneutik der Faktizität), Gesamtausgabe*, vol. 63, Frankfurt am Main: Vittorio Klostermann).

10 Jean Grondin, 1994, *Introduction to Philosophical Hermeneutics*, New Haven: Yale University Press, pp. 102–5.

11 This essay is contained in several volumes, among them: Rudolf Bultmann, 1985, *New Testament and Mythology: and other basic Writings*, translated by Schubert Miles Ogden, London: SCM Press; and Hans Werner Bartsch and Rudolf Bultmann, 1972, *Kerygma and Myth: A Theological Debate*, translated by Reginald Horace Fuller, London: SPCK (German: Rudolf Bultmann, 1985, *Neues Testament und Mythologie: Das Problem der Entmythologisierung der neutestamentlichen Verkündigung*, München: Chr. Kaiser).

12 The most important volumes are vols 1 and 2, which are translated into English. Hans-Werner Bartsch and Rudolf Karl Bultmann, 1953, *Kerygma and Myth: A Theological Debate*, London: SPCK; Hans Werner Bartsch and Rudolf Karl Bultmann, 1962, *Kerygma and Myth: A Theological Debate*, translated by Reginald Horace Fuller, vol. II, London: SPCK. Both volumes are together in: Hans Weiner Bartsch (ed.), 1972, *Kerygma and Myth: A Theological Debate*, London: SPCK.

13 Rudolf Bultmann, 'The Problem of Hermeneutics' (German: Rudolf Bultmann, 1952, 'Das Problem der Hermeneutik' *Glauben und Verstehen*, vol. II, Tübingen: J. C. B. Mohr (Paul Siebeck)).

14 Rudolf Bultmann, 1971, *The Gospel of John: A Commentary*, translated by G. R. Beasley-Murray, Oxford: Blackwell (NB the introduction in the English translation is not by Bultmann but by Walter Schmithals. Bultmann's text, which is very readable, begins with the interpretation of chapter 1, verse 1. Although

the assumptions on the dislocation of manuscript pages and the relation between Gnosticism and Johannine Christianity are out of date, this book provides a superb example of the application of the existentialist interpretation to biblical texts – German: Rudolf Bultmann, 1941, *Das Evangelium des Johannes*, 10th edn, Göttingen: Vandenhoeck & Ruprecht).

15 Rudolf Bultmann, 1952, *Theology of the New Testament*, translated by Kendrick Grobel, 2 vols, London: SCM Press (German: Rudolf Bultmann, 1948, *Theologie des Neuen Testaments*, Tübingen: J. C. B. Mohr (Paul Siebeck)).

16 Anthony C. Thiselton, 1980, *The Two Horizons: New Testament Hermeneutics and Philosophical Description with special Reference to Heidegger, Bultmann, Gadamer, and Wittgenstein*, Exeter: Paternoster.

17 Heidegger, *Being and Time*, pp. 182–203.

18 Heidegger, *Being and Time*, pp. 118–19.

19 Heidegger, *Being and Time*, p. 182.

20 Heidegger, *Being and Time*, p. 120.

21 Heidegger, *Being and Time*, pp. 119–20.

22 Heidegger, *Being and Time*, p. 120.

23 Heidegger, *Being and Time*, p. 120.

24 Heidegger, *Being and Time*, p. 172.

25 Heidegger, *Being and Time*, p. 174.

26 Heidegger, *Being and Time*, p. 174.

27 Heidegger, *Being and Time*, p. 176.

28 Heidegger, *Being and Time*, pp. 203–4.

29 Hans Jonas, 1958, *The Gnostic Religion: The Message of the Alien God and the Beginnings of Christianity*, Boston: Beacon Press, which is an abridged translation of Hans Jonas, 1934, *Gnosis und spätantiker Geist*, Göttingen: Vandenhoeck & Ruprecht.

30 Jonas, *The Gnostic Religion*, p. 334.

31 Bultmann, *New Testament and Mythology*, pp. 17–22.

32 Heidegger, *Being and Time*, pp. 203–4.

33 Heidegger, *Being and Time*, p. 188.

34 Heidegger, *Being and Time*, p. 195.

35 Heidegger, *Being and Time*, p. 192.

36 Heidegger, *Being and Time*, p. 199–200.

37 Bultmann, 'What does it mean to speak of God?', p. 53 (italics in the original).

38 Bultmann, 'What does it mean to speak of God?', p. 56.

39 Bultmann, 'What does it mean to speak of God?', p. 55.

40 Bultmann, 'What does it mean to speak of God?', p. 63.

41 Philipp Melanchthon, Martin Bucer et al., 1969, *Melanchthon and Bucer, The Library of Christian Classics*, vol. 19, Philadelphia: Westminster Press, p. 21.

42 Bultmann, 'What does it mean to speak of God?', p. 64.

43 Bultmann, *Theology of the New Testament*, vol. 1, part II, pp. 195–345, vol. 2, part III, pp. 3–75.

44 Rudolf Bultmann, 1972, 'New Testament and Mythology', in: Hans Werner Bartsch (ed.), *Kerygma and Myth*, pp. 17–43.

45 Bultmann, 'New Testament and Mythology', p. 18.

46 Bultmann, 'New Testament and Mythology', p. 18.
47 Bultmann, 'New Testament and Mythology', p. 22.
48 Bultmann, 'New Testament and Mythology', p. 43.
49 Bultmann, 'New Testament and Mythology', p. 22.
50 Rudolf Bultmann, 1972, 'The Case for Demythologizing', in: Bartsch (ed.), *Kerygma and Myth*, p. 192.
51 Bultmann, 'The Case for Demythologizing', pp. 192–3.
52 Karl Barth, 1972, 'Rudolf Bultmann – An Attempt to Understand Him', in: Bartsch (ed.), *Kerygma and Myth*, p. 114.
53 Barth, 'Rudolf Bultmann', p. 115.
54 Paul Ricoeur, 1980, 'Preface to Bultmann', in: *Essays on Biblical Interpretation*, Philadelphia: Fortress Press, pp. 65–6.
55 Ricoeur, 'Preface to Bultmann', p. 68.
56 Ricoeur, 'Preface to Bultmann', p. 72.

9

Existentialism II: The Path to Language

The German theologian Gerhard Ebeling (1912–2001) put the main insight of existentialist hermeneutics into a simple phrase. '*The primary phenomenon in the realm of understanding is not understanding* OF *language, but understanding* THROUGH *language.*'[1] Ebeling took up some important insights offered by the early Heidegger and Rudolf Bultmann, and developed their thought further. In this chapter, we will follow the thinking on the connection between language and meaning as proposed by Martin Heidegger in the later years of his career, his pupil Hans-Georg Gadamer (1900–2002), and Paul Ricoeur (1913–2005), who followed a Heideggerian approach in France quite independently of Gadamer. In this we will see how these thinkers avoided the two dangers highlighted by the critique of Bultmann. The first is the assumption that the object of theological hermeneutics and theology as a whole is only concerned with the human self before God, thus eclipsing a wider understanding of the human self as embedded in the wider world. The second is the notion that there is such a thing as 'innocent' language, which communicates the Christian *kerygma* without loss. We will see in this chapter how the authors featuring in the discussion overcome these problems.

Understanding through language

Heidegger in his later career

We saw in the previous chapter how Heidegger saw language expressing the speaker's or writer's interpretation of being. Consequently, Heidegger argued that assertions or apophantic statements were only derived from the more authentic form of language, which is interpretation of being.

In his later phase, Heidegger takes up this train of thought again, develops it further and elaborates on the relation between being and language. Heidegger's terminology is again somewhat confusing, which has led to many misunderstandings of his thought. For example, Antony Thiselton in his otherwise excellent study of existentialist hermeneutics finds that Heidegger's philosophy is in danger of 'word magic' and 'language mysticism'.[2] In order to avoid such misunderstanding of Heidegger's thought, it is necessary to distinguish carefully the terms he uses. Thus we shall approach Heidegger's later hermeneutical thinking by discussing the key terms, which Heidegger introduces in a number of lectures and essays throughout the 1950s, collected and published in the volume *On the Way to Language*.[3] These lectures are the main source for our understanding of Heidegger's later hermeneutical thought.

Heidegger distinguishes between language as *Geläut der Stille* (which can be translated as 'peal of stillness', as the English translator does,[4] or as 'sound of silence', which captures other important elements of Heidegger's phrase and, in addition, sounds more poetic) and as *Lauten des Wortes* (sounding of the word).[5] In short, 'sound of silence' is language not as spoken or thought, but as meaningful relation of being. 'Sounding of the word' is language as conceptual thought or spoken word. Furthermore, we will discuss the terms *Unter-Schied* (dif-ference)[6] and *Ereignis* (event – the English translation translates it as 'appropriation', which captures some of the meaning of the German, but omits other important connotations).[7]

Before we enter the discussion, it may be worthwhile pointing out that I believe that although the later Heidegger's theory of language and his hermeneutics are expressed in a highly idiosyncratic and obscure terminology, they can be understood in a much more straightforward way in the language of Augustine of Hippo's hermeneutics, which we have discussed in a previous chapter (see pp. 45–7).

Geläut der Stille *(sound of silence)* and Lauten des Wortes *(sounding of the word)*

Language as *Geläut der Stille* is not language as utterance or conceptual thought. It is language as meaningful relations of being which have not yet been conceptualized. Thus it must be carefully distinguished from spoken language, which Heidegger calls *Lauten des Wortes* (sounding of the word).

> The peal of stillness [sound of silence] is not anything human. But on the contrary, the human is indeed in its nature given to speech – it is linguistic. The word 'linguistic' as it is here used means: having taken place out of the speaking of language. What has thus taken place, human being, has been brought into its own by language, so that it remains given over or appropriated to the nature of language, the peal of stillness. Such appropriating takes place in that the very *nature*,

the *presencing*, of language *needs and uses* the speaking of mortals in order to sound as the peal of stillness for the hearing of mortals.[8]

Thus language as *Geläut der Stille* needs human language in order to be heard. It is the meaningful relationship of the individual and the totality in the world, the single thing and the whole. We saw earlier that Heidegger viewed language as the meaningful relationship of being already in *Being and Time*. There, Heidegger used the term 'significance' for the meaningful relationship of being, and 'discourse' for its expression in language. Here, in Heidegger's later work, the meaningful relationship of being is called *Geläut der Stille*, or, in another place, *Sage* (saying).[9]

Unterschied *(dif-ference)*

Language as *Geläut der Stille* originates in the *Unterschied* (dif-ference). The dif-ference is thought as a threshold, where the inside and the outside are ultimately close and yet definitely separated.[10] In the dif-ference, the individual thing is intimately close to the totality of being, but at the same time definitely separated. But it is at rest, that is, its meaningful relationship with the totality of the world is established.[11]

Moreover, the dif-ference gathers the world, in so far as the whole world is in meaningful relationship with the individual thing in the dif-ference. Thus it calls being into presence and 'grants' us things.[12] The 'granting' of things can be understood as disclosing to the human person, to the *Dasein*, the meaningful relationships by which the individual thing is related to the world and the world to the thing. Without language as *Geläut der Stille*, which originates in the dif-ference, the world would be meaningless because of the absence of meaningful relationships.

Ereignis *(event/appropriation)*

Language is disclosed in the event. It originates in the dif-ference, and is disclosed to the *Dasein* in the event. The event is not the result of a cause, an incident happening, but the granting of language.[13] In the event, the human being encounters language as *Sage* (saying) or *Geläut der Stille*, being is disclosed and *Dasein* is enabled to speak.[14]

Heidegger's *Ereignis* (event/appropriation) bears interesting resemblances to the religious experience as we found it in Schleiermacher's *Speeches* (see pp. 99–100). 'A manifestation, an event [NB Schleiermacher does not use the German term *Ereignis* here, but *Begebenheit*] develops quickly and magically into an image of the universe.'[15] For Schleiermacher, in the 'mysterious moment . . . before intuition and feeling are separated', the 'universe' – the totality of being – discloses itself to the beholder in a direct and immediate impression in relation to an individual 'manifestation' or 'event'.[16] The unity and separation between the totality and the individual are disclosed. Only after this moment the immediate impression is conceptualized through intuition and feeling.

Heidegger was familiar with Schleiermacher's work.[17] He uses a similar concept as Schleiermacher: in the event, the relation between the individual and the totality (the intimate closeness and yet definite separation which is expressed in the image of the dif-ference) is immediately (i.e. in an unmediated way) disclosed. In this understanding of the disclosure of being, Heidegger solves a problem in Augustine's hermeneutics and theory of mind, which the Church Father could not solve.

We recall that for Augustine the content of the mind, of the memory, was always complete, put there by God (see pp. 41–2). From this repository of memories thought would enter consciousness and there be translated into language. This neo-Platonic understanding of knowledge was not tenable in modern times, as it was generally assumed, at least since John Locke, that the mind is an empty slate that is gradually filled by sensory impressions. Thus the problem for any Augustinian hermeneutical theory is the origin of the memory. Heidegger, who had studied the relevant texts by Augustine thoroughly,[18] now offered an interesting solution: the pre-verbal thought does not originate from the memory as the repository of all knowledge, but from the self-disclosure of being in the event. In the event, the mysterious moment, meaningful relationships of being are disclosed, or, in other words, language as the *Geläut der Stille* or as 'saying' is 'heard' – 'to hear' is obviously used metaphorically here. Human language responds to the *Geläut der Stille*, and language (as *Geläut der Stille* or as 'saying') speaks through human language. Thus the inner word, the *verbum interius*, which the human has heard, is incarnate in the human word, the *verbum externum*. Thus, although he does not make this connection explicitly, Heidegger takes up Augustine's fundamental hermeneutical insight. In simple terms, the world is disclosed to the human beholder, and the human beholder responds to this disclosure by speaking. His or her speech then contains the revelation of the world. Thus Augustine's hermeneutics are married with Locke's assumption that the human mind is a *tabula rasa*, an empty slate, which is gradually filled.

Hans-Georg Gadamer

Hans-Georg Gadamer's hermeneutical thought follows that of his academic teacher Heidegger very closely in some respects. However, Heidegger's earlier work exerts the strongest influence over Gadamer, who develops those thoughts further and builds on them. Not surprisingly, there are a number of parallels between Gadamer's hermeneutical thinking and that of the later Heidegger. We will come back to these below. For now, it may suffice to observe that Gadamer's work is written in a much more approachable style and straightforward terminology than Heidegger's. It may be for this reason that Gadamer's hermeneutics are much more popular and more widely discussed and used than Heidegger's.

Gadamer's main work is his book *Truth and Method* (*Wahrheit und Methode*),[19] in which he deals with a number of philosophical questions, and discusses important hermeneutical issues extensively. Two issues raised in *Truth and Method* will be particularly relevant for our investigation: first, Gadamer's view of the relation between language and world, and second, the implications of his hermeneutical theory for textual interpretation.

Gadamer follows Heidegger in assuming that our understanding of the world takes place through language. He writes:

> Language is the universal medium in which understanding itself is realised. The mode of realisation of understanding is interpretation. . . . All understanding is interpretation, and all interpretation takes place in the medium of a language which would allow the object to come into words and yet is at the same time the interpreter's own language.[20]

Within this short quotation, we can already see an important difference between the thought of the later Heidegger and that of Gadamer. For Heidegger, it is language that speaks, that reveals the meaningful relationships of being. For Gadamer, it is the activity of the interpreter that generates language and understanding. In this respect, Gadamer follows the work of the early Heidegger rather than the later. This indicates that Heidegger's early philosophy could be developed in various directions, among them the hermeneutical thinking of the later Heidegger and that of Gadamer.

Much more explicit than for Bultmann and Heidegger, for Gadamer the foundation of his hermeneutical thinking is Augustine's distinction between the inner word and the spoken word. Gadamer himself once implied in a conversation that Augustine's teaching of the inner word was at the very heart of his own philosophy.[21] In *Truth and Method*, he dedicated a key section to the inner word in discussion with Augustine and Thomas Aquinas.[22] Following these hints and using the distinction between the inner and spoken word as the key to Gadamer's hermeneutics will provide a useful guide for the following discussion.

We have seen in the quotation above that humans understand the world through language. Language is the means by which meaningful relationships of being are established and understood. Thus, Gadamer can say that 'whoever has language "has" the world'.[23] World, for Gadamer, is the totality of meaningful relations, as opposed to the surrounding world or habitat (*Umwelt*), which is not interpreted and therefore meaningless. Humans gain mastery and understanding of their surrounding world or habitat through language, and it becomes world.

> To have a 'world' means to have an attitude towards it. To have an attitude towards the world, however, means to keep oneself so free from what one encounters in the world that one is able to present it to oneself as it is. This capacity is both the having of a 'world' and the having of language. Thus the concept of 'world' or 'environment' (*Welt*) is in opposition to the concept of 'surrounding world' or 'habitat' (*Umwelt*), as possessed by every living thing[24]

Thus, one crucial difference between human beings and other animals is that humans possess language, and as a result of language a world which can be understood. This understanding of the world can also be communicated.

We saw above that language, for Gadamer, is a human activity. It is the means by which the world is understood and meaningful. Language is, quite obviously, inherited. We learn to speak from parents and other members of our community. Thus we inherit the understanding of the world that is contained within the language that we learn to speak. Gadamer calls this 'linguistic tradition'.[25]

As humans, whose main property is the possession of language, we have inherited a particular understanding of the world once we learn language. Consequently, our understanding of the world is not neutral or objective, but always shaped by culture and society, by its values, presuppositions and prejudices. However, the understanding of the world is not static, it is open to change, be it by incremental development or revolutionary transformation. And as the understanding of the world changes, language changes, as it comes to contain new relationships of being.

The fusion of horizons

These fundamental hermeneutical insights regarding the nature of the world and language have important implications for the interpretation of texts. In the context of textual interpretation, Gadamer introduces the concept of the horizon.[26] In everyday language, horizon is the range of vision that includes everything that can be seen from a particular vantage point. In Gadamer's hermeneutical theory, it stands for the world as it is understood by a particular person. Thus the author of a text has his or her own horizon. The text itself has a horizon, too, which contains its own web of meaning enshrined in its language. This may be different from that of the author, because the author will not be able to include all of his or her horizon into the book. Obviously, the reader has his or her own horizon as well. In the interpretation of a text, the horizons of the text and the reader are fused. The 'fusion of horizons' stands for the enrichment of the understandings of the world, which takes place when the reader discovers meaningful relationships of being within the text, of which he or she was not aware before. A new horizon is formed, which is wider than the horizon of the text and that of the reader, which contains a new array of meaningful relationships. In short, the reader's understanding of the world has been broadened by the understanding of the world contained in the text.

It would be wrong to assume that the horizon of the text and that of the reader are completely separated. Of course, there are two horizons to start with, which means that the text is, in one respect, alien to the reader. In another aspect, however, the text and the reader belong to the same human culture; the text, through its 'effective history', that is, the impact it has had on the development of human thought, is more or less strongly connected with the interpreter. Homer's *Iliad*, for example, is a text that, even if not many have read it, has profoundly influenced European literature and other art forms, such as cinema and film. So if a reader takes up this text, he or she will find a degree of familiarity with the text. Gadamer puts this phenomenon this way: 'The place between strangeness and familiarity that a transmitted text has for us is that intermediate place between being a historically intended separate object and being part of a tradition. The true home of hermeneutics is in this intermediate area.'[27]

In this intermediate area between being a historically intended separate object and being part of a tradition, new truth can emerge. 'In as much as the tradition is newly expressed in language, something comes into being that had not existed before and that exists from now on.'[28]

This new understanding, the new meaningful relationships of being that had not existed before, is the new horizon which is the result of the fusion of the horizons of the text and the interpreter.

Gadamer takes up the insights of Heidegger and Bultmann regarding the pre-understanding of the subject matter of a text. Most readers take up a text with a particular purpose. For example, for the writing of this chapter I have taken my copy of *Truth and Method* from the bookshelf in order to refresh my knowledge of Gadamer's hermeneutics. So in order to learn about hermeneutics, of which I already have a moderate grasp, I approach a text that I think might be helpful. If I wanted to learn about something completely different, for instance whale hunting in the nineteenth century, then *Truth and Method* would be a bad choice. I might go and read Melville's *Moby Dick* instead. Thus I approach a text with one or more questions in mind. For Gadamer, every text is an answer to a question or a set of questions. 'But we found that this kind of understanding, "making the text speak," is not an arbitrary procedure that we undertake on our own initiative but that, as a question, it is related to the answer that is expected in the text.'[29] Obviously, the interpreter does not approach the text in a vacuum. The questions an interpreter may bring to a text are part of his or her world; they are part of the linguistic tradition.

Thus the questions themselves spring from the linguistic tradition of which reader and the texts are parts. For example, if I approach a religious text in order to deepen my understanding of religion, my preconceptions of religion are shaped by the Western Christian culture. And even someone who does not have any explicit knowledge about religion would still be deeply influenced by the same tradition. Thus even this relatively uninformed person will find a certain degree of familiarity with a text from the Western Christian tradition. So when a reader approaches a religious text in order to learn about religion, it is likely that the text will answer his or her question. When the text answers the reader's question and offers a new insight into the issue, then understanding, the fusion of horizons, is taking place.

Consequently, interpretation is a dialogue between the text and the reader, in which the reader approaches the text with a set of questions, which the text may or may not answer. In fact, the result of the interpretation may even be that the reader modifies his or her questions to more appropriate ones, which the text can answer better than the initial ones. In short, reading is dialogue.

An uncritical hermeneutic?

Much has been made of Gadamer's negative attitude towards methods in interpretation. Werner Jeanrond even suggests that 'the title of Gadamer's *magnum opus* should really be "Truth *or* Method" for he sees a radical conflict between his phenomenological approach to hermeneutics on the one hand and the host of modern methodological approaches for an adequate text-understanding on the other hand.'[30] This comment raises two serious questions. One is that of the significance of the passages on textual interpretation in the overall composition of the work, the other the question of Gadamer's attitude towards critical interpretation.

First, although Gadamer's comments on the interpretation of texts are highly significant and have influenced later thought on this issue in many ways, this is not the main point of Gadamer's book. It is an important step in Gadamer's argument, which culminates in his proposal of a hermeneutical ontology, in which language is the medium through which we understand the world. We have already discussed this aspect of Gadamer's hermeneutical thinking in the first part of this section. In this wider context, Gadamer's critical view of the use of methods in textual interpretation is only one aspect, and not the main one, in the thrust of the argument.

Second, Gadamer indeed argues against a hermeneutical theory that aims, through the careful use of methods, to recover the meaning of the text as the author intended it. In 1955, the Italian jurist Emilio Betti (1890–1968) suggested such a hermeneutical theory in his book *General Theory of Interpretation*.[31] Although Betti's book was translated into German only in 1967 (probably on Gadamer's instigation and by the same publisher who published *Truth and Method*),[32] he was known in Germany before that through a series of shorter polemical writings. Betti follows Dilthey's thinking in some key areas. With Dilthey, Betti sees entering the mind of the author as its final goal of interpretation, and careful application of methods as the means to this end. Much of Gadamer's work can be seen as a rejection of Betti's approach, which he replaces with a universal hermeneutical ontology.

In addition, Gadamer, although he diminishes the relevance of critical methods, does not envisage an uncritical reader. Gadamer's reader is the well-read and classically educated product of humanistic or liberal education in Germany. Gadamer refers to the *humanistische Gymnasium* – a German type secondary school in which the curriculum focuses on the classical languages Greek and Latin – in at least one place in *Truth and Method*.[33] In another place, Gadamer assumes that the learning of ancient languages (i.e. Greek and Latin) is a common experience he shares with the reader.[34] The interpreter whom Gadamer has in mind applies Gadamer's hermeneutics grounded within the old German liberal education. The person shaped by this education has enough critical intuition when reading ancient texts so that he or she is sufficiently educated, cultured and equipped with taste that the schematic application of methods may not be necessary. Alas, today this kind of education is available only to a small proportion of the population. Against this background, it would be misunderstanding Gadamer to assume that he dismisses critical reading altogether. His reader does it intuitively.

Having said this, Gadamer's basic hermeneutical insights, the fusion of the horizons and the turn to a hermeneutical ontology do not necessarily exclude the use of critical methods. Gadamer's younger French contemporary Paul Ricoeur shows that it is not only possible, but also a fruitful undertaking, to apply critical methods to the practice of reading within the framework of a hermeneutical ontology.

Paul Ricoeur

Paul Ricoeur developed his hermeneutical thought independently of Gadamer. In fact, we can assume that Ricoeur's main works of the 1960s and early 1970s were written without any knowledge of Gadamer's writings.[35] However, pursuing a rather different path than Gadamer, Ricoeur arrived at very similar conclusions.

Ricoeur's starting point is hermeneutics as the methodology for the interpretation of texts, not as the fundamental ontology of existence as for Heidegger. Thus Ricoeur stands in the tradition of Schleiermacher and Dilthey much more than in that of existentialism. In fact, he even criticizes the early Heidegger's move towards hermeneutics as the ontology of facticity as an illegitimate short cut. However, he also suggests that a consistent methodological approach will, in the end, also lead to a very similar result. The key to this long path to an ontology of existence via methodological hermeneutics is Ricoeur's understanding of symbol and metaphor. In his study of these figures of speech, Ricoeur arrived at his fundamental insight that language contains a 'surplus of meaning', layers of meaning beyond the immediate content of the utterance. Through this 'surplus of meaning', language is intrinsically bound up with human understanding of existence. We will explore this train of thought step by step in this section.

Sources and literature

The enormous range of Ricoeur's work spans everything from religious symbolism, psychology and theory of metaphor and narrative to a universal hermeneutical theory. For the purposes of a theological hermeneutics, the most important works by Ricoeur are *The Symbolism of Evil*, *Freud and Philosophy*, *The Conflict of Interpretations*, *The Rule of Metaphor*, *Interpretation Theory: Discourse and the Surplus of Meaning*, *Essays on Biblical Interpretation*, *Hermeneutics and the Human Sciences*, *Time and Narrative*, *Oneself as Another*, *Figuring the Sacred*.[36] For the reader unfamiliar with Ricoeur, *Interpretation Theory* will be a good first reading, as Ricoeur offers a good introduction of his work in this series of lectures. Dan Stiver's *Theology after Ricoeur* presents a helpful interpretation of and introduction to Ricoeur's hermeneutics.[37]

Critical method

One of Ricoeur's best-known concepts is the 'second naïvety'. This notion, which Ricoeur explored from the late 1960s, relates to a post-critical reading of the text. In short, when we read a text for the first time, we read it at a superficial level, and make an informed guess as to what the text may mean. This, however, constitutes only a naïve understanding. This needs to be followed by critical explanation of the text. In the process of this critical explanation, the reader moves, as it were, from 'in front of the text' to 'behind the text', and treats it with all the critical tools at the interpreter's disposal. Historical-critical methods may be employed, as may be structuralist analysis, psychoanalytical interpretation, Marxist critique of ideology, etc. Certainly, not every interpreter will use all methods, but a broad range of methods should be employed.

In the critical explanation of the text, the three masters of suspicion, whom we have already met above (see p. 109),[38] come into play. Ricoeur saw the significance of Freud, Nietzsche and Marx in their approach to texts guided by suspicion. In short, the text may say something else than it appears to at face value, something else than the author intended. Thus in Freudian psychological criticism, the text conveys the suppressed desires of the author as much as the intended subject matter. In Marxist critique of ideology, the text is understood to be primarily about the economic and social circumstances of the time and place of its writing. And for a Nietzschean interpretation, the text would tell of the author's will to power, or its suppression by the powerless. Thus, for all three masters of suspicion, the text conveys something more about the author and/or his or her time than meets the eye. It is this raising of the interpreter's critical awareness that Marx, Nietzsche and Freud contribute to Ricoeur's hermeneutical theory.

After having explained the text critically, the interpreter returns 'in front of the text', and reads it again at the surface level, but this time critically informed. Ricoeur calls this stage the second naïvety, in which a straightforward reading at the surface level is informed by the preceding critical explanation. This critically naïve reading may then, in turn, become the starting point for further critical explanation. Thus Ricoeur recognizes the fundamental circularity of understanding.[39]

The surplus of meaning

For Ricoeur, the task of interpretation does not stop with the mechanics of textual interpretation. On the contrary, this is only the starting point of the exploration of the surplus of meaning. As we have seen above, Ricoeur uses the masters of suspicion to show that there is a surplus of meaning in the text – the intended meaning plus the unintended meaning. Moreover, surplus of meaning entails not only unintended information about the speaker, but his or her whole world – because for Ricoeur, as for Gadamer, language is a web of meaningful relationships. 'Discourse refers to the speaker at the same time that it refers to the world.'[40] Discourse refers to the speaker in two ways, by conveying the intended meaning and also conveying information about the speaker. It refers to the world in so far as it 'tabs into' the pre-existing web of meaningful relationships within the language. At one point Ricoeur refers to this as the 'universe of logos'.[41] Thus language operates in two areas, on the one hand in 'real' life, referring to the author, on the other to discourse itself, that is, to the totality of meaningful relations contained within a language.

In this context, metaphor plays an important part in Ricoeur's hermeneutical thinking, because it demonstrates how language works and meaning is created. Ricoeur sees metaphor not merely as a trope or figure of speech, but a semantic device that bears meaning which could not be expressed in any other ways. It serves as an example for the way in which meaning arises.[42]

In a metaphor, two elements are combined that do not make sense together at the literal level. This leads to a creative tension between the two elements of the metaphor. They shed light on each other, and relationships of meaning applying to one element are brought into relation with the other.

What is at stake in a metaphorical utterance . . . is the appearance of kinship where ordinary vision does not perceive any relationship. . . . It is, in effect, a calculated error, which brings together things that do not go together and by means of this apparent misunderstanding it causes a new, hitherto unnoticed, relation of meaning to spring up between the terms that previous systems of classification had ignored or not allowed.[43]

So, as Ricoeur points out, when Shakespeare likens time to a beggar in the *Rape of Lucretia* this sheds an entirely new light on the human experience of time.[44] Through the newly established relationship between 'time' and 'beggar', new meaning is created, and the reader's understanding of the world is altered. 'A metaphor, in short, tells us something new about reality.'[45]

A metaphor, however, operates only in the 'already purified universe of the *logos*', that is, in discourse.[46] This means it only relates to other discourse, to pure language, without direct relation to *bios*, to life. This relation is made by the symbol. Ricoeur sees the symbol as hesitating on the 'dividing line between *bios* and *logos*'.[47] The symbol refers to something that occurs in the world, which can be seen, touched or experienced, and links it with additional meaning. Thus the symbol refers to more than is visible, it does not merely refer to the realm of *bios*, but to a whole range of meaningful relationships in the realm of *logos*. For example, if one speaks of a lion, this refers to the animal (or, to be more precise, to the mental image of the animal), as well as to a whole range of symbolic meanings, such as the lion as symbol of kingship, of strength and valour, and of a long list of other things.

Ricoeur brings the two concepts of metaphor and symbol together in the concept of the 'root metaphor'.[48] Root metaphors are metaphors that are rooted in other metaphors and symbols. They are thus deeply embedded in the web of meaningful relationships that is language. So a root metaphor evokes a whole field of meaning, which opens a wide field of relationships of being.

For Ricoeur, meaning is brought about not by individual words, but by the combination of words. We have discussed this in relation to metaphor and symbol. Such creation of meaning can also take place through narrative. Ricoeur sees the parable, for example, as an extended metaphor with a narrative element.[49] In his work *Time and Narrative*, Ricoeur discusses the creation of meaning through complex narratives. Basically, complex narratives reveal new meaning in a similar way as metaphor and symbol. The author puts his or her understanding of the world into plot (which Ricoeur creatively calls emplotment[50]) by means of mimicking life and shaping a narrative that contains his or her understanding of the world.

The conflict of interpretations

We saw earlier that Ricoeur finds a surplus of meaning in texts; they mean more than the author intended. In fact they may potentially contain an unlimited range of meaning. This implies, first of all, that authorial intention is only one aspect of the meaning of the text. Thus the text, as text, is a discrete identity, existing independently of the author and his or her intention. It is the reader who constructs meaning from the text, and each reader will do so in different ways and come to different conclusions. This, however, does not mean that interpretation is arbitrary and entirely subjective, as post-structuralism and deconstruction imply – we will discuss these approaches later (see pp. 166–70). Ricoeur argues that there are interpretations which are more plausible than others, and in the conflict of interpretations, interpreters discuss their various construals of the text and thus verify valid interpretations and falsify invalid ones. Thus through the conflict of interpretations, the field of valid interpretations of a given text is narrowed down.

This does not mean that the range of valid interpretations is closed; on the contrary, new interpretations of a text may emerge, and be discussed in the conflict of interpretation. If they survive as valid interpretations, they add to the field of meaning contained in the text.

Action and text

Finally, Ricoeur assumes that all meaningful action is to be understood as text. Action, as Ricoeur understands it here, is historical action, past events. Ricoeur assumes that historical events, such as the French Revolution, are in fact understood in analogy to texts. Events are interpreted, they are given meaning. The meaning of an event, like that of a text, is not determined by the author, or the agent.[51] This is not only because of the unintended consequences which human actions always bring with them, but also because it can be interpreted in different ways. Thus the French Revolution can be seen as a shining example of the power of reason and the ideals of liberty, equality and fraternity, leading to the development of a great nation, or it can be interpreted as an act of violation of ancient authority, a hasty overthrow of a regime, which led to barbarism and cruelty. The former interpretation is likely to be found in French history books, the latter in English popular literature, such as Baroness Emmuska Orczy's *The Scarlet Pimpernel*.

Furthermore, apparently accidental events may become highly significant, such as the sinking of the *Titanic* in 1912. As far as losses of ships go, this disaster was not a particularly big one, but it took on a great cultural significance, symbolizing the demise of the cultural optimism of the nineteenth century. And thus a great mythology has developed around this particular accident, which gained much more meaning for later generations than greater disasters. Thus, human action and events are in principle open works, open to ongoing interpretation and reinterpretation.[52]

The understanding of human action in analogy to the text leads to the understanding of the human self in analogy to a text. As Stiver points out:

> Ricoeur's understanding of the self is that all of us construe an ongoing narrative, or at least a protonarrative, of our lives, so the prefigured world in which we act as agents, while not written as text, already contains a protoplot.[53]

The way in which humans make sense of their lives is by constructing a narrative. This may be not in an explicit way, which is to what Stiver refers by the term 'protoplot'. However, as soon as one tells of one's life and of its meaning (or lack of it), the narrative structure becomes explicit. Or, to use the terminology of the early Heidegger, one's state-of-mind is expressed in narrative form.

The interpreter of this narrative reconstructs the world revealed by it, that is, the understanding of human existence that is contained in the narrative. As a result, the interpreter's understanding of existence, the interpreter's world, will be altered. The event that Gadamer calls the 'fusion of horizons' takes place. Or, in other words, the inner word of the text is recovered from within the external word.

We have seen that Ricoeur, although along another, longer path than the one Heidegger and Bultmann chose, arrives at an ontology of existence in his hermeneutical theory. Thus he builds a bridge between methodologically oriented hermeneutics such as Dilthey's and Betti's, and hermeneutics as the ontology of existence. In fact, as we will see in later chapters, his hermeneutical theory is eminently suited to facilitate discussion between diverse hermeneutical schools.

Ricoeur, unlike Heidegger and Gadamer, reflects critically on the issues raised by the textual nature of human understanding of reality. His concept of the surplus of meaning exposes the problems involved in the composition and interpretation of texts, and the resulting need for critical interpretation. Ricoeur went beyond Heidegger and Gadamer in supplementing the phenomenon of the inner word as the basis for the universal claim of hermeneutics by the universality of the text as basis for the human understanding of the world and the self. Having said this, it is important to keep in mind that for Ricoeur, although the world and existence are interpreted in analogy to text, the world is not text alone, because language builds the bridge between *bios* and *logos*.

Conclusion

In this chapter so far, we have followed the development of one important school of hermeneutics, which stands in the tradition of existentialism and which views the ontology of existence as an integral part of the hermeneutical endeavour. The key element in the thought of all thinkers discussed in this chapter is what Gerhard Ebeling expressed in the quote at the beginning of this chapter, that is that '*the primary phenomenon in the realm of understanding is not understanding* OF *language, but understanding* THROUGH *language*'.[54] In other words, the hermeneutical task is much more complex than only interpreting texts, because texts embody an interpretation of human existence, and interpretation of the human existence always takes place through language.

It may be worthwhile pointing out at this point that, although especially Gadamer and Ricoeur seem to understand language primarily as spoken and written, I would suggest that language be understood much more widely. Heidegger, for instance, used the work of art as an example for the workings of language.[55] In extension of this, one may also include other means by which existence can be interpreted within space and time. This would include music, mime, painting, sculpture and much more. But to include these other forms of interpretation of existence would be beyond the scope of this study.

Nevertheless, the widening of the task of hermeneutics from the interpretation of linguistic utterances to the fundamental ontology of existence, that is, the notion that all our understanding takes place through language, has far-reaching implications for all areas of theology, not only for the interpretation of biblical or other text.

Hermeneutical theology

The discussions of the preceding chapters are of great importance for theology – to the extent that a theology that takes them seriously will be a hermeneutical theology. This claim will be examined in this section. First, however, we will examine how the hermeneutical considerations of the later Heidegger, Gadamer and Ricoeur have been received by theologians, and second some general reflections on the shape of a hermeneutical theology will be offered. However, it is important to keep in mind that the approach offered in this chapter does not claim to be the only valid approach to theology. So subsequent chapters will discuss alternative approaches to theological hermeneutics and their implications for theology.

The new hermeneutics

A group of German theologians, known in German as *hermeneutische Theologie* or, in English, the 'new hermeneutic',[56] entered a close dialogue with the philosophical hermeneutics of the later Heidegger and Gadamer from the 1950s. Among them are Ernst Fuchs (1903–83) and Gerhard Ebeling (1912–2001).

Ernst Fuchs and the New Quest for the historical Jesus

The main sources for Fuchs' hermeneutical reflections are his two volumes *Hermeneutik* of 1954 and *Marburger Hermeneutik* of 1968.[57] In these, Fuchs seeks a conversation with Heidegger's later philosophy, and develops ways in which this can be applied to theology in general and New Testament interpretation in particular. Fuchs sees the human condition as being trapped in inauthentic language. We recall that, for the later Heidegger, language 'grants' us things, that is, it makes understanding possible and offers ways of understanding human existence. Fuchs sees the human understanding of existence as marred by inauthentic language, which does not disclose being.

Fuchs finds authentic language within the New Testament, and in particular in the authentic sayings of Jesus. Consequently, the identification of authentic sayings of Jesus becomes a priority for New Testament theology. This aim links in with the programme of the New Quest for the historical Jesus, which was instigated by a lecture given by Ernst Käsemann in 1953,[58] and which concentrated on identifying authentic sayings of Jesus. It is interesting to note at this place that both Fuchs and

Käsemann were pupils of Rudolf Bultmann. Bultmann had denied the theological significance of the historical Jesus. His pupils, however, while making use of the existentialist interpretation, rejected their teacher's position and embarked on the New Quest.

Those pursuing the New Quest would identify an authentic saying by Jesus using the criterion of difference, that is, those sayings that could not be derived from either Jewish thought or that of the early Church are likely to be authentic. Sometimes, an authentic saying would be identified within a longer saying or parable and reconstructed.[59]

This saying is then interpreted with a view to the understanding of existence that is embodied in it. The parables of Jesus were a particularly interesting group of texts, as they contain a small world within themselves. Thus the texts were seen as inviting the reader to enter the language world of the text, and to gain a new self-understanding and authentic language, enabling a new, more authentic understanding of existence in the process.

Thus, although moving away from Bultmann's rejection of research into the historical Jesus, the foundation of the New Quest is a modified form of the existentialist interpretation which takes seriously the significance of language for human interpretation of existence. The New Quest was popular among New Testament scholars, particularly in Germany and North America. Among the practitioners of the New Quest are, besides Käsemann and Fuchs, Günther Bornkamm, Norman Perrin, Robert Funk and James Robinson.

Although the New Quest for the historical Jesus was an important stage in the development of both New Testament Scholarship and hermeneutical reflection, a much wider approach to theological language is needed, as we will see in the discussion below (see the section 'A hermeneutical theology', pp. 212–21).

Gerhard Ebeling

Unlike his colleagues Fuchs and Käsemann, Gerhard Ebeling did not engage in the New Quest for the historical Jesus, but developed a more general approach to theological hermeneutics. His essays 'The Significance of the Critical Historical Method for Church and Theology in Protestantism' and 'Word of God and Hermeneutics'[60] give a good introduction into his thinking.

We have already seen in this chapter that Ebeling's key insight regarding hermeneutics is that '*the primary phenomenon in the realm of understanding is not understanding* OF *language, but understanding*

THROUGH *language*.[61] In the context of the hermeneutical considerations earlier in this chapter, the main thrust of this point ought to be clear; all understanding takes place through language, and language is something which is given to us, which we inherit from our surrounding culture. Thus we understand ourselves and the world through the matrix of existing language, although we can alter the matrix by altering the language, for example by inventing new metaphors or other means of expressing new, previously unknown relationships of being.

Keeping these insights in mind, we can now discuss Ebeling's thesis in its context.

> *The primary phenomenon in the realm of understanding is not understanding* OF *language, but understanding* THROUGH *language.* The word is not really the object of understanding, and thus the thing that poses the problem of understanding, the solution of which requires exposition and therefore also hermeneutics as the theory of understanding. Rather, the word is what opens up and mediates understanding, i.e. brings something to understanding. *The word itself has a hermeneutic function.* If the word-event takes place normally, i.e. according to its appointed purpose, then there is no need of any aid to understanding, but it is itself an aid to understanding. It is to my mind not unimportant for the proper grasp of the hermeneutic problem whether we set out from the idea that a verbal statement in itself is something obscure into which the light of understanding must be introduced, or whether, in the contrary, we set out from the fact that the situation in terms of which and into which the verbal statement is made is something obscure which is then illuminated by the verbal statement.[62]

In this passage, Ebeling raises the main issues with which a theological hermeneutic has to deal. First of all, there is the issue of the hindrance of the word-event. The word-event, to which Ebeling refers here, is the event of understanding, when the reader's (or hearer's) understanding of the world is altered by the word, that is, by the linguistic utterance. It is the fusion of horizons, in Gadamer's words, when text and reader come together and a new, wider horizon is established. In theology, the word-event is the encounter with the word of God, which is mediated through the human word of proclamation. The word, which has itself a hermeneutic function, makes the hearer or hearer understand his or her situation before God, which Ebeling, as a Lutheran theologian, takes to be that one is a sinner before God, yet justified without his or her own merit or worthiness. Thus the word interprets the hearer.

Whenever the word is heard and the word-event takes place, hermeneutical considerations are not necessary, for in this case the word fulfils its task. Hermeneutics is only needed if the word-event is hindered, and then, depending on the nature of the hindrance, measures need to be taken on a range from grammatical interpretation of the text to an analysis of what encounters us in the present, that is, the particular situation of the hearer or reader.

Furthermore, Ebeling sets his considerations on hermeneutics and theology firmly into the context of the existentialist interpretation as we have encountered it in our discussion of Rudolf Bultmann (see pp. 124–7). Ebeling remarks that 'the concept can be helpful and meaningful if it brings out the fact that existence is existence through word and in word. Then existentialist interpretation would mean *interpretation of the text with regard to the word-event.*'[63] Thus, the text is interpreted, is preached, in a way that facilitates the word-event, that is, so that the text is effective in performing its task. Or, in other words, that the word of God is heard in the text. Consequently, hermeneutics is for Ebeling, in the widest sense of the word, theology of the word of God.[64]

In his work, Ebeling formulated hermeneutics' claim to universality within the theological realm. If theology of the word of God is the foundation of theology, and hermeneutics is theology of the word of God, then all theology becomes hermeneutical. Theology, as Ebeling and those following him understand it, is necessarily hermeneutical theology.

We observe that hermeneutics has moved a long way. Once it was an ancillary science in the service of biblical interpretation. After Ebeling, hermeneutics claims to be at the very centre of all theological endeavour.

The hermeneutical debate was pursued vigorously until the late 1960s. Bultmann's existentialist interpretation and the hermeneutical reflections of the 'new hermeneutics' were broadly discussed in the theological world, until the debate subsided in the late 1960s. New issues, such as political and liberation theology, feminism and structuralism found interest among a younger generation of theologians. However, from the 1990s onwards, we can observe a renewed interest in hermeneutical questions, probably kindled by the issues raised by new challenges coming from biblical interpreters rejecting the historical-critical consensus and using a different set of methods, as well as by the debate of the various postmodern interpretative models. We will discuss these in later sections of this book.

Further reading

For Heidegger, see Further reading for Chapter 8, pp. 129–31.

Betti, Emilio, 1955, *Teoria Generale della Interpretazione*, 2 vols, Milano: Dott. A. Giuffrè Editore.

Betti, Emilio, 1967, *Allgemeine Auslegungslehre als Methodik der Geisteswissenschaften*, Tübingen: J. C. B. Mohr (Paul Siebeck).

Betti, Emilio, 1990, 'Hermeneutics as the General Methodology of the *Geisteswissenschaften*', in: Gayle L. Ormiston and Alan D. Schrift (eds), *The Hermeneutic Tradition: From Ast to Ricoeur*, Albany, NY: State University of New York Press, pp. 159–97.

Bourgeois, Patrick L. and Frank Schalow, 1990, *Traces of Understanding: A Profile of Heidegger's and Ricoeur's Hermeneutics, Elementa; Schriften zur Philosophie und ihrer Problemgeschichte*, vol. 53, Würzburg: Könighausen & Neumann.

Coltman, Rodney R., 1998, *The Language of Hermeneutics: Gadamer and Heidegger in Dialogue, SUNY Series in Contemporary Continental Philosophy*, Albany: State University of New York Press.

DiCenso, James, 1990, *Hermeneutics and the Disclosure of Truth: A Study in the Work of Heidegger, Gadamer and Ricoeur*, Charlottesville: University Press of Virginia.

Dostal, Robert J., 2002, *The Cambridge Companion to Gadamer, Cambridge Companions to Philosophy*, Cambridge: Cambridge University Press.

Ebeling, Gerhard, 1959, 'Hermeneutik', in: Kurt Galling (ed.), *Die Religion in Geschichte und Gegenwart*, vol. 3, 3rd edn, Tübingen: J. C. B. Mohr (Paul Siebeck), cols 242–62.

Ebeling, Gerhard, 1963, 'The Significance of the Critical Historical Method for Church and Theology in Protestantism', in: *Word and Faith*, London: SCM Press, pp. 17–61.

Ebeling, Gerhard, 1963, 'Word of God and Hermeneutics', in: *Word and Faith*, London: SCM Press, pp. 305–32.

Foster, Matthew Robert, 1991, *Gadamer and Practical Philosophy: The Hermeneutics of Moral Confidence*, Atlanta, Ga: Scholars Press.

Fuchs, Ernst, 1954, *Hermeneutik*, Bad Cannstatt: Müllerschön.

Fuchs, Ernst, 1968, *Marburger Hermeneutik, Hermeneutische Untersuchungen zur Theologie*, vol. 9, Tübingen: J. C. B. Mohr (Paul Siebeck).

Gadamer, Hans-Georg, 1959, 'Hermeneutik', in: Joachim Ritter (ed.), *Historisches Wörterbuch der Philosophie*, vol. 3, Darmstadt: Wissenschaftliche Buchgesellschaft, cols 1061–73.

Gadamer, Hans-Georg, 1960, *Wahrheit und Methode: Grundzüge einer philosophischen Hermeneutik*, Tübingen: J. C. B. Mohr (Paul Siebeck).

Gadamer, Hans-Georg, 1975, *Truth and Method*, London: Sheed & Ward.

Gadamer, Hans-Georg, 1989, 'Rhetoric, Hermeneutics and the Critique of Ideology', in: Kurt Mueller-Vollmer (ed.), *The Hermeneutics Reader: Texts of the German Tradition from the Enlightenment to the Present*, Oxford: Basil Blackwell, pp. 274–92.

Gadamer, Hans-Georg and Hugh J. Silverman, 1991, *Gadamer and Hermeneutics*, *Continental Philosophy*, vol. 4, New York; London: Routledge.

Gadamer, Hans-Georg and Lewis Edwin Hahn, 1997, *The Philosophy of Hans-Georg Gadamer*, *Library of Living Philosophers*, vol. 24, Chicago: Open Court.

Gadamer, Hans-Georg, Dieter Misgeld et al., 1992, *Hans-Georg Gadamer on Education, Poetry, and History: Applied Hermeneutics*, *SUNY Series in Contemporary Continental Philosophy*, Albany: State University of New York Press.

Grondin, Jean, 2001, 'Hans-Georg Gadamer und die französische Welt', in: *Von Heidegger zu Gadamer: Unterwegs zur Hermeneutik*, Darmstadt: Wissenschaftliche Buchgesellschaft, pp. 136–43.

Grondin, Jean, 2003, *Hans-Georg Gadamer: A Biography*, New Haven, Conn.; London: Yale University Press.

Grondin, Jean, 2003, *The Philosophy of Gadamer*, translated by Kathryn Plant, *Continental European Philosophy*, Chesham: Acumen.

Hahn, Lewis Edwin and Paul Ricoeur, 1995, *The Philosophy of Paul Ricoeur*, *Library of Living Philosophers*, vol. 22, Chicago: Open Court.

Harrington, Austin, 2001, *Hermeneutic Dialogue and Social Science: A Critique of Gadamer and Habermas*, *Routledge Studies in Social and Political Thought*, vol. 31, London: Routledge.

Käsemann, Ernst, 1962, 'The Problem of the Historical Jesus', in: *Essays on New Testament Themes*, London: SCM Press, pp. 23–65.

Kögler, Hans-Herbert, 1996, *The Power of Dialogue: Critical Hermeneutics after Gadamer and Foucault*, Cambridge, Mass. and London: MIT Press.

Michelfelder, Diane P. and Richard E. Palmer, 1989, *Dialogue and Deconstruction: The Gadamer–Derrida Encounter*, *SUNY Series in Contemporary Continental Philosophy*, Albany: State University of New York Press.

Palmer, Richard E., 1969, *Hermeneutics: Interpretation Theory in Schleiermacher, Dilthey, Heidegger, and Gadamer*, *Northwestern University Studies in Phenomenology & Existential Philosophy*, Evanston: Northwestern University Press.

Ricoeur, Paul, 1969, *The Symbolism of Evil*, *Beacon Paperback Ariadne*, vol. 18, Boston: Beacon Press.

Ricoeur, Paul, 1970, *Freud and Philosophy: An Essay on Interpretation*, translated by Denis Savage, *Terry Lectures*, New Haven; London: Yale University Press.

Ricoeur, Paul, 1974, *The Conflict of Interpretations: Essays in Hermeneutics*, *Northwestern University Studies in Phenomenology & Existential Philosophy*, Evanston: Northwestern University Press.

Ricoeur, Paul, 1975, 'Biblical Hermeneutics', *Semeia* 4, pp. 29–148.

Ricoeur, Paul, 1976, *Interpretation Theory: Discourse and the Surplus of Meaning*, Fort Worth: Texas Christian University Press.

Ricoeur, Paul, 1976, 'Language as Discourse', in: *Interpretation Theory: Discourse and the Surplus of Meaning*, Fort Worth: Texas Christian University Press, pp. 1–23.

Ricoeur, Paul, 1976, 'Metaphor and Symbol', in: *Interpretation Theory: Discourse and the Surplus of Meaning*, Fort Worth: Texas Christian University Press, pp. 45–69.

Ricoeur, Paul, 1977, *The Rule of Metaphor: Multi-disciplinary Studies of the Creation of Meaning in Language*, Toronto: University of Toronto Press.

Ricoeur, Paul, 1980, *Essays on Biblical Interpretation*, translated by Lewis Seymour Mudge, Philadelphia: Fortress Press.

Ricoeur, Paul, 1980, 'Preface to Bultmann', in: *Essays on Biblical Interpretation*, Philadelphia: Fortress Press, pp. 49–72.

Ricoeur, Paul, 1981, *Hermeneutics and the Human Sciences: Essays on Language, Action, and Interpretation*, translated by John B. Thompson, Cambridge and Paris: Cambridge University Press; Maison des sciences de l'homme.

Ricoeur, Paul, 1981, 'Metaphor and the Central Problem of Hermeneutics', in: *Hermeneutics and the Human Sciences: Essays on Language, Action, and Interpretation*, Cambridge and Paris: Cambridge University Press; Maison des sciences de l'homme, pp. 165–81.

Ricoeur, Paul, 1981, 'The Model of the Text: Meaningful Action considered as Text', in: *Hermeneutics and the Human Sciences: Essays on Language, Action, and Interpretation*, Cambridge and Paris: Cambridge University Press; Maison des sciences de l'homme, pp. 197–221.

Ricoeur, Paul, 1984, *Time and Narrative*, translated by Kathleen Blamey, 3 vols, Chicago; London: University of Chicago Press.

Ricoeur, Paul, 1992, *Oneself as Another*, Chicago; London: University of Chicago Press.

Ricoeur, Paul, 1995, *Figuring the Sacred: Religion, Narrative, and Imagination*, translated by Mark I. Wallace, Minneapolis: Fortress Press.

Risser, James, 1997, *Hermeneutics and the Voice of the Other: Re-reading Gadamer's Philosophical Hermeneutics, SUNY Series in Contemporary Continental Philosophy*, Albany: State University of New York Press.

Robinson, James McConkey and John B. Cobb, 1964, *The New Hermeneutic, New Frontiers in Theology*, vol. 2, New York: Harper & Row.

Stiver, Dan R., 2001, *Theology after Ricoeur: New Directions in hermeneutical Theology*, Louisville: Westminister John Knox Press.

Thiselton, Anthony C., 1977, 'The New Hermeneutic', in: I. H. Marshall (ed.), *New Testament Interpretation*, Exeter: Paternoster Press, pp. 308–33.

Wachterhauser, Brice R., 1999, *Beyond Being: Gadamer's post-Platonic Hermeneutical Ontology, Studies in Phenomenology & Existential Philosophy*, Evanston, Ill.: Northwestern University Press.

Warnke, Georgia, 1987, *Gadamer: Hermeneutics, Tradition, and Reason, Key Contemporary thinkers*, Cambridge and Oxford: Polity Press, in association with B. Blackwell.

Zuckert, Catherine H., 1996, *Postmodern Platos: Nietzsche, Heidegger, Gadamer, Strauss, Derrida*, Chicago; London: University of Chicago Press.

Notes

1   Gerhard Ebeling, 1963, 'Word of God and Hermeneutics', in: *Word and Faith*, London: SCM Press, p. 318 (italics in the original).

2   Anthony C. Thiselton, 1980, *The Two Horizons*, Exeter, Paternoster, p. 337.

3   Martin Heidegger, 1959, *Unterwegs zur Sprache*, Pfullingen: Neske, English: Martin Heidegger, 1971, *On the Way to Language*, New York: Harper & Row. Note that the English edition does not contain the first essay of the German edition 'Die Sprache'. This is published separately as Martin Heidegger, 1971, 'Language', in *Poetry, Language, Thought*, New York: Harper & Row; Martin Heidegger, 1986, and 'Language', in: David E. Klemm (ed.), *Hermeneutical Inquiry*, vol. 1, Atlanta: Scholars Press.

4   Heidegger, 'Language', p. 153.

5   Martin Heidegger, 1971, 'The Way to Language', in: *On the Way to Language*, New York: Harper & Row, p. 129.

6   Heidegger, 'Language', p. 150.

7   Martin Heidegger, 1959, 'Der Weg zur Sprache', in: *Unterwegs zur Sprache*, Pfullingen: Neske, p. 260, English: Heidegger, 'The Way to Language', p. 129.

8   Heidegger, *On the Way to Language*, p. 208 (italics in the original). The reprint of the same translation in Klemm, *Hermeneutical Inquiry* (p. 153) is unfortunately rendered unintelligible by a typographical error in a key place: 'Such appropriating takes place in the [!] the very *nature*, the *presencing*, of language *needs and uses* the speaking of mortals in order to sound as the peal of stillness for the hearing of mortals.'

9   Heidegger, 'The Way to Language', p. 127. In another place in the same essay, Heidegger identifies *Geläut der Stille* with *Sage*: 'Silence corresponds to the soundless tolling of the stillness [NB: This is translated by a different translator. The German uses *Geläut der Stille* here] of appropriating-showing saying.' Heidegger, 'The Way to Language', p. 131.

10   Heidegger, *On the Way to Language*, pp. 202–5.

11   Heidegger, *On the Way to Language*, pp. 206–7.

12   Heidegger, *On the Way to Language*, pp. 202–3.

13   Heidegger, 'The Way to Language', pp. 127–8. This translation uses 'appropriation' instead of 'event'.

14   Heidegger, 'The Way to Language', p. 129.

15   Friedrich Schleiermacher, 1996, *On Religion: Speeches to its Cultured Despisers*, edited by Richard Gouter, Cambridge and New York: Cambridge University Press, pp. 31–2.

16   Schleiermacher, *On Religion*, pp. 31–2.

17   Hugo Ott, 1993, *Martin Heidegger: A Political Life*, translated by Allan Blunden, London: HarperCollins, pp. 101–2.

18   Martin Heidegger, 1995, 'Augustinus und der Neuplatonismus', in: *Phänomenologie des religiöien Lebens, Gesamtausgabe*, vol. 60, Frankfurt am Main: Klostermann, pp. 157–299.

19   Hans-Georg Gadamer, 1975, *Truth and Method*, London: Sheed & Ward, German: Hans-Georg Gadamer, 1960, *Wahrheit und Methode: Grundzüge einer philosophischen Hermeneutik*, Tübingen: J. C. B. Mohr (Paul Siebeck).

20   Gadamer, *Truth and Method*, p. 350.

21   Jean Grondin, 1994, *Introduction to Philosophical Hermeneutics*, New Haven: Yale University Press, p. xiv.

22 Gadamer, *Truth and Method*, pp. 378–87.

23 Gadamer, *Truth and Method*, p. 411.

24 Gadamer, *Truth and Method*, p. 402.

25 Gadamer, *Truth and Method*, p. 351.

26 Gadamer, *Truth and Method*, pp. 269–70.

26 Gadamer, *Truth and Method*, pp. 262–3.

28 Gadamer, *Truth and Method*, p. 419.

29 Gadamer, *Truth and Method*, p. 341.

30 Werner Jeanrond, *Theological Hermeneutics: Development and Significance*, London: SCM Press, p. 69 (italics in the original).

31 Emilio Betti, 1955, *Teoria Generale della Interpretazione*, 2 vols, Milano: Dott. A. Giuffrè Editore. This book is, to my knowledge, not translated into English. The only writing by Betti of which I was able to find an English translation is Emilio Betti, 1990, 'Hermeneutics as the General Methodology of the *Geisteswissenschaften*', in: Gayle L. Ormiston and Alan D. Schrift (eds), *The Hermeneutic Tradition: From Ast to Ricoeur*, Albany, NY: State University of New York Press.

32 Emilio Betti, 1967, *Allgemeine Auslegungslehre als Methodik der Geisteswissenschaften*, Tübingen: J. C. B. Mohr (Paul Siebeck). Grondin, *Introduction to Philosophical Hermeneutics*, pp. 125–9.

33 Gadamer, *Wahrheit und Methode*, p. 271. The English translation omits this reference and replaces it with a more general reference to 'liberal education' (Gadamer, *Truth and Method*, p. 255).

34 'We know this from the learning of ancient languages' (Gadamer, *Truth and Method*, p. 259).

35 Jean Grondin, 2001, 'Hans-Georg Gadamer und die französische Welt' *Von Heidegger zu Gadamer: Unterwegs zur Hermeneutik*, Darmstadt: Wissenschaftliche Buchgesellschaft, p. 139.

36 Paul Ricoeur, 1969, *The Symbolism of Evil*, Boston: Beacon Press; Ricoeur, *Freud and Philosophy*; Paul Ricoeur, 1974, *The Conflict of Interpretations: Essays in Hermeneutics, Northwestern University Studies in Phenomenology & Existential Philosophy*, Evanston: Northwestern University Press; Paul Ricoeur, 1976, *Interpretation Theory: Discourse and the Surplus of Meaning*, Fort Worth: Texas Christian University Press; Paul Ricoeur, 1977, *The Rule of Metaphor: Multi-disciplinary Studies of the Creation of Meaning in Language*, Toronto: University of Toronto Press; Paul Ricoeur, 1980, *Essays on Biblical Interpretation*, translated by Lewis Seymour Mudge, Philadelphia: Fortress Press; Paul Ricoeur, 1981, *Hermeneutics and the Human Sciences: Essays on Language, Action, and Interpretation*, translated by John B. Thompson, Cambridge and Paris: Cambridge University Press; Maison des sciences de l'homme; Paul Ricoeur, 1984, *Time and Narrative*, translated by Kathleen Blamey, 3 vols, Chicago; London: University of Chicago Press; Paul Ricoeur, 1992, *Oneself as Another*, Chicago; London: University of Chicago Press; Paul Ricoeur, 1995, *Figuring the Sacred: Religion, Narrative, and Imagination*, translated by Mark I. Wallace, Minneapolis: Fortress Press.

37 Dan R. Stiver, 2001, *Theology after Ricoeur: New Directions in Hermeneutical Theology*, Louisville: Westminister John Knox Press.

38 Ricoeur, *Freud and Philosophy*, p. 32.

39   Paul Ricoeur, 1981, 'Metaphor and the Central Problem of Hermeneutics', in: *Hermeneutics and the Human Sciences*, p. 171.

40   Paul Ricoeur, 1976, 'Language as Discourse', in: *Interpretation Theory*,
p. 22.

41   Paul Ricoeur, 1976, 'Metaphor and Symbol', in: *Interpretation Theory*,
p. 59.

42   For a concise overview of Ricoeur's theory of metaphor and symbol, see
Ricoeur, 'Metaphor and Symbol'.

43   Ricoeur, 'Metaphor and Symbol', p. 51.

44   Ricoeur, *The Rule of Metaphor*, p. 211.

45   Ricoeur, 'Metaphor and Symbol', p. 53.

46   Ricoeur, 'Metaphor and Symbol', p. 59.

47   Ricoeur, 'Metaphor and Symbol', p. 59.

48   Ricoeur, 'Metaphor and Symbol', p. 64.

49   For Ricoeur's treatment of parable, see Paul Ricoeur, 'Biblical Hermeneutics', *Semeia*, 4 (1975), 29–148.

50   Cf., for example, Ricoeur, *Time and Narrative*, vol. I, p. 52

51   Paul Ricoeur, 1981, 'The Model of the Text: Meaningful Action considered as Text', in: *Hermeneutics and the Human Sciences*, pp. 206–7.

52   Ricoeur, 'The Model of the Text', pp. 208–9.

53   Stiver, *Theology after Ricoeur*, p. 67.

54   Ebeling, 'Word of God and Hermeneutics', p. 318 (italics in the
original).

55   Martin Heidegger, 1971, 'The Origin of the Work of Art', in: *Poetry,
Language, Thought*, New York: Harper & Row.

56   James McConkey Robinson and John B. Cobb, 1964, *The New Hermeneutic*, *New Frontiers in Theology*, vol. 2, New York: Harper & Row, which
presents a good introduction to the thinking of the 'new hermeneutic'.

57   Ernst Fuchs, 1954, *Hermeneutik*, Bad Cannstatt: Müllerschön; Ernst
Fuchs, 1968, *Marburger Hermeneutik*, *Hermeneutische Untersuchungen zur
Theologie*, vol. 9, Tübingen: J. C. B. Mohr (Paul Siebeck). Unfortunately, none
of these volumes is translated into English.

58   Ernst Käsemann, 1962, 'The Problem of the Historical Jesus', in: *Essays
on New Testament Themes*, London: SCM Press.

59   For the methods of the New Quest for the historical Jesus, see Gerd Theissen and Dagmar Winter, 2002, *The Quest for the Plausible Jesus: The Question
of Criteria*, Louisville; London: Westminster John Knox Press, pp. 112–40.

60   Gerhard Ebeling, 1963, 'The Significance of the Critical Historical Method for Church and Theology in Protestantism' in: *Word and Faith*, London:
SCM Press; Ebeling, 'Word of God and Hermeneutics'.

61   Ebeling, 'Word of God and Hermeneutics', p. 318 (italics in the
original).

62   Ebeling, 'Word of God and Hermeneutics', p. 318 (italics in the
original).

63   Ebeling, 'Word of God and Hermeneutics', p. 331.

64   Ebeling, 'Word of God and Hermeneutics', p. 332.

10

The Universality of the Sign I:
Open Sign Systems

In the preceding sections, the history of hermeneutics was presented as if it moved straight towards the hermeneutic tradition, culminating in a critical hermeneutical theology. This narrative, I must admit, left out alternative developments. Some of these alternative developments are the object of the following passages. Hermeneutical approaches are not isolated from others. On the contrary, they develop in critical interaction with each other, and we find the result of this interaction in the way in which the different approaches influence each other.

In this chapter and the next, we are going to investigate the various models that are based on theories of signs. These can be separated into two categories, on the one hand those who consider texts an open system of signs, such as structuralism, post-structuralism, and deconstruction. We shall discuss these approaches in this chapter. On the other hand, there are models based on theories of signs that assume that texts are closed systems of signs. Adherents of these models see texts as closed systems, which generate meaning within themselves. Karl Barth's hermeneutics, canonical criticism, new biblical theology and literary approaches fall into this category. Adherents of these approaches will usually mainly focus on the interpretation of texts and, where appropriate, on the application of these texts to the reader's life. These approaches which are based on closed sign systems will be discussed in the following chapter.

Approaches based on open sign systems assume that an individual text, such as this present text on theological hermeneutics, is an individual instance of a wider language system. In this, they go back to Ferdinand de Saussure's (1857–1913) *Course in General Linguistics*, in which Saussure develops the theory that would become famous after his death as structuralism. Structuralism became increasingly influential, especially among French thinkers, in the period from the Second World War until the late 1960s, and in places even into the 1970s, when it was gradually replaced by post-structuralism and deconstruction. The latter movements constitute what is commonly known as postmodernism or postmodernity. This transition is commonly connected with the names of Roland Barthes (1915–80), Jacques Derrida (1930–2004) and Michel Foucault (1926–84).

Structuralism

Ferdinand de Saussure: the founder of structuralism

In the final words of his lectures that were to be published as *Course in General Linguistics*, Ferdinand de Saussure formulates the main aim of the structuralist project: 'The true and unique object of linguistics is language studied in and for itself.'[1] Conventionally, language had been studied with a view to its reference. Saussure suggests that the more appropriate approach is to study language as a self-contained system regardless of its reference. Building on this basic insight, he postulates that meaning is not generated by reference to external objects, but by difference within the linguistic system.

Saussure distinguishes between two ways in which the term language can be understood. On the one hand, language can be understood as an individual utterance. Saussure calls this type of language *parole*, 'speech'. On the other hand, language can be understood as the formal system of language, on which the speaker draws in order to speak. This type of language Saussure calls *la langue*, 'language'. *Langue* is abstract; it is a formal system of signs, which does not refer to anything outside itself. It is the totality of all possible utterances in a given language. Within language (*langue*) there is no outside reference. It is a self-contained whole. Meaning within language is generated by the difference between a given sign and neighbouring signs.

> Everything that has been said up to this point boils down to this: in language there are only differences. Even more important: a difference generally implies positive terms between which the difference is set up; but in language there are only differences without positive terms. Whether we take the signified or the signifier, language has neither ideas nor sounds that existed before the linguistic system, but only conceptual and phonic differences that have issued from the system. The idea or phonic substance that a sign contains is of less importance than the other signs that surround it.[2]

Thus it is by negative relation that signs have their meaning. This can be seen, for example, by the definition of colours – 'orange', for example, is not defined by its reference to an external 'orangeness', but by its opposition to 'red' and 'yellow'. Another example would be 'father', which is defined by its opposition to 'mother' and 'child'. In Saussure's words, 'the entire mechanism of language . . . is based on oppositions of this kind and on the phonic and conceptual differences that they imply'.[3]

This linguistic system determines the utterance an individual can make. All speech (*parole*) can only draw on language (*la langue*). And as human mental concepts are formed through language, we perceive the world in the way that is prescribed to us by language. Our mental concepts are a product of language, thus our thought is to some degree predetermined by the possibilities contained within language. Or, in other words, the linguistic system determines the individual.

It may be worthwhile pointing out some of the differences between the system suggested by Saussure and that which was developed throughout the preceding chapters. The guiding principle of the hermeneutic tradition, including Schleiermacher, Heidegger, Gadamer and Ricoeur, is the inner word, the meaning of the utterance. Be it through methodical interpretation or existentialist analysis, the interpreter of texts aims at recovering the inner word contained in the text. This, in turn, is related to the interpretation of the world, which takes place through language. In the latter part, there is some congruence between the structuralist and the hermeneutic school – both agree that the way in which we interpret the world is determined by the language we employ in doing so. The main difference lies in the former part. The hermeneutic tradition is interested in the inner word, while structuralism is interested in language as a system without necessarily considering external reference. In fact, we will see in the later development of structuralism into post-structuralism that in the last consequence, the structuralist approach will deny the possibility of any extra-lingual meaning at all.

Saussure's *Course in General Linguistics* laid out the methodological grounding of structuralism, but Saussure did not develop the implications of the approach he founded. This was left to a later generation of thinkers in a great variety of subject areas, to authors such as Claude Lévi-Strauss in anthropology, Jacques Lacan in psychology, Roland Barthes in literary criticism and cultural studies, Michel Foucault in sociology and Julia Kristeva in psychology and (feminist) philosophy.

Claude Lévi-Strauss: structuralist interpretation of myth

Claude Lévi-Strauss' (born 1908) anthropological studies led him to apply structuralist methods to the discipline. In his investigations into the myths and customs of primitive tribes, he did not attempt to understand them at the conceptual level, but in their deep structure. So the myths are not interpreted on the level of their straightforward meaning, but as a string of *mythemes*, of elements of myths that, in their totality, make up the mythological vocabulary – or, in other words, they are like the individual signs from which *la langue* is made. Lévi-Strauss analyses the way in which the individual mythemes are organized within a given myth and thus identifies the deep structure of the myth. For example, in this interpretation of the Oedipus myth, Lévi-Strauss organizes the various elements of the myth into four groups, those that have to do with the overrating of blood relations, the underrating of blood relations, fights with monsters and characters that appear to be earth-born.[4] This leads Lévi-Strauss to the structuralist interpretation of the myth:

> The myth has to do with the inability, for a culture which holds the belief that mankind is autochthonous . . . to find a satisfactory transition between this theory and the knowledge that human beings are actually born from the union of man and woman. Although the problem obviously cannot be solved, the Oedipus myth provides a kind of logical tool which relates the original problem – born from one or born from two? – to the derivative problem: born from different or born from same? By a correlation of this type, the overrating of blood relations is to the underrating of blood relations as the attempt to escape autochthony is to the impossibility to succeed in it. Although experience contradicts theory, social life validates cosmology by its similarity of structure. Hence cosmology is true.[5]

Thus, Lévi-Strauss finds a way of interpreting myths at a deeper level than the literal. This must not be confused with traditional allegorical interpretation, because Lévi-Strauss' interpretation presupposes that there are deep structures in the human mind and in human culture which find expression in myths. The deeper meaning of the text does not point towards the divine, but towards the human. As we will see, later post-structuralists will discard the notion that texts point at a deeper meaning.

In a similar fashion, Lévi-Strauss interprets certain customs, such as kinship systems and food laws, as something similar to myths. They are a way of imposing order on an otherwise chaotic world, and thus they reveal the structure in the human mind according to which humans will always organize themselves. Marriage laws, for example, are not arbitrary rules, but are governed by a small number of simple principles, which work like individual signs within a language system. In fact, they work analogous to language. Their function is to organize society, to define belonging and separation, and thus give meaning to human community. Without it, human society would not be possible.

In all these instances, the driving force behind the myth is the human desire to mediate between contradictions and oppositions, which are an inevitable part of human life. Telling myths, establishing kinship structures and having totems make these contradictions and oppositions bearable. These strategies reveal the mental structures according to which we make sense of the world in which we live.

Jacques Lacan: structuralist psychoanalysis

Jacques Lacan (1901–81) applied structuralist thinking to psychoanalysis. He contends that the 'unconscious is structured like a language',[6] thus allowing for psychological symptoms to be interpreted analogously to speech. A psychological symptom, such as a compulsive behaviour, is, according to Lacan, like a metaphor or symbol, which refers to a signified beyond itself, such as suppressed desire. This signified, however, cannot be unambiguously discerned. As the concept in Saussure's *la langue*, the signifier, that is, the symptom, must be understood in relation to other signifiers within the language system. Thus a conscious utterance or action (in analogy to *parole*) is, for the purposes of psychoanalysis, to be understood within the language of the unconscious (*langue*). In fact, the conscious utterance or action is only a manifestation of the language of the unconscious – the language of the unconscious speaks through the individual action or utterance. Consequently, the notion that the conscious could be in control over unconscious, that the self is in control of itself, is only an illusion.

Lacan's application of structuralism to psychoanalysis, as well as Lévi-Strauss' use of structuralism in anthropology, demonstrates the ability of structuralist theory and practice to be used in various areas, way beyond the interpretation of linguistic utterances. Structuralism, as a hermeneutic tradition, can claim that its approach to interpretation is universally applicable.

This, obviously, has important implications for theology and particularly for biblical interpretation. There are methods of structuralist textual interpretation, often known as 'formalism' and connected with the name of the Russian Vladimir Propp (1895–1970). These can be applied to biblical interpretation in a straightforward manner, analysing the deep structures of the text.[7] On a more interesting level, Lévi-Strauss' structuralist analysis of myths and Lacan's structuralist psychoanalysis can be applied to biblical texts, theological writings and ecclesiastical practice, with interesting results.[8]

However, as mentioned before, structuralism has since been superseded by post-structuralism. This development followed, to some extent, the inner logic of structuralism. If signifiers refer to a signified which is a mental concept, but mental concepts, as we have seen in Lacan's psychology, are only signifiers to another signified within the language of the unconscious, where can we find a final signified? Where does the chain of signification stop? The answer that post-structuralism offers is simple: nowhere.

Post-structuralism and deconstruction

In this section, probably appropriately for the discussion of postmodern hermeneutics, I shall discuss the relevant authors in reverse chronological order. Roland Barthes, although the oldest of the authors discussed in this section, came to post-structuralism last, and his post-structuralist work is deeply influenced by Jacques Derrida and Michel Foucault. However, it is in Barthes' work that we can follow the transition from structuralism to post-structuralism best and understand the key issues of this transformation. With the understanding gained in the discussion of Barthes, we will then move backwards and discuss the work of Foucault and Derrida in the light of the insights gained in Roland Barthes' work.

Post-structuralism

In his early work, up to the late 1960s, Barthes applied the structuralist method to a wide range of objects. Literary texts, images, fashion, social practices and conventions, etc. can all be analysed in this way. For Barthes, everything is a sign referring to other signs. Thus Barthes interprets everyday cultural phenomena, such as the attitude of the French middle classes towards drinking wine, places like striptease clubs or the title page of the *Paris Match* showing a black soldier saluting the flag. All these practices and occurrences are interpreted as myths, which function to legitimize bourgeois society and make it operate better. The mythological meaning of these myths is not too hidden, according to Barthes – 'Myth hides nothing: it distorts.'[9] It does so by transforming history into nature, by pretending that a social construct is something natural and that the interest of the bourgeoisie is universal.[10] In Barthes' universe, everything is a sign, because everything is loaded with meaning. Greta Garbo's face in the film *Queen Christina*,[11] or the mental concept of vines – these, for example, evoke associations of Mediterranean countries, idealized rural life, wine harvest and celebration – in short, vines are a signifier, pointing at a number of social conventions and aspirations.

From this attitude, it is only a small step towards post-structuralism. In structuralism as we have discussed it so far, signifiers signify a more or less identifiable signified. In post-structuralism, towards which Barthes moved in the late 1960s, the signifier does not point to any more or less fixed signified, it potentially points to every other sign. This invalidates the quest for any ultimate meaning of a text or any other sign – one signifier points to another, which points to another, which points to another. Vines as a signifier, for example, signify all the things mentioned above, which, in turn, signify an even greater number of other signifieds. They may also be interpreted as a psychological symptom, so that my pondering on vines may be a sign for some suppressed Bacchanalian desire, which in turn points at other signifiers within the language of the unconscious. And so forth.

As a result, the concept of the author of a text as its ultimate meaning becomes problematic. In 'The Death of the Author',[12] Barthes draws this consequence.

> We know that a text is not a line of words releasing a single 'theological' meaning (the message of the Author-God) but a multi-dimensional space in which a variety of writings, none of them original, blend and clash. The text is a tissue of quotations drawn from innumerable centres of Culture ... The writer can only imitate a gesture that is always anterior, never original. His only power is to mix writings, to counter the ones with others, in such a way as never to rest on one of them.[13]

Thus a text is a quotation from or reference to other texts. Authorial intention is absolutely insignificant in this free play of signification and quotation. The text does not have an ultimate meaning; it refers in random ways to other texts and to the world as a text. All these random significations and references come together in the reader.

> The reader is the space on which all the quotations that make up writing are inscribed without any of them being lost; a text's unity lies not in its origin but in its destination. Yet this destination cannot any longer

be personal: the reader is without history, biography, psychology; he is simply the *someone* who holds together in a single field all the traces by which the written text is constituted.[14]

Thus the reader is, as Barthes points out in a later essay, the co-producer of the text.[15] Barthes suggests that the reader 'plays' the text in analogy to a musician who plays a score, intimately involved in the production of the piece of music or the text. The reader collaborates in the production of the text by re-producing it, not as an internalized appropriation or mimesis, but by looking for a practice that re-produces it.[16] The text becomes part of the reader's life. Texts understood in this way are without boundaries. They can be broken, that is, read in fragments, partially, and at the same time the text is part of a greater, intertextual whole of reference and signification. The text is like a field, on which the play of and with signification, quotation, reference and allusion takes place (way beyond what an author could envisage, and without regard for the historical situation of the author – after all, the author is dead, according to Barthes). Julia Kristeva coined the term 'intertextuality' for this phenomenon, which 'suggests that each text is situated for each reader in an ever-changing web composed of innumerable texts'.[17] This excludes the possibility of a more or less definable meaning of texts – there are as many meanings in the text as there are readings.

For the post-structuralist, the world is a text. There is no clear separation between texts and human life and environment. As we have seen above, all mental concepts, every sight we see and all we encounter, are signifiers which signify other signifiers. Thus life refers to text, texts to life in a way that the distinction between them is impossible. In the end, everything is text.

Finally, during the last period of his work (if this term is permissible with reference to him), Barthes developed an even more radical view of language. He grew to see that language imprisons the free play of association and signification. Barthes said in his inaugural lecture at the Collège de France that 'Language is legislation, speech is code. We do not see the power which is speech because we forget that all speech is classification, and that all classifications are oppressive: *ordo* means both distribution and commination.'[18] So ultimately, speech is oppressive. Consequently, 'freedom can exist only outside language. Unfortunately, human language has no exterior: there is no exit.'[19] As a result, Barthes suggested that we need to cheat speech with speech.[20] He goes on to assert that we need a multitude of languages, 'as many languages as there are desires'.[21] Barthes demands that literature be developed, which will at least bring closer the utopia of speech without power. Here, Barthes comes very close to Michel Foucault's analysis of power.

Michel Foucault applied structuralist method – albeit in a very free manner – to the sociological and historical analysis of cultural institutions. His main focus in this is the way in which these institutions are a product of power: 'power produces; it produces reality; it produces domains of objects and rituals of truth. The individual and the knowledge that may be gained of him belong to this production.'[22] Power is not a group of institutions and mechanisms that ensure the subservience of the citizens of a given state, and also not a mode of subjugation or a general system of domination exerted by one group over another.[23] Rather, it is the 'multiplicity of force relations immanent in the sphere in which they operate and which constitute their own organization',[24] the processes that maintain or reverse these forces and the strategies by which they work. Therefore, within the system of Foucault's thought, power is omnipresent, because it is exercised at every point of the social body. It is an abstract concept which is present in every human social body. It is 'not built up out of "wills" (individual or collective), nor is it derivable from interests. Power is constructed and functions on the basis of particular powers, myriad issues, myriad effects of power.'[25] Institutions and their historical development demonstrate the increasing power over human life, power that administers life, but prevents the anarchic play of desire and the will to power.

Discourse is, for Foucault, yet another instrument of power. 'We must conceive discourse as a violence that we do to things, or, at all events, as a practice we impose upon them.'[26] The basis of this insight is that 'we should not imagine that the world presents us with a legible face, leaving us merely to decipher it . . . there is no prediscoursive fate disposing the world in our favour'.[27] In other words, the world is meaningless and only the arena for human desire and will. In this, Foucault takes up Friedrich Nietzsche's fundamental claim (see pp. 110–11). On this primordial chaos, discourse imposes order and thus is an act of violence. This is exactly the point that Roland Barthes picks up some years later in his Inaugural Lecture.

In sum, Foucault perceives the world as chaos, and humanity as a set of undisciplined bodies upon which power has imposed order and created a space within which the permanent death-threat of natural life has been lifted to some degree. The whole task of a 'genealogy' of institutions serves only to unmask that institutions are, as a matter of fact, only a function of power which gains or maintains control over bodies, orders the social body and administers life. Apart from this function in the game of power, there is no meaning, no truth in any human construct. Thus the world is a text, which can be read and decoded, but in the end, the result is that there is no such thing as meaning. The code is empty.

Barthes and Foucault show how the structuralist method, developed into post-structuralism, can function to interpret not only texts, but all aspects of human life. Everything is a signifier, and signifiers signify other signifiers, but at no stage do they signify anything like fixed meaning.

Deconstruction

Deconstruction is closely related to post-structuralism, although its starting point differs from that of post-structuralism. It is the consequence of Jacques Derrida's critique of phenomenological philosophy, especially that of Martin Heidegger. As we have seen above, Heidegger assumed that language 'grants us things' (see p. 137). We recall that 'granting' of things is the disclosure of the meaningful relationships by which an individual thing is related to the world and the world to the thing. Through language and its 'granting', the world is a meaningful whole. This does not only apply to things that are physically present. Language can also make present something that is physically absent by speaking of it, by disclosing the meaningful relationships of being in which the thing dwells. In short, language is *logos*, which gives meaning to the world and which also communicates being. Derrida is vehemently opposed to this logocentrism. He disputes that language 'grants', or that it makes present. Derrida uses a theory of signs similar to that of post-structuralism, thus proposing that the presence that has been brought about by language is merely a signifier in itself, which, in turn, points to an endless array of further signifiers.

The starting point of the deconstruction of a text is the identification and undermining of binary oppositions – A and not-A, such as male/female, transcendent/immanent, spirit/body, inside/outside, etc. Within these oppositions, one is always seen as superior to the other, they stand in hierarchical violence rather than equal partnership.[28] Deconstruction is set to undermine, to deconstruct these oppositions by showing that they are not as clear cut as it is assumed. As the literary theorist Terry Eagleton puts it,

> Deconstruction tries to show how such oppositions, in order to hold themselves in place, are sometimes betrayed into inverting or collapsing themselves, or need to banish to the text's margins certain niggling details which can be made to return and plague them.[29]

Thus the interpreter seizes on those elements that undermine the binary oppositions on which the text is built, and uses them to deconstruct the text's internal system of oppositions. This is more than a mischievous reading of certain texts – it points at the very essence of writing itself (if one may use these terms in the context of postmodernity). Or, in Eagleton's words,

> There is something in writing itself which finally evades all systems and logics. There is a continual flickering, spilling and defusing of meaning – what Derrida calls 'dissemination' – which cannot be easily contained within the categories of the text's structure, or within the categories of a conventional critical approach to it.[30]

Consequently, it becomes clear that a text's structure is something superficial, something that is always open to be undermined, deconstructed. A structure requires 'a centre, a fixed principle, a hierarchy of meanings and a solid foundation, and it is just these notions which the endless differing and deferring of writing throws into question'.[31] Thus the text is de-centred and opened to eccentric and playful readings. In the end, every reading of the text is equally legitimate, as bizarre and absurd as it may appear to other readers. There is no limit to the way in which signs may refer to other signs, within the text and beyond, to other texts and to the world, which is a text, too. In short, the text is freed from the limitations and the oppression of conventional perceptions of meaning.

Postmodern theology

Obviously, post-structuralist hermeneutics are relevant for theology in a number of ways. The most apparent way is the interpretation of biblical and non-biblical texts. A wide variety of authors interpret biblical texts deconstructively. For example, Stephen D. Moore presents an interesting reading of the passage of the woman at the well in John 4 and the crucifixion narrative of John's Gospel in his book *Poststructuralism and the New Testament*.[32] As is typical for post-structuralist readings, the tone of the interpretation is light-hearted and humorous. Moore identifies a two-storey ironic structure in John 4.[33] On one level, the woman is trapped in her incomprehension of the deeper levels of meaning.

> Above is a higher level of meaning, a second floor of which the woman is unaware, unlike the reading or listening audience, who have just now taken up residence there along with Jesus and the Johannine narrator, who share a double bed.[34]

Moore proceeds to identify the binary oppositions on which the Gospel is based – knowledge/ignorance, spiritual/literal, spirit/flesh, etc. It is the task of deconstruction to deconstruct these binary oppositions. Moore identifies the main opposition governing this particular text as that between male and female.[35] We cannot follow through Moore's complex argument here, in which he deconstructs this and a number of other oppositions. It will suffice to quote his conclusion, a conclusion which is typical in style for post-structuralist readings:

> For many who have written on the scene at the Samaritan well, the woman's oblivion to her own need, assumed to be so much greater than that of Jesus, is the pivot on which the irony of their dialogue turns. Deeper by far, however, is the irony that Jesus' own need – not to mention that of his Father – is just as the woman's. 'The well is deep', as the woman says; desire, however, is bottomless.[36]

This type of reading may appear somewhat arbitrary to the uninitiated. And indeed, if there are endless legitimate readings, it becomes the responsibility of the reader to read the text in ways that do not support oppressive or exploitative practices. Thus post-structuralist reading is, as joyful, playful and anarchic as it may appear, a deeply ethical undertaking. When the reader plays a decisive role in the creation of meaning, then 'there are no neutral, innocent readings; every reading is an ethical and ultimately political act'.[37] Consequently, reading is part of political practice. The playful yet responsible reading of the text must become part of the reader's life and practice.[38]

Yet the significance of post-structuralism and deconstruction for theology does not stop here. Foucault's archaeology of social institutions has provided an important tool for the study of the Church, both in history and present. It has provided the methodological foundation for important criticism of the way in which the Church has wielded and still wields social power, consciously or unconsciously.

More important, however, is the impact of this way of thinking on the understanding of God. One way of appropriating this thought is through nonrealism, which, in the theological sphere, is usually connected with the Cambridge theologian Don Cupitt and a network called *The Sea of Faith*.

> SoF is often identified with what commentators on postmodernity call the 'linguistic turn' in philosophy: the growing consensus that ideas – including religious ideas such as 'God' and 'heaven' – cannot be

understood apart from the language systems that created them. Where religious conservatives find the linguistic turn threatening and heretical (because it undermines notions of reality and subverts comforting certainties), Sea of Faith thinkers like Don Cupitt, Stephen Mitchell and Jude Bullock have joined with the linguistic philosophers in celebrating the liberating effects of the twentieth century's revolutionary understanding of 'the word made flesh'. In this sense, *Sea of Faith is philosophically 'nonrealist'*.[39]

Nonrealism assumes that religious utterances do not refer to an external reality at all, but work only within the language system. We cannot discuss the philosophical foundation of nonrealism here, but its stance is hermeneutically interesting as it assumes that there is no reality in religious utterances at all. All that is there, to use a term coined by Ludwig Wittgenstein, are language-games, which we play, and which may be helpful for us to cope with life and its complications, but which do not have any relation to an extra-lingual reality.[40]

However, nonrealism is not the necessary conclusion from deconstruction and post-structuralism. Stephen Moore makes an interesting connection between Derrida's thought and negative or apophatic theology. We saw in an earlier section of this book that negative theology assumed that the reality of the divine is too great to be expressed in language, so that all we can say about God is what God is not (see p. 55). Moore observes that Derrida's thought on the relation between language and being moved more and more towards an apophatic approach.[41] Although this passage is somewhat elusive, I understand that Moore suggests that Derrida was unable to avoid apophatic theology, that is, the notion that being is too great to be expressed in language. So, although we will never be able to express it, there is an ultimate signified, there may even be ultimate meaning, but this is inaccessible to human language. This use of deconstruction would then be a deconstruction of all false human certainties and superficial meanings, clearing the field for the encounter with the reality that is beyond language, and therefore beyond comprehension.

A similar approach seems to be taken by Mark C. Taylor, who develops 'a/theology', a theology that carries its negation within itself, and which deals with the God who is beyond being and not-being. This is a negative theology of the death of God and the death of the self.

In sum, the consequence of the serious application of post-structuralism and deconstruction to theology is not necessarily the nihilism of Michel Foucault, who assumes a primordial chaos on which power has imposed order. In theology, they can lead to a playful and anarchic yet ethically serious reading of biblical texts, based on an understanding of God beyond being and non-being, an understanding that stands in the same apophatic tradition as mystical theology.

However, we cannot conclude this section of post-structuralism and deconstruction without a few critical remarks. Both approaches, in so far as they can be distinguished, assume that the reader is a co-producer of the meaning of the text. The text is not an authority over the reader, but the reader is co-author of the text. The first fundamental question raised by this is if a text then can tell the reader anything new. If the reader creates the meaning of the text, and reading therefore is a purely ethical activity, leading to non-oppressive or liberating action, then there is little space for the text to contain something new, something that had not been part of the reader's horizon before. In postmodern reading, the text is in danger of providing the reader merely with a mirror image of herself or himself. Reading is an enjoyable game, making intertextual references across a wide range of other texts according to the taste of the reader, but there cannot be anything new in a text thus read. This may be part of the agenda of post-structuralism and deconstruction, in so far as it denies the author or the text any power over the reader. However, it excludes the possibility of the text telling the reader something completely new.

If the Christian proclamation is something new, if the word of the cross is foolishness to the world, that is, not part of common enlightened wisdom, even that kind of wisdom which focuses on peace, justice and an end to oppression, then it must be able to alter the reader's horizon in unexpected ways. However, if one follows a postmodern approach, the text does not have an inner word, it cannot tell the reader or hearer anything he or she did not know before. Therefore a postmodern Christianity is reduced to ethics, to action. Traditional Pauline theology, from Paul via Augustine to Luther, and even to a liberal theologian like Friedrich Schleiermacher and to ecumenical documents such as the recent *Joint Declaration on the Doctrine of Justification*[42] between the Roman Catholic Church and Lutheran churches, has always asserted that Christianity is not about right action, or morals, but it is about receiving something which is not part of fallen human nature, about experiencing something which we cannot tell ourselves. In short, it is about gift, gift from beyond the human self. The very possibility of this is denied by the postmodern approaches discussed here.

Furthermore, the complete de-coupling of 'reality' from language may be problematic. In post-structuralism and deconstruction, discourse exclusively refers to language, and language refers only to language. Any extra-linguistic reality is completely irrelevant.

It must be admitted, however, that reality, the environment we encounter and even the bodies we inhabit, are always already interpreted. We have seen this in the discussion of the hermeneutic tradition, which in this case agrees with the postmodern approaches discussed in this chapter. However, it may be said that the denial of any relation between language and extra-linguistic reality throws out the baby with the bath water.

We recall that for the early Heidegger, any apophantic statement, such as 'The hammer is heavy', is derived from the interpretation of the speaker's *Dasein* in relation to this object. Thus, if I say 'The hammer is heavy', it means that I understand the hammer as too heavy for the task at hand. That I understand the object in question as a hammer and know what to do with it, as well as the fact that people manufacture these things, is also culturally conditioned. However, despite all this interpretation and cultural condition, the physical object makes a connection between physical life and language. Here, Paul Ricoeur's concept of the symbol is helpful. The symbol, we recall, makes a connection between *bios*, physical life, and the universe of *logos*, language. The hammer thus functions as a symbol, which connects *bios* with *logos*. Its place in the physical world becomes obvious when I drop it on my foot. The resulting pain is a raw creaturely reality, although it, too, is always interpreted. But the impact on the muscle tissue of the foot, the signals sent through the nerve system to the brain and the resulting brain activity are basic physical realities. They function as symbols, even while the pain is interpreted and is given a place in the meaningful relations within the world. Yet it remains pain. The final reality of this is if the injury with the hammer leads to my death – then all interpretation is at an end, all social construction is overtaken by the naked fact that my physical life has come to an end.

Further reading

Barthes, Roland, 1982, 'The Face of Garbo', in: *A Barthes Reader*, London: Jonathan Cape, pp. 82–4.

Barthes, Roland, 1982, 'Inaugural Lecture, Collège de France', in: *A Barthes Reader*, London: Jonathan Cape, pp. 457–78.

Barthes, Roland, 1982, 'Myth Today', in: *A Barthes Reader*, London: Jonathan Cape, pp. 93–149.

Barthes, Roland, 1984, 'The Death of the Author', in: *Image Music Text: Essays*, London: Fontana Paperbacks, pp. 142–8.

Barthes, Roland, 1984, 'From Work to Text', in: *Image Music Text: Essays*, London: Fontana Paperbacks, pp. 155–64.

Bible and Culture Collective, 1995, *The Postmodern Bible*, edited by George Aichele et al., New Haven; London: Yale University Press.

Coward, Harold G. and Toby Foshay (eds), 1992, *Derrida and Negative Theology*, Albany, NY: State University of New York Press.

Derrida, Jacques, 1976, *Of Grammatology*, Baltimore, Md: Johns Hopkins University Press.

Derrida, Jacques, 1987, *The Post Card: From Socrates to Freud and Beyond*, Chicago: University of Chicago Press.

Derrida, Jacques, 1990, *Writing and Difference*, London: Routledge.

Derrida, Jacques, 1995, *The Gift of Death*, Religion and Postmodernism, Chicago: University of Chicago Press.

Foucault, Michel, 1972, 'The Discourse on Language', in: *The Archaeology of Knowledge & The Discourse on Language*, New York: Pantheon, pp. 215–37.

Foucault, Michel, 1977, *Discipline and Punish: The Birth of the Prison*, New York: Pantheon.

Foucault, Michel, 1980, 'The History of Sexuality', in: *Power-Knowledge: Selected Interviews and other Writings, 1972–1977*, Brighton, Sussex: Harvester Press, pp. 183–93.

Foucault, Michel, 1981, *The History of Sexuality*, vol. 1, Harmondsworth: Penguin.

Galland, Corina and Alfred M. Johnson, 1976, *The New Testament and Structuralism: A Collection of Essays, Pittsburgh Theological Monograph Series*, vol. 11, Pittsburgh: Pickwick Press.

Lacan, Jacques, 1979, *The Four Fundamental Concepts of Psycho-Analysis*, Harmondsworth: Penguin.

Lévi-Strauss, Claude, 1963, *Structural Anthropology*, New York: Basic Books.

Moore, Stephen D., 1994, *Poststructuralism and the New Testament: Derrida and Foucault at the Foot of the Cross*, Minneapolis: Fortress Press.

Polzin, Robert, 1977, *Biblical Structuralism: Method and Subjectivity in the Study of Ancient Texts, Semeia supplements*, Philadelphia: Fortress Press.

Saussure, Ferdinand de, 1966, *Course in General Linguistics*, translated by Wade Baskin, New York: McGraw-Hill.

Sea of Faith, 2005, 'What SoF is about . . .' (website, accessed 22 April 2006). Available from http://www.sofn.org.uk/Firsttim.html.

Thiselton, Anthony C., 1995, *Interpreting God and the Postmodern Self: On Meaning, Manipulation and Promise*, Edinburgh: T & T Clark.

Notes

1 Ferdinand de Saussure, 1966, *Course in General Linguistics*, translated by Wade Baskin, New York: McGraw-Hill, p. 232.

2 Saussure, *Course in General Linguistics*, p. 120.

3 Saussure, *Course in General Linguistics*, p. 121.

4 Claude Lévi-Strauss, 1963, *Structural Anthropology*, New York: Basic Books, pp. 206–31.

5 Lévi-Strauss, *Structural Anthropology*, p. 216.

6   Jacques Lacan, 1979, *The Four Fundamental Concepts of Psycho-Analysis*, Harmondsworth: Penguin, p. 20

7   For examples of this, see Corina Galland and Alfred M. Johnson, 1976, *The New Testament and Structuralism: A Collection of Essays*, Pittsburgh Theological Monograph Series, vol. 11, Pittsburgh: Pickwick Press; Robert Polzin, 1977, *Biblical Structuralism: Method and Subjectivity in the Study of Ancient Texts*, *Semeia supplements*, Philadelphia: Fortress Press. See also Bible and Culture Collective, 1995, *The Postmodern Bible*, edited by George Aichele et al., New Haven; London: Yale University Press, pp. 70–4.

8   Bible and Culture Collective, *The Postmodern Bible*, pp. 73–85, 196–210.

9   Roland Barthes, 1982, 'Myth Today', in: *A Barthes Reader*, London: Jonathan Cape, p. 116.

10   Barthes, 'Myth Today', p. 116.

11   Roland Barthes, 1982, 'The Face of Garbo', in: *A Barthes Reader*, London: Jonathan Cape; the following illustration is my own.

12   Roland Barthes, 1984, 'The Death of the Author', in: *Image Music Text: Essays*, London: Fontana Paperbacks.

13   Barthes, 'The Death of the Author', p. 146.

14   Barthes, 'The Death of the Author', p. 148 (italics in the original).

15   Roland Barthes, 1984, 'From Work to Text', in: *Image Music Text: Essays*, p. 163.

16   Barthes, 'From Work to Text', p. 162.

17   Bible and Culture Collective, *The Postmodern Bible*, p. 130.

18   Roland Barthes, 1982, 'Inaugural Lecture, Collège de France', in: *A Barthes Reader*, p. 460.

19   Barthes, 'Inaugural Lecture, Collège de France', p. 461.

20   Barthes, 'Inaugural Lecture, Collège de France', p. 462.

21   Barthes, 'Inaugural Lecture, Collège de France', p. 467.

22   Michel Foucault, 1977, *Discipline and Punish: The Birth of the Prison*, New York: Pantheon, p. 194.

23   Michel Foucault, 1981, *The History of Sexuality*, vol. 1, Harmondsworth: Penguin, p. 92.

24   Foucault, *The History of Sexuality*, vol. 1, p. 92.

25   Michel Foucault, 1980, 'The History of Sexuality', in: *Power-Knowledge: Selected Interviews and other Writings, 1972–1977*, Brighton, Sussex: Harvester Press, p. 188.

26   Michel Foucault, 1972, 'The Discourse on Language', in: *The Archaeology of Knowledge & The Discourse on Language*, New York: Pantheon, p. 229.

27   Foucault, 'The Discourse on Language', p. 229.

28   Bible and Culture Collective, *The Postmodern Bible*, p. 122.

29   Terry Eagleton, 1996, *Literary Theory: An Introduction*, 2nd edn, Oxford: Blackwell, p. 133.

30   Eagleton, *Literary Theory*, p. 134.

31   Eagleton, *Literary Theory*, p. 134.

32   Stephen D. Moore, 1994, *Poststructuralism and the New Testament: Derrida and Foucault at the Foot of the Cross*, Minneapolis: Fortress Press.

33   Moore, *Poststructuralism and the New Testament*, p. 45.

34   Moore, *Poststructuralism and the New Testament*, p. 45.

35   Moore, *Poststructuralism and the New Testament*, p. 46.

36   Moore, *Poststructuralism and the New Testament*, pp. 63–4.

37   Bible and Culture Collective, *The Postmodern Bible*, p. 135.

38   Barthes, 'From Work to Text', p. 162.

39   Sea of Faith, 2005, 'What SoF is about . . .'. Available from http://www.sofn.org.uk/Firsttim.html (italics in the original) (accessed 22 April 2006).

40   Ludwig Wittgenstein, 1967, *Philosophical Investigations*, Oxford: B. Blackwell, No. 7.

41   Moore, *Poststructuralism and the New Testament*, pp. 36–41.

42   Lutheran World Federation and The Catholic Church, 1999, 'Joint Declaration on the Doctrine of Justification'. Available from http://www.vatican.va/roman_curia/pontifical_councils/chrstuni/documents/rc_pc_chrstuni_doc_31101999_cath-luth-joint-declaration_en.html (accessed 7 November 2006).

11

The Universality of the Sign II: Closed Sign Systems

Karl Barth

Most likely, Karl Barth would have been surprised at being listed under the heading of 'closed sign systems'. However, the proponents of the canonical approaches to the Bible, which represent what I would call 'closed sign system' approaches, call upon him as their theological inspiration.[1] And, as it will become apparent, the description will fit Karl Barth's thinking better than one might anticipate.

Hermeneutics and theology: speaking of God

We already mentioned Karl Barth and the beginnings of dialectical theology in an earlier chapter (see pp. 115–16). We recall that the dialectical theology movement insisted on the infinite qualitative difference between God and creation, or, in other words, on God's absolute transcendence. This was polemically summarized in the battle cry 'God is in heaven, and thou art on earth.'[2] This meant that there can hardly be any relation between God and the world – God's world is absolutely separate from the created order – except in one point in which they meet, in the resurrection. 'In the resurrection the new world of the Holy Spirit touches the old world of the flesh, but it touches it as a tangent touches a circle, that is, without touching it.'[3] Thus even revelation is inaccessible to human activity, including theology. From this, Karl Barth concludes that the activity of the Church, its teaching, ethics and worship, can seek 'to be no more than a void in which the Gospel reveals itself'.[4] Thus human activity, including human language, can never be directly related to the word of God itself, which, Barth insisted, would always come 'straight from above'.[5]

Barth gives some ideas how this revelation straight from above may take place. For example, in the preface to the second edition of the *Epistle to the Romans*, he describes his wrestling with the text of the letter:

> When an investigation is rightly conducted, boulders composed of fortuitous or incidental or merely historical conceptions ought to

179

disappear almost entirely. The Word ought to be exposed behind the words. Intelligent comment means that that I am driven on till I stand with nothing before me but the enigma of the matter; till the document seems hardly to exist as a document; till I have almost forgotten that I am not its author; till I know the author so well that I allow him to speak in my name and am even able to speak in his name myself.[6]

Thus true interaction with a text, in this case the biblical text of Paul's Letter to the Romans, leads to a break through the words, leads to a direct disclosure of the subject matter of the text to the reader. This is a revelation that takes place behind the letters of the text. The text is merely the void in which revelation may take place, in which God may speak directly to the hearer.

Elsewhere Barth reaffirms the problem that humans cannot speak about God: '[as] theologians we are supposed to talk about God. Yet we are human beings and as such we are unable to talk about God.'[7] Only God is able to talk about God.[8] Consequently, the only option for theology is to allow God to talk himself.[9] Theology provides the void in which God speaks.

Until not too long ago, the commonest interpretation of Karl Barth's theology was that, after the controversy with Erik Peterson, Barth shifted away from the dialectical approach towards an approach based on analogy, which was seen to be much more in line with traditional theology. This interpretation can be traced back to Hans Urs von Balthasar's work on Karl Barth.[10] It is this interpretation of Karl Barth's work that brought him the reputation of being neo-orthodox. However, it has been acknowledged in more recent Barth scholarship that Barth actually never changed his mind fundamentally, but that his theology continued to be based on the metaphysical distinction between the divine and the human.[11]

In line with this newer interpretation, which brings out the radical nature of Karl Barth's theology and hermeneutics much better than von Balthasar's, we can find in Barth's mature and late work the same distinctions. The divine is absolutely separated from the human, and human language can never contain the word of God, or speak of God directly. In his *magnum opus*, the *Church Dogmatics*, Barth distinguishes three forms of the word of God, revelation, Scripture and the proclamation of the Church. These three forms of the word of God, however, are merely mirror images of the one word of God, which cannot be expressed in human words.[12] Thus human talk of God, and Karl Barth talks about God quite eloquently in the many volumes of the *Church Dogmatics*, this is only the means by which the space is created in which God will talk.

Analogy of faith

Theological language, for Karl Barth, is analogical language. However, Barth rejects the *analogia entis*, the analogy of being, and introduces a new concept, the *analogia fidei*, analogy of faith.

> Theology is *modest* because its entire logic can only be a human *ana-logy* to that Word; analogical thought and speech do not claim to be, to say, to contain, or to control the original word. But it gives a reply to it by its attempt to co-respond with it; it seeks expressions that resemble the ratio and relations of the Word of God in a proportionate and, as far as feasible, approximate and appropriate way. Theology's whole illumination can be only its human reflection, or mirroring . . . and its whole production can only be a human reproduction.[13]

Thus human language is a response in faith to the self-revelation of God. Human language cannot contain or express in any way God's word, but it can seek to correspond to it. In short, it can point in the direction in which revelation is to be found, it can provide the space in which God may speak. This is very different from the classical concept of analogy in the *analogia entis*, which, as we recall, assumed a structural analogy between the being of God and created being (see pp. 58–60).Thus, when we attribute something to God, such as 'goodness', then we draw on these structural similarities, yet are aware that there are even greater dissimilarities. So there is a certain correspondence between human goodness and God's goodness, yet the two are not the same, but very different. Barth's analogy of faith, however, does not assume any structural similarity between creator and creation. They are totally different, and thus we cannot speak of God using the analogy of being. We can only reflect what has been revealed to us, but never ever 'catch' it in human language.

> Theology is not called in any way to interpret, explain, and elucidate God and his Word. Of course, where its relationship to the witnesses of the Word is concerned, it must be an interpreter. But in relation to God's Word itself, theology has nothing to interpret. At this point the theological response can only consist in confirming and announcing the Word as something spoken and heard prior to all interpretation.[14]

God speaks for godself, and theology only announces this.

It is also worth emphasizing Barth's notion that the word of God comes before all interpretation. We recall that the hermeneutic tradition, from

Augustine onwards, assumed that understanding takes place through interpretation. The inner word, the thought, is pre-verbal, and needs to be translated into spoken language, into the external word in order to be understood (see pp. 45–7). Thus the external word contains (although with a certain loss) the internal word. Barth does not agree with this approach. He assumes that the word of God cannot be translated into human language – analogical speech does not contain the original word. Using Augustine's distinction, it is always inner word and can never be translated into the external word. If this is the case, we might even be able to say that, if we follow Barth, we cannot understand the word of God.

Biblical hermeneutics

Karl Barth's hermeneutical theory obviously has a number of consequences for reading the Bible and the practice of the proclamation of the Church. First of all, in reading the Bible, the reader will not find the word of God within its pages, but will need to break through the words in order to wrestle with its ultimate content, which is the word of God.

Furthermore, Barth asserts that the Church must accept the authority of the Bible.[15] The Church cannot go beyond this authority, because the Church is founded on the biblical testimony to Jesus Christ. Only because the Church accepts this testimony as normative is the Church the Church. Thus Barth can say that the Bible 'imposes itself' as normative upon the Church, and the Church 'can only register this event as such, as the reality in which the Church is the Church'.[16] This argument may appear circular; the Bible is an authority over against the Church, and the Church is the Church because it recognizes this authority. There is no need for an external validation of this authority. Consequently, biblical interpretation as a theological discipline is a task exclusively for the Church, as it is the reading of the Bible as the mirror image of the one word of God, and not a secular reading with historical or philological interest at heart. This would exclude any dialogue between theology and other academic disciplines, and indeed, Barth was always hostile towards Rudolf Bultmann's dialogue with existentialist philosophy. For Barth, such a thing would only pollute the purity of the Church's theology.[17]

This position is understandable if we recall that the Bible is a mirror image of the word of God. In other words, it is a sign that signifies the word of God, and thus refers to God. As a sign pointing at God, it is a complex sign, made up of a huge variety of signs within it, the various texts, passages, etc.

> Nevertheless, . . . theology confronts in Holy Scriptures an extreme-
> ly polyphonic, not a monotonous, testimony to the work and word
> of God. Everything that can be heard is differentiated – not only the
> voices of the Old and New Testament as such, but also the many voices
> that reverberate through both.[18]

This polyphonic testimony or sign correlates with the word of God.
Those who wrestle with the sign, the Bible, will come to wrestle with
what it signifies, the word of God. There are no extra-biblical references
necessary in order to read the sign. Its internal multitude of voices, its
contrasts and tensions, form a complex sign, which refers the reader to
God, who is the reality behind the sign. Barth seems to follow Augustine
here, who, as we recall, saw the Bible as a whole as a sign pointing to God
(see p. 44). Only that for Barth, the knowledge of God is not mediated by
the text, but in the end immediate and straight from above.

Canonical approaches and new biblical theology

Brevard Childs

Karl Barth's hermeneutical approach has re-emerged in a curious alli-
ance with postmodernism. As Harrisville and Sundberg astutely observe,
in the postmodern environment no discourse is supposed to dominate
another one. So the historical-critical discourse, it may be said, has lost
its claim to be the universally valid and thus privileged discourse in the
realm of biblical studies. Thus other discourses, even faith-based ones,
can assert themselves as equally valid within the academic arena.[19]

This chance has been recognized by the American theologian Brevard
S. Childs (born 1923), the founder of the canonical approach to Scripture. His approach is based on the rejection of the notion that a text
must be interpreted within its original context, and asserts that it is to
be interpreted within the context of the canon of the Bible in its received
form.

> Interpretation begins with the canonical form of the text. . . . The move
> is obvious because to speak of the New Testament canon is to identify
> that corpus received as scripture. The canonical form marks not only
> the place from which exegesis begins, but also it marks the place at
> which exegesis ends. The text's pre-history and post-history are both
> subordinated to the form deemed canonical.[20]

Thus all historical-critical work, if it needs to be done at all – and Childs is ambiguous on this question – is subordinated to the interpretation of the final form. This is justified, according to Childs, because he demands that the Bible must be read first and foremost as Scripture of the Church, as the book in which God's will is to be found and discerned.

> The theological issue turns on the Christian church's claim for the integrity of a special reading which interprets the Bible within an established theological context and toward a particular end, namely the discerning of the will of God, which is constitutive of the hermeneutical function of the canon.[21]

Consequently, the proper context for the interpretation of the Bible is the Church as the Christian community shaped by these texts. The Church has received these texts in their canonical form, and thus it is this form in which the texts are to be interpreted. This allows the discovery of intertextuality between the canonical writings even beyond that which a historical-critical reading may find permissible. Having said this, it is important to emphasize that Childs restricts intertextuality to the limits described by the canon.[22] References to extra-biblical texts, such as the critical use made of the Babylonian creation myth *Enuma Elish* in the priestly creation account in the book of Genesis, the use of 1 Enoch in the Letter of James or the use of the Stoic concept of *logos* in the prologue to John's Gospel, are thus irrelevant. For Childs, the Bible is a closed system of texts (and signs) within which lively intertextuality takes place, but where references to the outside are cut off. This becomes particularly interesting when Childs detaches the texts even from historical reference:

> The canonical approach to the New Testament concerns itself with authorship, but in a fashion different from the debates generally engaged in between conservatives and liberals. It seeks to pay close attention to the theological function of eyewitness claims (Luke 1.3; John 21.24) without immediately translating the biblical testimony into a question of historical referentiality.[23]

This shows that Childs is indeed not trying to return to a pre-modern exegesis, but that his approach is deeply indebted to postmodernism. At the same time, this raises the problem of reference. If there is not necessarily a historical reference to historical claims, and the existentialist referentiality of the hermeneutic school is rejected, what does the Bible in its canonical form refer to? Child assumes that the biblical writings are witnesses, and their witness is to a common subject matter, which is the reconciliation of the world to God in Jesus Christ. Theological reflection in a canonical context means, for Childs, to move 'from a description of the biblical witness to the object towards which these witnesses point, that is, to their subject matter, substance, or *res*'.[24]

We recognize in this language, which Childs employs frequently in this work, the hermeneutical language of Karl Barth. We saw above that Barth assumed that the reader would wrestle with the text until he or she would break through the text and wrestle with the subject matter of the text directly (see p. 182). In his later work, we saw that Barth did not identify the biblical texts with the word of God directly, but saw them as mirror images, as witnesses to the one word of God. The reader would wrestle with these and then the word of God would reveal itself to him or her.[25] Thus for Childs, as for Barth, the Bible is a closed system of signs, which in its totality signifies the word of God.

This is certainly a legitimate point of view, but it brings with it a number of difficulties. The first is that theology cuts itself off from the debate with other disciplines and world-views. If the Bible is a closed system of signs, which confirms itself for the believing community, then there is no reason to be in a debate with anyone who does not share this presupposition. The fruitful dialogue between theology and philosophy, which began even at the time of the biblical authors, is ignored and cut off. It is a return to the catacombs.

Furthermore, Barth himself, even if he never acknowledged it, was deeply influenced by certain philosophical schools. For example Hegel's influence is quite evident in Barth's work. Barth, unaware of his own philosophical presuppositions, is happy, however, to criticize Bultmann for being influenced by existentialist philosophy. One may be forgiven for thinking that it would be difficult for him to counter accusations of a lack of intellectual integrity.

Finally, the Barthian approach is far from being as neo-orthodox as its followers would like. All human language is only a reflection of revelation, which in itself is reduced to the size of a mathematical point. The Bible is not and does not contain the word of God, theological language merely mirrors it, and all activity of the Church provides only the space for revelation to happen without mediation. If one wants to embrace this extreme separation between the eternal and the temporal, between God and creation, it is certainly a tenable position. But one needs to be aware what one is taking on board.

Literary criticism

Another group of contemporary approaches is based on the application
of literary theory to the biblical texts. Some of these are modelled on
the way in which the Bible would be studied within an English literature department, and thus do not fall under the category of theological
hermeneutics.[26] Others, however, attempt to integrate the insights of Literary studies into the field of theology. An interesting attempt in this
direction has been made by Mark Alan Powell, who develops a genuinely
theological approach to literary theory.[27] His approach is a good example
to discuss, as it highlights the issues arising not only from his approach,
but from all literary approaches to the Bible.

Background

Powell sets narrative criticism, which is the name he uses for his literary
approach, in the context of a number of literary theories. First of all,
he quotes the new criticism of the mid twentieth century approvingly.[28]
This was a movement which approached a given text as a self-contained
whole. This means that the text for the new critic is self-sufficient and
independent of other texts. Consequently, it is interpreted without reference to its author, historical and social setting, etc.[29] The basis of new
criticism is then a 'close reading' of the text, which is a detailed analysis
of the interrelations of the elements of the text. Powell follows new criticism in so far as he, too, approaches the text as a self-contained whole,
which can be interpreted without reference to the circumstances of its
composition.

Powell makes it clear that his narrative criticism is developed in opposition to historical criticism. Against historical criticism, Powell establishes
some basic rules for narrative criticism: 'literary criticism focuses on the
final form of the text'; 'literary criticism emphasizes the unity of the text
as a whole'; 'literary criticism views the text as an end in itself'.[30]

Powell then develops the main features of narrative criticism in interaction with structuralism, rhetorical criticism and reader-response criticism. Powell agrees with structuralism that interpretation must be text-
centred and objective.[31] With rhetorical criticism he shares an interest in
the effect that the text has on the reader, and in investigating how the text
achieves this effect.[32] From reader-response criticism Powell learns the
way in which the text guides the reader through a narrative.[33]

Principles

Powell's approach to narrative criticism is based on a theory of communication that assumes an author, the text, and the reader. He finds, however, that these are assumed within the text. This means that there is an implied author, who may be different from the real author. He uses the example of Robert Louis Stevenson, who wrote both *Treasure Island* and *Dr. Jekyll and Mr. Hyde*. Both books have a narrator who claims to be the author of the story, and in both cases this implied author is very different, although the real author of the works is the same.[34] So the text implies an author, who may be very different from the real author. Not every text is as explicit about the intended author as those that have a first-person narrator. However, we can discern a lot about the person of the implied author, his or her knowledge and viewpoint.

In the same way we can discern an 'idealized implied reader who is presupposed by and constructed from the text'.[35] From the text we learn that the implied reader knows certain things, which are clearly presupposed, and is ignorant of others, which need to be explained. The reader should be familiar with what the implied reader knows, and 'forget' everything that the implied reader does not know.[36] Thus Powell is able to treat the text as a self-contained and autonomous whole, without falling into the formalism of structuralist interpretation.

The details of Powell's method which flows from his hermeneutical theory are of no concern for this discussion. The main question we need to discuss, however, is the question of reference. Powell seems to assume that reference is always historical – that texts refer to historical events – and that historical-critical interpretation aims solely at reconstructing these events. 'The "end" for historical criticism is a reconstruction of something to which the text attests, such as the life and teaching of Jesus, the interests of the early Christians who preserved the traditions concerning him, or the concerns of the evangelists and their communities.'[37] It is this understanding of reference that he has in mind when he describes the hermeneutical foundation for his approach, and it is this kind of historical reference that Powell rejects.[38] Instead, he suggests that if 'God is able to speak through story as well as through history, then the poetic witness of these narratives is no less significant for us today than their referential witness'.[39]

In the light of our earlier hermeneutical investigations, Powell's assertion of a 'poetic' witness over against a 'referential witness' seems difficult to maintain. At best, it is a straw-man which he builds in order to tear down. We may recall from Chapters 8 and 9 that in the hermeneutic tradition, the tradition of Heidegger, Bultmann, Gadamer, Ebeling and Ricoeur, a text refers to the self-understanding of the author or, in Gadamer's words, to his or her world. Karl Barth suggested that the reference of the biblical text is in that it points away from itself, towards its subject matter, towards the word of God. The reader, wrestling with the testimony of the text, will break through the words of the text and come to wrestle with the subject matter, the word within the words (see p. 180). A pure historical or factual reference, which Powell rejects, is not something that plays a part in serious hermeneutical discourse.

Furthermore, as we have seen, the reference of the text is necessary for it to be meaningful at all. Once the text is separated from reference, as we saw happen in the movement from structuralism to post-structuralism, the text becomes unable to tell the reader anything new. The reader constructs the meaning of the text. Thus reading is a purely ethical practice, which must be exercised in a way that enables the reader to act ethically by rejecting oppressive ideologies. But the text is devoid of an inner word.

Consequently, it is a fundamental problem with literary approaches to the Bible that they cannot satisfactorily answer the question of the text's reference. We see this when Powell avoids the problem of reference by a short mention of Luther's insight that the proclamation brings about faith in the hearer, or that the biblical texts are intended to evoke responses in line with the will of God.[40] So he appears to identify the text with the word of God. Such naïve identification may make literary criticism look attractive as a short cut to a conservative exegesis. The reader is relieved of the burden of historical-critical research, and can read the text with a supposedly pre-modern naïvety. But this ignores the issue of the external reference of the text. A text without reference is without a *verbum interius*, and so it can only be the template around which the readers construct their ethical praxis. The text may even be helpful in constructing the ethical praxis, or in evoking a response in line with the perceived will of God, but it is nothing more than a language-game without any external reference.

In sum, narrative criticism as proposed by Powell highlights some of the fundamental difficulties of literary hermeneutical approaches in biblical studies – although they may look attractive on a superficial level, they pose fundamental problems in relation to reference. In the context of this section, we can say that they treat the text as a closed sign system, which is precisely the opposite of post-structuralism and deconstruction. However, narrative approaches carry with them the same assumption, which is that the text does refer to anything beyond text – only that in post-structuralism and deconstruction the text refers to an endless multitude of texts, while in literary approaches it does not refer to anything beyond itself at all. When opting for such approaches, students need to be aware that they buy into these hermeneutical assumptions.

Further reading

Alter, Robert, and Frank Kermode, 1987, *The Literary Guide to the Bible*, Cambridge, Mass.: Belknap Press of Harvard University Press.

Balthasar, Hans Urs von, 1971, *The Theology of Karl Barth*, translated by John Drury, New York: Holt, Rinehart and Winston.

Balthasar, Hans Urs von, 1992, *The Theology of Karl Barth: Exposition and Interpretation*, translated by Edward T. Oakes, San Francisco: Communio Books Ignatius Press.

Barth, Karl, 1933, *The Epistle to the Romans*, translated by Edwyn Clement Hoskyns, Oxford: Oxford University Press.

Barth, Karl, 1936, *Church Dogmatics*, translated by Geoffrey William Bromiley, edited by Thomas Forsyth Torrance and G. T. Thomson, Edinburgh: T & T Clark.

Barth, Karl, 1962, 'Das Wort Gottes als Aufgabe der Theologie', in: Jürgen Moltmann (ed.), *Anfänge der dialektischen Theologie*, vol. 1, München: Kaiser, pp. 197–218.

Barth, Karl, 1963, *Evangelical Theology: An Introduction*, London: Weidenfeld & Nicolson.

Barth, Karl, 1972, 'Rudolf Bultmann – An Attempt to understand him', in: Hans Werner Bartsch (ed.), *Kerygma and Myth: A Theological Debate*, vol. 2, London: SPCK, pp. 83–132.

Barth, Karl, 1989, *Der Römerbrief*, 14th edn, Zürich: Theologischer Verlag.

Childs, Brevard S., 1984, *The New Testament as Canon: An Introduction*, London: SCM Press.

Childs, Brevard S., 1993, *Biblical Theology of the Old and New Testaments: Theological Reflection on the Christian Bible*, Minneapolis: Fortress Press.

Hunsinger, George, 1991, *How to Read Karl Barth: The Shape of his Theology*, Oxford: Oxford University Press.

Jensen, Alexander S., 2004, *John's Gospel as Witness: The Development of the early Christian Language of Faith*, Ashgate New Critical Thinking in Religion, Theology, and Biblical Studies, Aldershot: Ashgate.

McCormack, Bruce L., 1995, *Karl Barth's Critically Realistic Dialectical Theology: Its Genesis and Development, 1909–1936*, Oxford; New York: Oxford University Press.

Noble, Paul R., 1995, *The Canonical Approach: A Critical Reconstruction of the Hermeneutics of Brevard S. Childs, Biblical Interpretation Series*, vol. 16, Leiden: E.J. Brill.

Peterson, Erik, 1971, 'Was ist Theologie?', in: Gerhard Sauter (ed.), *Theologie als Wissenschaft: Aufsätze und Thesen, Theologische Bücherei*, vol. 43, München: Kaiser, pp. 132–51.

Powell, Mark Allan, 1990, *What is Narrative Criticism?, Guides to Biblical Scholarship, New Testament Series*, Minneapolis: Fortress Press.

Notes

1   Alexander S. Jensen, 2004, *John's Gospel as Witness: The Development of the Early Christian Language of Faith*, Ashgate New Critical Thinking in Religion, Theology, and Biblical Studies, Aldershot: Ashgate, pp. 7–9.

2   Karl Barth, 1933, *The Epistle to the Romans*, translated by E. C. Hoskyns, Oxford: Oxford University Press, p. 10.

3   Barth, *The Epistle to the Romans*, p. 30.

4   Barth, *The Epistle to the Romans*, p. 36.

5   The first occurrence of the famous 'straight from above' is in Barth, *Der Römerbrief*, p. 6. The English translation translates it as 'vertically from above' (Barth, *The Epistle to the Romans*, p. 30).

6   Barth, *The Epistle to the Romans*, p. 8.

7   Karl Barth, 1962, 'Das Wort Gottes als Aufgabe der Theologie', in: Jürgen Moltmann (ed.), *Anfänge der dialektischen Theologie*, vol. 1, München: Kaiser, p. 199.

8   Barth, 'Das Wort Gottes als Aufgabe der Theologie', p. 217.

9   Barth, 'Das Wort Gottes als Aufgabe der Theologie', p. 215.

10   Hans Urs von Balthasar, 1971, *The Theology of Karl Barth*, translated by John Drury, New York: Holt, Rinehart and Winston. A new translation is published as Hans Urs von Balthasar, 1992, *The Theology of Karl Barth: Exposition and Interpretation*, translated by Edward T. Oakes, San Francisco: Communio Books Ignatius Press. The German original appeared in 1951.

11   This re-evaluation of Karl Barth's theology is connected with the work of George Hunsinger (George Hunsinger, 1991, *How to Read Karl Barth: The Shape of his Theology*, Oxford: Oxford University Press) and Bruce McCormack (Bruce L. McCormack, 1995, *Karl Barth's Critically Realistic Dialectical Theology: Its Genesis and Development, 1909-1936*, Oxford; New York: Oxford University Press).

12   Karl Barth, 1936, *Church Dogmatics*, translated by Geoffrey William Bromiley, edited by Thomas Forsyth Torrance and G. T. Thomson, Edinburgh: T & T Clark, vol. 1/1, p. 132. Barth takes up the image of the mirror image again in his last book (Karl Barth, 1963, *Evangelical Theology: An Introduction*, London: Weidenfeld & Nicolson, p. 33).

13   Barth, *Evangelical Theology*, p. 17 (italics in the original).

14   Barth, *Evangelical Theology*, p. 18.

15   Barth, *Church Dogmatics*, 1/1, pp. 106–8.

16   Barth, *Church Dogmatics*, 1/1, pp. 107.

17   Barth, 'Rudolf Bultmann', p. 121.

18   Barth, *Evangelical Theology*, p. 33.

19   Roy A. Harrisville and Walter Sundberg, 2002, *The Bible in Modern Culture: Baruch Spinoza to Brevard Childs*, 2nd edn, Grand Rapids, Mich.: W. B. Eerdmans, pp. 304–9.

20   Brevard S. Childs, 1984, *The New Testament as Canon: An Introduction*, London: SCM Press, p. 48.

21   Childs, *The New Testament as Canon*, p. 37.

22   Childs, *The New Testament as Canon*, p. 48.

23   Childs, *The New Testament as Canon*, p. 52.

24   Brevard S. Childs, 1993, *Biblical Theology of the Old and New Testaments: Theological Reflection on the Christian Bible*, Minneapolis: Fortress Press, p. 80.

25   The influence of Karl Barth on Brevard Childs has been frequently observed. Harrisville and Sundberg, *The Bible in Modern Culture*, p. 323.

26   For example, Robert Alter and Frank Kermode, 1987, *The Literary Guide to the Bible*, Cambridge, Mass.: Belknap Press of Harvard University Press.

27   Mark Allan Powell, 1990, *What is Narrative Criticism?*, *Guides to Biblical Scholarship. New Testament Series*, Minneapolis: Fortress Press.

28   Powell, *What is Narrative Criticism?*, pp. 4–5.

29   M. H. Abrams, 1999, *A Glossary of Literary Terms*, 7th edn, Fort Worth, Tex.: Harcourt Brace College, pp. 180–2.

30   Powell, *What is Narrative Criticism?*, p. 7.

31   Powell, *What is Narrative Criticism?*, pp. 12–14.

32   Powell, *What is Narrative Criticism?*, pp. 14–16.

33   Powell, *What is Narrative Criticism?*, pp. 16–18.

34   Powell, *What is Narrative Criticism?*, p. 5.

35   Powell, *What is Narrative Criticism?*, p. 15.

36   Powell, *What is Narrative Criticism?*, p. 20.

37   Powell, *What is Narrative Criticism?*, p. 9.

38   Powell, *What is Narrative Criticism?*, p. 99.

39   Powell, *What is Narrative Criticism?*, p. 100.

40   Powell, *What is Narrative Criticism?*, p. 98–9.

12

Critical Theory, Feminism and Postcolonialism

In this chapter, we are going to discuss the hermeneutical approaches based, however loosely, on critical theories. These include the work of Jürgen Habermas (born 1929) and feminist and postcolonial hermeneutics. However, before we can discuss these thinkers and movements, we need to shed some light on their intellectual background, which we will find in the neo-Marxist philosophy of the Frankfurt School, which is commonly known as Critical Theory.[1] Habermas himself is a second-generation product of this school, and, directly or indirectly, much of feminist, postcolonial and other critical theory has been influenced by it.

Critical Theory

The Frankfurt School

The Frankfurt School is a school of thought connected with the Institute for Social Research (*Institut für Sozialforschung*) of the University of Frankfurt am Main in Germany. The Institute was founded in 1923, and from the very beginning was dedicated to the development of a Marxist understanding of society. It gained outstanding influence under the directorship of Max Horkheimer (1895–1973), which began in 1931, and which was handed on to Theodor Adorno (1903–69) in 1958/59.[2]

The Institute developed Marxist thought in non-orthodox ways in so far as it differed from the Communist Party and the Socialist International by not accepting the orthodox thesis that the working class was becoming increasingly impoverished and that the Revolution would inevitably take place as a result of proper training of the working class in Marxist doctrine. Instead, the Critical Theorists of the Frankfurt School developed an independent analysis and critique of capitalist economy and society. Their aim was, from the very beginning of the school, the emancipation of the individual from oppression, in particular from oppression by capitalist and bourgeois society. At a later stage they came to see that this oppression was exercised by Western society as a whole.

An important part of the critical approach of the Frankfurt School is the 'critique of ideology' (*Ideologiekritik*). This is based on the Marxist concept of ideology, which understands that every society has a base, which consists of the means of production, and a superstructure, which consists of the society's ideology, its legal system, political system, and its religions. According to this model, the base determines the super-structure (see p. 109). Consequently, in a capitalist society, where the means of production are controlled by the capitalists, the superstructure reflects the interests of the ruling class. The ideology of a society is a means of obscuring the real conditions of the working class by creating a 'false consciousness', such as the fetish for commodities, religion, etc. It is the task of *Ideologiekritik* to unmask these false consciousnesses, and the ideologies behind them, in order to bring about the emancipation of the individual.

The Institute for Social Research was forced to leave Germany during the Third Reich, and went into exile in the USA, where it exerted some considerable influence on American social and philosophical thought. During this time, the philosophy of Horkheimer and Adorno became increasingly pessimistic and disillusioned with Western civilization as a whole. In *The Dialectic of Enlightenment*[3] they moved beyond a critique of the forces and relations of production in capitalist society and aimed their critique at Western civilization as a whole. Self-destruction, as em-bodied in the Third Reich and the Second World War, are intrinsic to the development of human society. Instrumental reason, which is the basis for human domination of nature, inevitably leads to Fascism.

After the Second World War, the institute moved back to Frankfurt, where its members were instrumental in shaping the Western-German post-war political discourse. It was during this time that Jürgen Haber-mas became associated with the Institute. In due course, he would become the leading figure of the second generation of Critical Theory. We need to turn to his work now, because Habermas develops Critical Theory in a way that has an important impact on the development of hermeneutical theory and praxis.

Jürgen Habermas

Jürgen Habermas (born 1929) is the leading protagonist of the second generation of the Frankfurt School. His work has brought Critical Theory into dialogue with the hermeneutic tradition, and later developed it into a critical hermeneutical theory. Habermas developed his hermeneutical thinking in a debate with Hans-Georg Gadamer from 1967 to 1971. As far as I can see, his hermeneutical thinking did not take any important new turns after this, but was incorporated into a broader social theory in *The Theory of Communicative Action*.[4]

The debate with Gadamer

Habermas opened the debate with Gadamer in a review of (then) recent literature, which was published as *On the Logic of the Social Sciences* in 1967.[5] Gadamer responded to this with the essay 'Rhetoric, Hermeneutics and the Critique of Ideology'.[6] Habermas responded to this with 'On Hermeneutics' Claim to Universality'.[7] In the context of this debate, Habermas also published 'Towards a Theory of Communicative Competence'.[8] This debate with Gadamer helped Habermas to shape his own hermeneutical thinking.

Habermas attacked Gadamer by pointing out that hermeneutics is not an end in itself, but a means towards the overarching enterprise of the emancipation of the individual – he is, after all, a product of the Frankfurt School. Habermas explained his view of the relation between hermeneutics and Critical Theory (as the means of emancipation) in the appendix of *Knowledge and Human Interest*.[9] Here, Habermas distinguishes between three guiding principles or interests, which form the frame of reference that prejudge the meaning of statements. The first is the scientific or empirical-analytic frame of reference, which aims to establish objective knowledge with a view to establish technical control over the environment.

The second frame of reference is historical-hermeneutical. It is governed by a practical cognitive interest, that is, the interpreter aims to comprehend 'the substantive content of the tradition by applying tradition to himself and his situation'.[10] Thus the objective is to establish intersubjective understanding, for which Habermas frequently uses the term consensus. In other words, 'the understanding of meaning is directed in its very structure toward the possible attainment of consensus between actors in the framework of a self-understanding derived from tradition'.[11]

The third frame of reference is that of the sciences of social action (economics, sociology and political science). As critical social sciences, they aim at the emancipation of the individual.

The systematic sciences of social action, that is economics, sociology, and political science, have the goal, as do the empirical-analytic sciences, of producing nomological objects and knowledge. A critical social science, however, will not remain satisfied with this. It is concerned with going beyond this goal to determine when theoretical statements grasp invariant regularities of social action as such and when they express ideologically frozen relations of dependence that can in principle be transformed. To the extent that this is the case, the critique of ideology, as well, moreover, as psychoanalysis, take into account that information about lawlike connections sets off a process of reflection in the consciousness of those whom the laws are about. Thus the level of unreflected consciousness, which is one of the initial conditions of such laws, can be transformed.[12]

In other words, critical social sciences bring to the fore the false understanding that is at the root of oppressive relationships, and, having made the false understanding explicit, work to transform it. Habermas sees this as the task of psychoanalysis with regard to the individual, and of critique of ideology with regard to societies. Both unmask unconscious motivations, which govern individual or social actions beneath the surface. Without critique, the power of these unconscious motivations is obscured because their influence is rationalized and masked with acceptable explanations. Unmasking them will open the possibility of transformation of oppressive relationships, which, at the conscious level, may not even be realized as such, and thus bring about emancipation. This emancipatory commitment lies at the very heart of Habermas' philosophy. It is the key to his hermeneutics.

From this starting point, Habermas criticized Gadamer's hermeneutical philosophy for not taking into account the possibility that speech situations may be distorted by power relations that have not been recognized.

> Language is also a medium of domination and social power. It serves to legitimate relationships of organized force. Insofar as the legitimations do not articulate the power relationships whose institutionalization they make possible, insofar as that relationship is merely manifested in the legitimations, language is also ideological. In that case it is not so much a matter of deceptions in language as of deception with language as such. Hermeneutic experience, encountering this dependence of symbolic context on actual relationships, becomes a critique of ideology.[13]

Consequently, Habermas believes that Gadamer's hermeneutical philosophy lacks a methodologically grounded reflection, because it does not question beyond the explicit tradition and does not criticize the ideologies contained within the tradition.[14] In short, Gadamer is too uncritical towards the tradition, from which he assumes our understanding flows.

Habermas elaborates his thinking in 'On Hermeneutics' Claim to Universality' and 'Towards a Theory of Communicative Competence'. Habermas introduces the term 'systemically distorted communication' for discourse that is built on false consensus and unconscious motivations. In fact, Habermas suspects all discourse to be systemically distorted.[15] The remedy that Habermas suggests against the systemic distortion of discourse is depth-hermeneutics. This approach does not take an utterance at face value, but analyses it critically, by using psychoanalysis to identify the sources of distortion in individuals, and critique of ideology in societies. Thus critically aware hermeneutics will always bear in mind the possible sources of systematically distorted communication.

Consequently, a critical hermeneutical theory will be aware that knowledge of truth cannot be achieved in systemically distorted communication, which potentially includes all real existing discourse. Truth can only be guaranteed 'by that consensus which might be reached under the idealized conditions to be found in unrestrained and dominance-free communication'.[16] Dominance-free communication is thus the ideal speech situation. Interestingly, Habermas is ambiguous about the reality of dominance-free communication. On the one hand, he says that dominance-free communication 'could, in the course of time, be affirmed to exist'.[17] On the other hand, even within the same text he can speak of it as 'the idea of the true life', which we anticipate in our critically informed discourse. Such an idea is counterfactual, it does not exist but ought to exist.[18] Although it is generally assumed that Habermas sees dominance-free communication as a utopia, a certain ambiguity remains.[19]

This brings Habermas to the key aim of his emancipatory hermeneutics: we anticipate the idealized conversation against the dominant systematically distorted communication. This anticipation enables us to criticize false consensus as based on false consciousness.[20] Or, in other words, Habermas' hermeneutic is really a moral appeal to anticipate the ideal speech situation, which, conversely, involves building the ideal forum for communication, which means transforming society.[21]

Critical remarks

Habermas' hermeneutics is based on the Marxist distinction between a society's base, that is, the means of production, and its superstructure (see p. 109). Habermas includes language in this social superstructure, which is determined by the means of production. Habermas makes this quite explicit:

> A change in the mode of production entails a restructuring of the linguistic world view. . . . Certainly, revolutions in the conditions of the reproduction of material life are in turn linguistically mediated. But a new practice is not set in motion by a new interpretation. Rather, old patterns of interpretation are also attacked and overthrown 'from below' by new practices.[22]

Thus the critique of ideology must understand the linguistic tradition as an expression of the modes of production and the relations of power within a society, and unmask the wrong consensus that has emerged at the hermeneutical level.

Consequently, Habermas sees the aim of hermeneutics not in the achievement of self-understanding within the linguistic tradition in which we live, but in the critique of ideology. His ultimate aim is the establishment of a situation in which communication is not distorted by power any more, but where a real, unconstrained consensus is possible. The only way of doing this, although he does not say this explicitly, is the transformation of society.

This distinguishes Habermas' critical theory from a critically informed hermeneutic such as that of Paul Ricoeur. As we saw above, Ricoeur used the hermeneutics of suspicion in order to understand the text, or, more accurately, to understand the human self better in the light of the self-understanding contained within the text (see p. 145) . Ricoeur explains the text using critical methods, including psychoanalysis, critique of ideology, etc. Yet the aim in this explanation is to allow a deeper understanding of the text in the second reading, the second naïvety. Such a critical method is in the service of the understanding of the text. For Habermas, the explanation of the text, or reflection as he prefers to call it, is in the service of emancipatory action. The text is analysed in order to unmask systematically distorted communication.

Behind Habermas' critical hermeneutics lies the vision of the ideal speech situation, when people will be able to communicate with each other truly as peers, without domination impeding true understanding. As we have seen, Habermas is ambiguous with regard to the nature of the ideal speech situation. Is it something that can be brought about in the future, or is it a utopian ideal which we pursue, even anticipate, without being able to realize it in the world?

It is interesting to recall at this point that Augustine of Hippo envisaged an ideal speech situation, when language would not be necessary any more to communicate thoughts imperfectly. But for Augustine, this was located in the heavenly Jerusalem, in the new creation after the current transitory world will have perished. We said at the time that hermeneutics is an expression of human finitude. It is impossible to say if Habermas is as modest.

Feminism

If discourse can be systematically distorted by the power relations within a political system and its means of production, it is also possible that other social factors may distort communication. Feminists view the power structures that underlie the relations between genders within society as the crucial distorting force. This area of investigation became particularly pertinent with the rise of the second-generation women's liberation movement in the 1960s which challenged the systemic oppression of women in Western societies.[23]

In Church and theology, the beginnings of feminist critique can be found in the debate about women's ordination in the Roman Catholic Church at the time of the Second Vatican Council. The most notable writing of that period is Mary Daly's *The Church and the Second Sex*[24] of 1968, which has even been called the 'beginning point' of feminist theological literature.[25] The argument of Daly's book goes beyond the arguments in favour of and against women's ordination and addresses the marginalization of women within the Church. It exposes how the Church, especially the Roman Catholic Church, has institutionally supported marginalization of women and misogyny throughout its history. The critique of sexist and patriarchal structures in Church and society has been an integral part of feminist literature.

However, the feminist critic may have to analyse oppression at a deeper level – it may well be that oppression and marginalization of women is sanctioned and possibly even presupposed in the foundational writings of Christianity, in the Bible, the theological classics and the language and praxis of liturgy, to name but a few.

Mary Daly thought that the churches and Christianity as a whole were sexist beyond redemption and turned her back on it. Others, however, work to reclaim the foundational texts of Christianity for women.

Feminist interpretation

Elisabeth Schüssler-Fiorenza is one of the authors working to reclaim women's place in the biblical tradition. She describes the aim of such explorations in the introduction to *In Memory of Her*:

> They attempt to reconstruct early Christian history as women's history in order not only to restore women's stories to early Christian history but also to reclaim this history as the history of women and men . . . The Bible is not just a historical collection of writings but also Holy Scripture, gospel, for Christians today. As such it informs not only theology but also the commitment of women today. Yet as long as the stories and history of women in the beginnings of early Christianity are not theologically conceptualized as an integral part of the proclamation of the gospel, biblical texts and traditions formulated and codified by men will remain oppressive to women.[26]

Schüssler-Fiorenza follows this agenda by using historical-critical methods in order to identify the stories of women which were left out in the composition of the biblical writings. She goes behind the text in order to rediscover the 'history and theology of struggle, life and leadership of Christian women who spoke and acted in the Spirit'.[27] In recovering these, she aims to 'reconstitute' the world of the Christian beginning.[28] Thus Schüssler-Fiorenza makes a critical move behind the text, where she finds material that will empower women in the Church.

In a later book, *Jesus: Miriam's Child, Sofia's Prophet*,[29] Schüssler-Fiorenza critiques the Christological discourses of the Church as inherently patriarchal and kyriocentric, and constructs a feminist Christology, which avoids the systemic distortion of traditional Christology.

So feminist hermeneutics are, on one level, the identification of systemic distortion of theological discourse, its critique and the establishing of alternative, inclusive discourses. This can take place in biblical interpretation, in dogmatic theology or any other area. The move towards an inclusive language, not only in the wider society but also in the Church, is part of this movement. If one refers to God consistently as 'He', it implies a maleness of God, which may serve the oppression of women in Church and society. Despite its occasionally eccentric manifestations, 'inclusive language' is an important element in the eradication of the male-centred distortion of discourse.

A slightly different approach can be found in the work of Sandra M. Schneiders. In her study *The Revelatory Text*, Schneiders follows the hermeneutic tradition of biblical interpretation. She follows Gadamer in describing understanding as the 'fusion of horizons', which brings about a transformation in the reader.[30] She also takes seriously Ricoeur's insight that the methodical explanation of the text contributes an important critical perspective.[31] Her approach is feminist in so far as a 'feminist critical strategy' is prominent in the critical explanation of the text.[32] Thus the aim of interpretation is not merely going behind the text and finding useful perspectives and traces of eradicated narratives, which may aid the empowerment of women, but to allow the self to be transformed in the encounter with the text. This encounter is critically informed by feminist critical strategy, which prevents the possibly androcentric perspective of the text to dominate the discourse. In short, while the text is a source for Schüssler-Fiorenza, it is the bearer of meaning for Schneiders.

The construction of gender

In some respects, gender theory goes back to the early days of post-war feminism. Already in the 1950s Simone de Beauvoir assumed that gender was constructed by society and acquired, rather than inborn. Or, in de Beauvoir's words, 'One is not born, but rather becomes a woman.'[33] Thus the distinction was established between sex, which is the biological state of a person, and gender, which are the signs, roles and behaviours that society attaches to the sex.[34] This basic insight, which in itself is not relevant for our discussion, took on a new dimension when it was combined with post-structuralist theory. We recall that post-structuralists see everything as a sign, which points towards an indefinite number of other signs, which in turn point at signs again (see p. 167). Gender theory has applied this insight to the notion of gender. If everything is constituted by signs, and, at the same time, is a sign itself, then what about gender?

Thus our socially and semantically constructed perception of gender does, or at least has done in the past, enforce patriarchal privilege. It is, as it were, the 'embodiment' of the androcentric ideology of a society. Monique Wittig, for example, compares the opposition of 'man' and 'woman' as structurally parallel to 'master' and 'slave'.[35] This opposition is an expression of a power relation: 'master' and 'slave' define each other. Without 'master' there can be no 'slave', and vice versa. If one abolishes slavery, then there will be not only no slaves any more, but also the concept of 'master' will have disappeared. Conversely, if patriarchy is abolished, then 'sex' will disappear as a category to distinguish people. Thus for Wittig, all gender differentiation is socially, and therefore linguistically constructed.

In viewing gender as linguistically constructed, the distinction between feminist hermeneutics and feminist theory has been abolished. A post-structuralist hermeneutic serves as the basis for feminist theory.

The atomization of feminism

Another consequence of the notion that the unified human self is problematic is the fragmentation of feminism. Feminism came under attack for assuming that the subject of feminist theory is the white, middle-class, heterosexual woman.[36] Consequently, other feminist voices, such as African American, Latina, Asian American, lesbian and other groups made their voices heard.[37] Thus new theologies emerged, such as womanist theology, which begins with the perspective of African American women, and mujerista theology, which takes the experience of Hispanic American women as its starting point. Other non-Western women's theology came into being as well.

For our hermeneutical investigations this means that the interpretative community is fragmented and even atomized. Readings must thus be relevant for a very narrow context, otherwise one will opt out of that discourse and find another one, which one finds more congenial. The notion of a common female experience, not to mention a common human experience, seems to be excluded. Reading becomes a highly localized ethical activity.

Feminism as a unified field of enquiry has thus become problematic. Its great contribution to a wider field of study, however, will probably have lasting influence. Discourse is distorted not only by class perspective and means of production, as the Frankfurt School assumed, but also by inequality and oppression in gender relations. An awareness of this must be part of every interpretation, and feminist criticism should be an important item in the interpreter's toolbox.

Postcolonialism

Once it is accepted that discourse constructs otherness and opposition, then one must recognize that there is an unlimited number of exclusions and oppressions that will distort discourse. More recently, postcolonialism has attracted some attention. R. S. Sugirtharajah summarizes the concern of postcolonial readings.

Colonial reading can be summed up as informed by theories concerning the innate superiority of Western culture, the Western male as subject, and the natives, heathens, women, blacks, indigenous people, as the Other, needing to be controlled and subjugated. It is based on desire for power/domination . . . Colonial intentions were reinforced by the replacement of indigenous reading practices, negative representations of the 'natives', and the employment of exegetical strategies in the commentarial writing and hermeneutical discourses that legitimized imperial control.

The current move towards a postcolonial biblical criticism, seeks to overturn colonial assumptions.[38]

In other words, imperial power is exercised not only by force, but much more effectively by means of imposing a discourse that legitimizes imperial control. From the use of the language of 'the desire for power/domination', we can identify that postcolonialism is deeply influenced by Foucault's view of the will to power as the driving force of humankind.[39] In colonialism, the will to power manifests itself in cultural imperialism. This colonial mindset was first identified and criticized by Edward Said in his highly influential book *Orientalism*,[40] which established postcolonialism as a field of study. Because of its Foucaultian origin, postcolonialism as a theory suffers similar weaknesses as Foucault's hermeneutics and philosophy. We saw above that Foucault assumed that power is the all-permeating force, which disciplines human bodies. All institutions and ideologies are only functions of power and, apart from its function in relation to power, there is no reference in any utterance (see pp. 169–70). Thus, if one takes over postcolonialism in its Foucaultian form, one will need to be aware of the ideological baggage it carries with itself. However, within the context of a critical hermeneutical theory, the identification of colonialism as a distortion of discourse will be an important critical tool in the interpreter's toolbox. It raises the awareness that the view of other cultures, Western as well as non-Western, may be influenced by a perception of one's own cultural superiority, and that as a result, discourse may be distorted by it. The construction of the 'other', in cultural or other terms, is always fraught with the danger of distortion, and the desire to dominate the 'other' is also real. However helpful these insights may be, it may be less helpful to build a universal theory on them.

The same applies to all forms of critical theory that we have discussed in this chapter. The insight that discourse may be systemically distorted is important and powerful. It is essential for the interpreter to identify such distortion, be it as a result of class interest, gender inequality, cultural imperialism at the level of societies, or neurosis and desire at the level of the individual. If one ignores them, the interpreter is in danger of being influenced by them unconsciously, without being able to control them.

When we turn to a general discussion of theological hermeneutics in the next chapter, we will have to take these insights very seriously.

Further reading

Critical theory

Adorno, Theodor W. and Max Horkheimer, 1986, *Dialectic of Enlightenment*, 2nd edn, London: Verso.

Friedeburg, Ludwig v., 'History of the Institute of Social Research' (accessed 27 September 2006). Available from http://www.ifs.uni-frankfurt.de/english/history.htm.

Habermas, Jürgen, 1971, *Knowledge and Human Interests*, Boston: Beacon Press.

Habermas, Jürgen, 1984, *The Theory of Communicative Action*, 2 vols, Boston: Beacon Press.

Habermas, Jürgen, 1986, 'On Systemically Distorted Communication', in: David E. Klemm (ed.), *Hermeneutical Inquiry*, vol. 2, Atlanta: Scholars Press, pp. 209–19.

Habermas, Jürgen, 1986, 'Towards a Theory of Communicative Competence', in: David E. Klemm (ed.), *Hermeneutical Inquiry*, vol. 2, Atlanta: Scholars Press, pp. 222–34.

Habermas, Jürgen, 1988, *On the Logic of the Social Sciences*, Cambridge, UK: Polity Press.

Habermas, Jürgen, 1989, 'On Hermeneutics' Claim to Universality', in: Kurt Mueller-Vollmer (ed.), *The Hermeneutics Reader: Texts of the German Tradition from the Enlightenment to the Present*, Oxford: Basil Blackwell, pp. 294–319.

How, Alan, 2003, *Critical Theory, Traditions in Social Theory*, Houndmills, Hampshire; New York: Palgrave Macmillan.

Marx, Karl, 1859, 'Economic Manuscripts: Preface to A Contribution to the Critique of Political Economy', in: *Marx & Engels Internet Archive* (website, accessed 14 September 2006). Available from http://www.marxists.org/archive/marx/works/1859/critique-pol-economy/preface.htm.

Marx, Karl, 1977, *A Contribution to the Critique of Political Economy*, Moscow: Progress Publishers.

Feminism

Beauvoir, Simone de, 1953, *The Second Sex*, translated by H. M. Parshley, New York: Knopf.

Cahill, Ann J., 2005, 'Continental Feminism', in: *The Stanford Encyclopedia of Philosophy* (website, Fall 2005), edited by Edward N. Zalta. Available from http://plato.stanford.edu/archives/fall2005/entries/femapproach-continental.

Daly, Mary, 1985, *The Church and the Second Sex*, Boston: Beacon Press.

McClintock Fulkerson, Mary, 2003, 'Feminist Theology', in: Kevin J. Vanhoozer (ed.), *The Cambridge Companion to Postmodern Theology*, Cambridge; New York: Cambridge University Press, pp. 109–25.

Messer-Davidow, Ellen, 2005, 'Feminist Theory and Criticism: 1. From Movement Critique to Discourse Analysis', in: Michael Groden, Martin Kreiswirth and Imre Szeman (eds), *The Johns Hopkins Guide to Literary Theory & Criticism*, 2nd edn, Baltimore, Md.: Johns Hopkins University Press, pp. 299–305.

Meyers, Diana, 2004, 'Feminist Perspectives on the Self', in: *The Stanford Encyclopedia of Philosophy* (Spring 2004), edited by Edward N. Zalta. Available from http://plato.stanford.edu/archives/spr2004/entries/feminism-self.

Schneiders, Sandra Marie, 1991, *The Revelatory Text: Interpreting the New Testament as Sacred Scripture*, San Francisco: HarperSanFrancisco.

Schüssler Fiorenza, Elisabeth, 1994, *Jesus: Miriam's Child, Sophia's Prophet: Critical Issues in Feminist Christology*, New York: Continuum.

Schüssler Fiorenza, Elisabeth, 1995, *In Memory of Her: A Feminist Theological Reconstruction of Christian Origins*, 2nd edn, London: SCM Press.

Tuana, Nancy, 2004, 'Approaches to Feminism', in: *The Stanford Encyclopedia of Philosophy* (website, Winter 2004), edited by Edward N. Zalta. Available from http://plato.stanford.edu/archives/win2004/entries/feminism-approaches/.

Walsh, Mary-Paula, 1999, *Feminism and Christian Tradition: An annotated Bibliography and critical Introduction to the Literature, Bibliographies and indexes in religious studies, no. 51.*, Westport, Conn.: Greenwood Press.

Postcolonialism

Moore, Stephen D. and Fernando F. Segovia, 2005, *Postcolonial Biblical Criticism: Interdisciplinary Intersections, The Bible and Postcolonialism*, London; New York: T & T Clark.

Said, Edward W., 1978, *Orientalism*, London: Routledge & Kegan Paul.

Sugirtharajah, R. S., 1998, *The Postcolonial Bible, Bible and Postcolonialism*, vol. 1, Sheffield: Sheffield Academic Press.

Sugirtharajah, R. S., 1999, *Asian Biblical Hermeneutics and Postcolonialism: Contesting the Interpretations, Biblical Seminar*, vol. 64, Sheffield: Sheffield Academic Press.

Sugirtharajah, R. S., 1999, *Vernacular Hermeneutics, Bible and Postcolonialism*, vol. 2, Sheffield: Sheffield Academic Press.

Sugirtharajah, R. S., 2001, *The Bible in the Third World: Precolonial, Colonial, Postcolonial Encounters*, Cambridge: Cambridge University Press.

Sugirtharajah, R. S., 2003, *Postcolonial Reconfigurations: An Alternative Way of Reading the Bible and Doing Theology*, London: SCM Press.

Notes

1 In the following, I will use 'Critical Theory' capitalized when referring to the thought of the Frankfurt School, and 'critical theory' in lower case when referring to critical schools of thought influenced by it or similar.

2   For the history of the Institute for Social Research, Ludwig v. Friedeburg, 'History of the Institute of Social Research'. Available from http://www.ifs.uni-frankfurt.de/english/history.htm (accessed 27 September 2006).

3   Theodor W. Adorno and Max Horkheimer, 1986, *Dialectic of Enlightenment*, 2nd edn, London: Verso.

4   Jürgen Habermas, 1984, *The Theory of Communicative Action*, 2 vols, Boston: Beacon Press.

5   Jürgen Habermas, 1988, *On the Logic of the Social Sciences*, Cambridge, UK: Polity Press.

6   Hans-Georg Gadamer, 1989, 'Rhetoric, Hermeneutics and the Critique of Ideology', in: Kurt Mueller-Vollmer (ed.), *The Hermeneutics Reader: Texts of the German Tradition from the Enlightenment to the Present*, Oxford: Basil Blackwell.

7   Jürgen Habermas, 1989, 'On Hermeneutics' Claim to Universality', in: Kurt Mueller-Vollmer (ed.), *The Hermeneutics Reader*. A shorter version of this is Jürgen Habermas, 1986, 'On Systematically Distorted Communication', in: David E. Klemm (ed.), *Hermeneutical Inquiry*, vol. 2, Atlanta: Scholars Press.

8   Jürgen Habermas, 1986, 'Towards a Theory of Communicative Competence', in: David E. Klemm (ed.), *Hermeneutical Inquiry*, vol. 2, Atlanta: Scholars Press.

9   Jürgen Habermas, 1971, *Knowledge and Human Interests*, Boston: Beacon Press, pp. 308–15.

10   Habermas, *Knowledge and Human Interests*, p. 309.

11   Habermas, *Knowledge and Human Interests*, p. 309.

12   Habermas, *Knowledge and Human Interests*, p. 310.

13   Habermas, *On the Logic of the Social Sciences*, p. 172.

14   Habermas, *On the Logic of the Social Sciences*, p. 170.

15   Habermas, 'On Hermeneutics' Claim to Universality', p. 314.

16   Habermas, 'On Hermeneutics' Claim to Universality', p. 314.

17   Habermas, 'On Hermeneutics' Claim to Universality', p. 314.

18   Habermas, 'On Hermeneutics' Claim to Universality', p. 315.

19   Alan How, 2003, *Critical Theory, Traditions in Social Theory*, Houndmills, Hampshire; New York: Palgrave Macmillan, p. 137; and David E. Klemm (ed.), 1986, *Hermeneutical Inquiry: Volume 2: The Interpretation of Existence, AAR Studies in Religion*, vol. 44, Atlanta: Scholars Press, p. 208.

20   Habermas, 'On Hermeneutics' Claim to Universality', p. 314.

21   Habermas, 'On Hermeneutics' Claim to Universality', p. 314.

22   Habermas, *On the Logic of the Social Sciences*, p. 173.

23   For the development of feminist criticism within the context of the women's liberation movement, see Ellen Messer-Davidow, 2005, 'Feminist Theory and Criticism: 1. From Movement Critique to Discourse Analysis', in: Michael Groden, Martin Kreiswirth and Imre Szeman (eds), *The Johns Hopkins Guide to Literary Theory & Criticism*, 2nd edn, Baltimore, Md.: Johns Hopkins University Press; and Nancy Tuana, 2004, 'Approaches to Feminism', in: *The Stanford Encyclopedia of Philosophy* (website, Winter 2004), edited by Edward N. Zalta. Available from http://plato.stanford.edu/archives/win2004/entries/feminism-approaches/.

24   Mary Daly, 1985, *The Church and the Second Sex*, Boston: Beacon Press.

25 Mary-Paula Walsh, 1999, *Feminism and Christian Tradition: An Annotated Bibliography and Critical Introduction to the Literature, Bibliographies and Indexes in Religious Studies*, vol. 51, Westport, Conn.: Greenwood Press, p. 15.

26 Elisabeth Schüssler Fiorenza, 1995, *In Memory of Her: A Feminist Theological Reconstruction of Christian Origins*, 2nd edn, London: SCM Press, pp. xliv–xlv.

27 Schüssler Fiorenza, *In Memory of Her*, p. 36.

28 Schüssler Fiorenza, *In Memory of Her*, p. 29.

29 Elisabeth Schüssler Fiorenza, 1994, *Jesus: Miriam's Child, Sophia's Prophet: Critical Issues in Feminist Christology*, New York: Continuum.

30 Sandra Marie Schneiders, 1991, *The Revelatory Text: Interpreting the New Testament as Sacred Scripture*, San Francisco: HarperSanFrancisco, p. 16.

31 Schneiders, *The Revelatory Text*, pp. 17, 20.

32 Schneiders, *The Revelatory Text*, p. 183.

33 Simone de Beauvoir, 1953, *The Second Sex*, translated by H. M. Parshley, New York: Knopf, p. 267

34 For a more comprehensive discussion of this issue, see Ann J. Cahill, 2005, 'Continental Feminism', in: *The Stanford Encyclopedia of Philosophy* (website, Fall 2005), edited by Edward N. Zalta. Available from http://plato.stanford.edu/archives/fall2005/entries/femapproach-continental; Diana Meyers, 2004, 'Feminist Perspectives on the Self', in: *The Stanford Encyclopedia of Philosophy* (Spring 2004), edited by Edward N. Zalta. Available from http://plato.stanford.edu/archives/spr2004/entries/feminism-self. See also Mary McClintock Fulkerson, 2003, 'Feminist Theology', in: Kevin J. Vanhoozer (ed.), *The Cambridge Companion to Postmodern Theology*, Cambridge; New York: Cambridge University Press.

35 Cahill, 'Continental Feminism'.

36 McClintock Fulkerson, 'Feminist Theology', p. 111.

37 McClintock Fulkerson, 'Feminist Theology', p. 111.

38 R. S. Sugirtharajah, 1998, *The Postcolonial Bible, Bible and Postcolonialism*, vol. 1, Sheffield: Sheffield Academic Press, p. 15.

39 'Postcolonial Studies,' in: Abrams, *A Glossary of Literary Terms*.

40 Edward W. Said, 1978, *Orientalism*, London: Routledge & Kegan Paul.

13

Towards a Hermeneutical Theology

Preliminary considerations

In the previous chapters, we followed the development of hermeneutical thought from antiquity to the present. In this final chapter, we will draw some conclusions from the historical survey, and develop a critical hermeneutic as a basis for theology and scriptural interpretation. Some of these conclusions and observations regarding the nature and problems of theological hermeneutics will be, in my opinion, generally applicable. And even if not everyone will agree with the answers proposed here, every theological hermeneutic will have to find answers to the questions raised in this chapter.

First of all, we have to acknowledge that understanding is a complex and problematic business. Unreflected hermeneutics will easily fall prey to unacknowledged prejudices, and there is no such thing as a natural or God-given way of understanding. Second, certain basic theological attitudes will always inform, if not determine, one's hermeneutics. These need to be brought to the fore and made explicit. Only then can one begin to construct one's own theological hermeneutics, on the basis of which one will be able to develop methodologies for the various fields of theological study. Finally, one can then establish appropriate methods for the theological tasks.

As the focus of this investigation is hermeneutical, we will not discuss all of these steps. We will focus on the influence of fundamental theological questions on hermeneutics, and touch on some methodological issues.

Overcoming naïve realism

As we have seen above, the common modern attitude towards reality and truth has been shaped by the empiricist and mechanist world-view as exemplified in the work of Francis Bacon and the Royal Academy (see pp. 82–4). In the English-speaking world, this view has been supplemented and mediated by Scottish common-sense philosophy, which insisted that reality – the things 'as they really are' – are perceived directly by our senses and understood immediately (see p. 83). The resulting concept of reality assumes that reality, the world, can be perceived objectively. There is one reality, and every reasonable person can gain objective knowledge of this reality by making use of his or her senses. Consequently, the truth of an utterance is determined by its truthfulness to the objective fact. Thus myths, such as the *Iliad* or the *Odyssey*, although they may give us some valuable insight into human psyche and behaviour, are, at the most basic level, simply not true. Conversely, if a text is true, then the facts it describes must depict what 'really happened' quite accurately and objectively.

Much of modern criticism of Christianity and religion in general is based on the presupposition that, if the foundational texts of a religion do not reflect 'reality' adequately, then they are worthless. At the same time, modern fundamentalism is based on the same presupposition. If the revered texts are to be true, then they must describe objective reality accurately, and one must insist that they are absolutely reliable at the literal-historical level. Between categorical rejection and acceptance of the texts at the literal-historical level there are intermediate positions, which would accept parts (those which are deemed essential) as true, while others (those which are taken to be peripheral) may be historically untrue. However, in terms of their hermeneutical approach, these positions do not avoid the shortcomings of the extremes – they rely on a naïve view of language and reality.

The discussion within this book so far should have shown that such a simplistic notion of truth and reality neglects the complexity of human understanding, the nature of human language and the impossibility of a direct, immediate access to what we call reality. All understanding is interpretation, and all interpretation is linguistically mediated.

Theological foundations

Even when disregarding naïve realism as a viable hermeneutical approach, there is still a vast range of possible and legitimate approaches. The theologian needs to keep in mind that his or her hermeneutical approach, both in biblical and wider theological hermeneutics, is informed, if not determined by certain fundamental theological decisions. These decisions are not always made deliberately or even consciously – the theologian's tradition, denomination and culture will bear on them. It is therefore important for the theologian to be aware of his or her presuppositions and, wherever possible, make them explicit, reflect on them and, where appropriate, criticize them.

First and foremost, what one sees as the ultimate reference of theological language is of utmost importance. Theologians' attitudes toward this question will inevitably determine their hermeneutics. The ultimate reference of theological language is, at the same time, what one would believe to be the basis of Christian faith, that beyond which one cannot question any more.

Furthermore, the theologian must be clear about the way in which he or she believes God's revelation in Jesus Christ is mediated. Is it by certain historical events, by the word of God encountering the hearer in the human word, or by direct revelation 'straight from above', to name but a few options?

Finally, the theologian must have addressed the relation between meaning and language, the inner word and the spoken word, or, in theological language, the human word and the word of God. The answer to this question will be informed by one's view on the relation between the infinite and the finite, eternity and time, God and creation.

These three questions are interrelated, that is, one's view on one of them will affect one's view on the others, and together they form an important aspect of what I suggest make the heart of theology. Furthermore, the way in which one answers these three questions will determine one's hermeneutics. I shall illustrate this with a number of examples.

Some theologians assume that faith is based on certain historical events, which we interpret and then draw conclusions from. This does not necessarily mean a fundamentalist approach, which, as we have seen, would involve a view of the biblical texts as direct and accurate mediators of historical 'facts'. Avoiding this, and taking a more critical approach, this may mean that one takes certain events as validated by historical-critical research, as certain features of Israel's history and of Jesus' ministry, death and resurrection, and bases faith and theology on them.

This does not presuppose either a liberal or conservative approach. Marcus Borg, for example, suggests that a historically reliable picture of Jesus, his teaching and his action, stripped of all dogma and mythology, would give us an example by which to live, and on which we can ground life and faith.[1] N. T. Wright takes a similar approach from a more conservative angle; he assumes that large parts of Jesus' ministry, and his resurrection, including the empty tomb, as historical facts, can be reliably established and form the basis of faith.[2] Both theologians, from very different starting points and theological outlooks, find historically reliable facts behind the biblical text, be it the authentic sayings of Jesus or the resurrection and empty tomb. These 'facts' behind the text form the basis of their faith and theology.

Another approach would see the word of God revealing itself independently of the text. In this view, which is most prominently held by Karl Barth (see p. 180), the text is only a mirror image of the word of God, and by wrestling with the text, the reader breaks through the words of the text and engages directly and without mediation with the word behind the words, with the word of God. Again, the source of faith and theology is to be found behind the text, although this time not in the 'historical facts' that the text conveys, but in the divine reality that lies behind the text, and reveals itself independently of the text.

In all these cases, the text does not contain the word of God, but points at something behind itself – be it the authentic teaching of Jesus, historical facts or the unmediated divine revelation.

Yet another approach assumes that faith and theology are grounded in religious experience, which is somehow mediated by language. According to this view, faith is grounded in the inner life, be it the speaker's or writer's feeling, self-understanding or world (as the meaningful totality of being as perceived by the human self), which language is able to communicate. We recall that Friedrich Schleiermacher saw the feeling of the author as the ultimate reference, be it his or her intuition and feeling of the universe, or his or her feeling of absolute dependence (see pp. 99–101). (Note that, for Schleiemacher, feeling is not primarily emotion, but a form of self-consciousness.) The text communicates the author's feeling, and the reader interprets the text in order to relive this feeling. In case of Christian texts, the Bible or other Christian literature, the feeling contained in the text is religious feeling, that is, faith. The reader will interpret the text and understand it, thus reliving the author's feelings. In this way, the reader shares in the author's religious self-consciousness, and makes it his or her own. So religion is passed on through the medium of language.

The same principle applies to Rudolf Bultmann's approach, with the difference that he sees the transition from life without faith to life in faith as more radical (see pp. 125–6). For Schleiermacher, the shift from life without faith to life in faith is gradual, and what is needed in order to realize one's religious potential is proper guidance. For Bultmann, faith is not a human possibility, but something that is brought about by grace alone. Faith is a response to the challenge posed in the encounter with the word of God, with the *kerygma*. There is no gradual process towards faith, but ultimate discontinuity. Theological language is a testimony to the encounter with the *kerygma*, which describes the transformation of human self-understanding in the encounter and acceptance of the word of God. The reader, interpreting the text using the existentialist interpretation, will understand the transition that took place in the author's self-understanding, and hear the challenge of the word of God directed at himself or herself. All theological language, be it that of the Bible, of dogmatic theology, of praise or of promise, refers to the change in human self-understanding, and the challenge that brings about this change. Thus human language can embody the word of God, because the reader is addressed by the words of the text, and hears the challenge, the call to life in faith in the words of the text.

For approaches such as Schleiermacher's or Bultmann's, faith is not grounded in facts or events behind the text, but in the transformation that takes place in the encounter with the text. For Schleiermacher, the feeling that constitutes faith is communicated from one person to another, without necessary reference to a third agency. Or, as the young Schleiermacher wrote in the *Speeches*, 'one religion without God can be better than another with a God'.[3]

Bultmann sees the challenge that the text (or speech) poses to the reader (hearer) as grounded in the life, death and resurrection of Jesus Christ. The challenge of the Christian proclamation, the *kerygma*, is precisely that it proclaims that God has acted decisively in the man Jesus of Nazareth, and that his crucifixion is God's redeeming act for humankind. So the *kerygma*, which is contained in the proclamation, refers to a particular historical event. However, it is part of the challenge of the *kerygma* that the significance of the event, namely, that the crucifixion was the decisive act of God, is not independently verifiable. According to Bultmann, as the resurrection cannot be established by historical-critical methods, the acceptance of its truth is an act of faith. To have faith in the resurrection is the consequence of the acceptance of the *kerygma*.

The subject matter of the *kerygma*, however, is not the historical event, but the transformation of the inner life which is brought about by the encounter with the *kerygma*. It does not communicate historical facts, but it calls to the existential decision by showing the alternatives of living inauthentically and living authentically.

Very different from the approaches outlined above are the so-called postmodern ones. They see the text merely as a template, in which the reader can find a playful and never-ending web of reference. In this view, the text does not have to say anything new to the reader, it does not contain an inner word at all. The reader produces the meaning, using reading practices that will encourage non-oppressive praxis in life (see pp. 172–3). Consequently, the underlying theology is that there is no meaning in a chaotic world, at least no discernible meaning. The notion that there is the word of God in or behind the text is also abandoned; there is only the meaning that the reader constructs. This is either based on the absence of God as in the negative theology of mysticism, which sees God as absolutely inaccessible by human language, or on nihilism, which does not accept any meaning in a world that is merely the playing field for the human will to power. From the previous discussions of post-modern approaches, it appears that Derrida leans to the former position (p. 173), while Foucault leans to the latter (p. 169).

These are only a few examples of fundamental theological decisions and their implications for hermeneutics. The list is far from being comprehensive, and some positions may be depicted in a simplified manner. However, the reader can refer back to previous chapters, in which these approaches were discussed in more detail. Here, I trust, they serve the purpose of illustrating the intimate connection between theology and hermeneutics. One's hermeneutics flow from the basic theological decisions. The theologian's hermeneutics will then determine the methodology for his or her theological subject area, biblical interpretation, systematic theology, ethics, Church history or practical theology. On the basis of this the theologian will develop methods in order to apply them to a task at hand. Theological hermeneutics, therefore, plays an essential bridging role between theology on the one hand and methodology and methods on the other.

A hermeneutical theology

In this section, we are going to apply the insights gained not only from the earlier considerations in this chapter, but also from the discussion of the development of hermeneutics and current positions, and construct an approach to theological hermeneutics. This will be a deliberately broad-brush approach, serving to highlight the range of theological questions that need to be considered in the hermeneutical debate. After the previous discussions, it should be clear that I do not assume this approach to be the only valid one. I am offering it here as a starting point for discussion and reflection.

A linguistically constituted experience

Dietrich Bonhoeffer suggested in his lectures on Christology that the beginning of all theology is the presence of Christ mediated through word and sacrament.[4] The communal experience of the presence of Christ is the basis of all theology, it is the 'given', beyond which the theologian cannot question. It either has to be accepted or rejected, and this acceptance or rejection will, in most cases, not be rationally explainable.

According to Bonhoeffer, the presence of Christ in the Church is not an immediate divine presence, but is mediated through the proclamation of the word and the celebration of the sacraments. These actions of the Church make the presence of Christ manifest and discernible. It is not the Church that brings about this presence, but God. For all Christian denominations, this is the starting point for their theology and Church life.

Certainly, different Christian traditions lay the emphasis on the means of mediation in various ways. Some denominations stress the sacraments more, others the word. Admittedly, the Pentecostal and Charismatic traditions are different in so far as they allow for an element of immediate ecstatic experience. But even this is related to the proclamation of the word and not independent of it.

The experience of the presence of Christ is mediated through language, the spoken language of proclamation or the symbolic language of the sacraments. The mediation through language is not only important in so far as it makes known the presence, but also in so far as it identifies the risen Christ who is present with the crucified Jesus of Nazareth and recalls his ministry, life and death. The one who is present in the Church is the same as the one who died on the cross – this is at the heart of the specifically Christian proclamation.

For the first Christians, their encounter with the risen Jesus Christ, whom they had known in his earthly life and ministry, brought about a radical transformation of their lives. Their understanding of God, of the meaning of life, of the world, of their relationship with other people, all changed dramatically by the presence of the risen Christ among them. A whole new set of meaningful relationships of being was established. Or, in Gadamer's terms, their world was fundamentally changed when their horizon fused with that of the Christian language-world. Consequently, the way in which they spoke about Jesus changed, as their new understanding of the world shaped their narratives.

The agent of this radical change is what we call the word of God. Jesus Christ is the incarnate word of God in so far as the encounter with him brought about this radical change. When the Church proclaims the word of God, it is through its proclamation, in word, sacrament and communal life, that people encounter Christ present and thus enter the Christian world.

The new world, the new creation which the early Christians experienced and began to understand, was enshrined in the new way in which they told stories about Jesus, in which they prayed and in which they formulated theology. This took place through developing symbols, metaphors and narratives in order to understand the new world of Christianity, in order to interpret their lives anew. The different religious languages of Judaism and its various groupings, the languages of Hellenistic learning and culture, were all employed in order to make sense of the new experience.[5]

Through the language of theology, praise and promise, as well as through the life of the community shaped by it, newcomers were able to share the experience of the risen Christ. They took over the narratives, symbols and metaphors of the early Church, and contributed their own, shaped by their own linguistic background. In this way, different churches developed different languages of faith, which is reflected, for example, in the varying languages and theologies of the different writings of the New Testament. Thus the collective experience of the presence of the risen Christ was enshrined and mediated through the language of worship and theology, in the narratives about Jesus, in theological controversy and the symbols of the sacraments.

Christianity can be understood as the almost 2,000-year-long process of receiving and passing on the language of Christian faith, the language of theology, worship, proclamation in word and sacrament, and the life of the community. Each generation of Christians has its world shaped by the language of faith. It participates in the presence of Christ which is mediated through the language of faith, and interprets its existence within the world in the light of this experience as well as in the light of the changing understanding of human existence in Christ and before God. Thus the language of Christian faith is reshaped by every generation, incorporating the received language of the foundational narratives and the ongoing worship, but finding new expressions in theology, worship and Christian life.

In this ongoing process of receiving, reshaping and passing on, it is the task of the theologian (not only the academic, but everyone who is talking and reasoning about God, that is every Christian) to understand the Christian faith through a careful interpretation of the Christian language past and present, and to translate it so that it can be understood in the theologian's own community, so that it interprets the life of the contemporary community. Theology is therefore translation, *hermeneia*.

Critical interpretation of texts

This translation must be critical, and hermeneutical theology must be critical theology. We have seen in the discussion of Paul Ricoeur's hermeneutical thought that language always contains a surplus of meaning.

Ricoeur's understanding of the surplus of meaning raises the need for suspicion and criticism. Does the text include something that is the result of an unwanted influence of psychological, sociological or other realities? Is a theological text coloured by the socio-economic circumstances at the time and place of its writing? For instance, this could well be the case in the passages regarding slavery in the New Testament, which seem to take the institution of slavery for granted. Furthermore, it is quite possible that Anselm of Canterbury's view of God in his treatise *Cur deus homo* (*Why God became man*),[6] which contains the seminal formulation of the substitutionary model of the atonement, is deeply influenced by the medieval social and economical system. Anselm's description of God may be seen to resemble a medieval feudal overlord, whose honour is violated and must be restored by retribution. Finally, the dialectical theology movement of the early twentieth century was a direct reaction to the collapse of the social, economical and political order in Germany after the First World War. These are only three particularly obvious examples, but the same will apply, to varying extent, to every theology. Such socio-economic influences on the formation of different theologies do not invalidate their content, yet they need to be taken into account when translating them for one's own community – otherwise their understanding may be grossly distorted.

A text may also be influenced by the psychological condition of the author. For example, quite a lot of Martin Luther's writings and elements of his theology are profoundly influenced by his ongoing struggle with depression.[7] It has also been observed that some of the strong sensual language of medieval mysticism may have been influenced by the suppressed sexuality of the mystical authors. And I believe that Freud does have a point when he suggests that certain religious practices are the result of obsessional neurosis.[8]

In addition to these examples, there are many other possible distortions – some of these we discussed in an earlier chapter (see Chapter 12). Marxist critique of ideology, feminism and postcolonialism are only a few of the perceived distortions of the text. In this context, it is interesting to observe that distortions are 'discovered' when social circumstances change. For example, before the advent of feminism, sexism contained in texts did not pose an obstacle to understanding. It was not perceived as offensive. Only when women's liberation took root, and society and the collective consciousness became sensitive to these issues, did sexist distortion of language become an obstacle. In the same way, that an imperialist agenda may distort the language regarding non-Western cultures was identified only in the late 1970s, and has since become a major field of study as postcolonial criticism. This, again, is a reflection of the changing political order in the world, and a changing consciousness. In the same way, as society continues to change, new obstacles to understanding will be identified and criticized.

Moreover, since it is more or less generally accepted that discourse can be systematically distorted, an uncritical reading of texts will rightly be suspected of being captive to agendas beyond the author's and reader's control.

Finally, critical interpretation serves also to avoid the dangers stemming from uncritical familiarity with the text. For instance, different Christian traditions have their theological discourse shaped by their denominational literature, most chiefly the great classics of the Christian tradition, such as the Anglican *Book of Common Prayer*, the *Geneva Psalter*, Luther's Bible translation and his *Smaller Catechism*, to name just a few of the most obvious. These texts have become common currency within religious language within their respective traditions. They, together with the denominational socialization within a particular tradition, shape the understanding of the Christian faith in line with that denominational tradition. This will often not have been consciously reflected.

The connection with the biblical text through a particular tradition is an important link between the interpreter and the texts, for instance the biblical texts. Gadamer has shown that this link is essential for understanding (see p. 142). However, the immersion in a particular tradition of biblical interpretation will exclude other, conflicting or complementary interpretations. A Lutheran, for example, brought up listening to Luther's Bible translation, and knowing by heart Luther's *Smaller Catechism*, will always read the Bible through a Lutheran lens, and, not surprisingly, find Lutheran theology in it.

So a critical approach to biblical and other texts will enable the interpreter to overcome prejudices with regard to the text, and find new and fresh meaning in it, to allow the text to alter the interpreter's language world in ever new ways. Critical interpretation does not only remove obstacles to understanding, but also makes new, creative understandings of the text possible. It opens new horizons.

Speaking within the theologian's context

Theology is translation. We have seen in the previous section how theology must interpret texts in a critical way in order to make them speak. Likewise, the theologian must interpret his or her own context in order to find adequate theological language. Someone wearing sandwich-boards saying 'Repent, the End is Nigh!' will probably not find much comprehension in a twenty-first century Western city. The message is meaningless to the audience. Thus a careful analysis of the context into which the theologian is going to speak or to write or to communicate by any other means, is necessary. A good example of the form this can take is Eberhard Jüngel's *God as Mystery of the World*,[9] in which Jüngel first analyses the context of modern atheism and its origin, and of the legitimate critique of theism by atheist thinkers, and then formulates a way of speaking of God that responds to this context. In the same way, Bultmann's existentialist interpretation, as we have seen above, was an attempt to translate the Christian *kerygma* for the modern world (see pp. 127–8).

More often than not the theologian will do this intuitively and instinctively. Most people are aware of the context in which they live at least to some level, and thus will speak in a way comprehensible to their contemporaries. However, a critical theology involves a deeper understanding of the context than only at the intuitive level. It must make explicit the issues which face the community to which the theologian speaks. It must understand its own context critically. Using Jüngel's book as an example again, the theologian will deliberately explore the origin and function of modern atheism. The interpreter will need to understand the context, in this case modern atheism, better than the average modern atheist does. The same applies for all aspects of the interpreter's context, be it patriarchal structures, economic conditions, social inequality or prevalent ideology. Only if the theologian understands his or her context at a profound level will he or she be able to speak or write not only meaningfully, but also authoritatively within his or her context. Then the theologian will be able to translate what he or she has learned in interaction with the Christian tradition into a language that can be understood by his or her environment.

The nature of theological language

So far, we have treated theological language without distinguishing its different genres. The same hermeneutical principles certainly apply to all theological language, but there are some significant differences in their modes of reference. All theological language ultimately refers to human religious experience, as Schleiermacher pointed out, and objectifying language, which talks about the properties of God or the world, is derived from the primary form of the theological language. Although aspects of

Schleiermacher's dictum are open to criticism, the main thrust remains valid: all religious language refers to the experience of the presence of Christ in the Christian community. Yet different genres of language do so differently.

For the purposes of this discussion, I am going to distinguish between four forms of theological language. These are dogmatic language, narrative, praise and promise. Dogmatic language is quite distinguished from other genres of theological language, because it attempts to conceptualize the experience of Christian faith and discusses it in abstract technical language. Non-dogmatic language can be grouped into genres in various ways. The distinction proposed here has the advantage of being simple and able to highlight the hermeneutical issues. As a result of the different modes of reference of the four genres of theological language, the interpreter will need to choose suitable methodologies when interpreting them.

Dogmatic language

We have seen above in the discussion of both Friedrich Schleiermacher and Rudolf Bultmann that theological language is not objectifying language. It always refers back to religious experience.

If we take God's transcendence seriously, namely, that God is beyond time and space, beyond the realm of creation, we cannot speak of God univocally. All terms and concepts that we apply to God cannot apply to God directly, but indirectly, metaphorically or analogically. In fact, all theological language, be it that of academic theology or the language of worship and proclamation, is language that relates to the self-understanding of the speaker within the Christian community. This does not mean that there is only one legitimate experience. On the contrary, a variety of worlds, of self-understandings, are compatible with the mainstream Christian experience. Theology's task is to safeguard the collective experience against false interpretations.

For example, the Arian controversy of the fourth century, although at the surface about abstract theological concepts, had at its very heart the Christian self-understanding before God. If, as Arianism assumed, Christ is a creature, albeit the highest, then salvation is brought about in a fundamentally different way from that in which Nicene orthodoxy understands it. For the Arian, salvation is brought about through obedience to God, whereas for the Nicene Christian, salvation is brought about by God's saving action and the resulting deification of the believer. Consequently, the situation of the Church and of the believer before God is very different in Arianism and Nicene Christianity. This leads to incompatible religious language systems. The difference between these two was perceived to be so fundamental that they could not coexist.

The challenge for Nicene Christianity was to find a formula that expressed the understanding of the human self before God in language. As there was no ready language available to express this, it was left to the Cappadocian Fathers to develop a theological and philosophical language in order to express this. They met this challenge by introducing a new distinction between the terms *ousia* (being) and *hypostasis* (manifestation of being/person). This distinction had been unknown in conventional philosophical discourse, and violated accepted philosophical terminology.[10]

Thus even the highly specialized and abstract language of trinitarian theology has its origin in the expression of a particular self-understanding and world-view. Dogmatic language is derived from the expression of human self-understanding. It is secondary in nature and is subordinated to the primary form of theological language, which is the expression of religous self-understanding. In short, it does not say univocally how God is in godself, but expresses a particular understanding of human existence before God in rejection of another, competing self-understanding.

This brings us back to Christos Yannaris' understanding of dogmatic language as defining, that is, delimiting the boundaries of acceptable descriptions of shared religious experience (see p. 57). When interpreting dogmatic language, be it the language of some of the letters in the New Testament, of the ancient creeds, of Thomas Aquinas' *Summa Theologiae* or that of Reformation confessions or of the Second Vatican Council, the theologian must refer back to the religious self-understanding contained in them.

Narrative, praise and promise

The language of dogma is not the only genre of theological language. In fact, it is a highly specialized form of language, which, apart from the liturgical recitation of the Nicene Creed in some traditions, is not commonly used by average Christians. The genres of language that most Christians encounter frequently are those of narrative, praise and promise. In addition, the liturgical enactment is another important expression of Christian faith, although this does not fall into the scope of our investigation.

The hermeneutical principles for the understanding of narrative, praise and promise are the same as for dogmatic language – they refer to the human religious experience, to human self-understanding before God, within the Christian community and in the world. Only they do so not by defining, as dogmatic language does, but by indirect reference.

We have seen in the discussion of Paul Ricoeur's hermeneutic that he assumed that human beings make sense of their life by constructing a narrative (see p. 149). This narrative may be close to 'factual' or contain misconceptions and imaginary elements. It may also be distorted by psychological, socio-economic or other factors. Finally, the narrative does not even need to be factual or intend to be factual – fictional story can also be used to express religious self-understanding.

Narrative expresses one's interpretation of the self, God and the world as story. All religious narrative needs to be understood along these lines, be it an evangelical conversion account, a medieval life of a saint, a biblical story or any other narrative.

There are certainly other legitimate interests in the text – the Church historian may be interested in how far the narratives in the Acts of the Apostles are an accurate reflection of the early Church, the archaeologist may be interested in the description of sites in the Jewish Scriptures, the New Testament scholar may investigate which actions attributed to Jesus may be actions of the 'historical Jesus', etc. Besides these legitimate interests, interpretation becomes a genuinely theological enterprise when it is aimed at understanding the religious self-understanding contained in the text. Nevertheless, all other questions that can be asked of the text are important for the critical explanation of the text, which will lead to a new, post-critical understanding of the text, to the second naïvety.

Language of praise needs to be understood in the widest sense – it does not only contain praise, but also lament, petition and all other language directed to God. It can take the forms of prayer, prose, verse or hymnody, to name but a few. This, too, is an expression of the human self-understanding before God and within the world. One's joy, gratitude, pain, anxiety or any other emotion is put into words addressed to God. We must not forget that we saw in the discussion of Martin Heidegger that the state-of-mind, or moods and emotion, are an unarticulated expression of our self-understanding.

Finally, promise is a performative form of language. Performative language, according to the speech-act theory of J. L. Austin, brings about what it refers to.[11] When a police officer tells a suspect 'You are arrested!' then the person in question is arrested. His or her status in relation to society has changed. Without being able to go into the details of Austin's theory, it is a helpful concept for understanding the theological genre of promise. In the language of promise, the understanding of the relation between humankind and God is expressed in making performative declarations. 'Your sins are forgiven.' When the confessor says this to the penitent, the relation between the penitent, the Christian community and God has changed – an obstacle to a healthy relationship is removed and the relationship restored.

Based on the fundamental understanding of the human situation before God, as experienced through the presence of Christ in the Christian community, one Christian expresses this to another or to a group in the form of a promise. Different denominations may have requirements as to who may make such promises in certain contexts, but the principle remains the same. A promise like 'Go in peace, the Lord is with you' expresses in a nutshell the relationship of the human person to God.

Apart from these examples of short promises, they can take longer and more complex forms. A sermon, for instance, can be an extended promise, which draws on other genres of theological language; it may teach, tell a story, include prayer and so forth, but all this is drawn together in the promise of salvation. Another mixed form of theological language is the Eucharist. The eucharistic prayer includes both praise (in its wider sense) and narrative, and the eucharistic action culminates in a promise: 'The body of Christ, given for you.'

We have examined, although very briefly, four genres of theological language. Each of them refers to the Christian religious experience in different ways, and thus requires different methodologies and methods – both for formulating them and for interpreting them.

Conclusion

In this chapter, we have highlighted the intimate relation between fundamental theological decisions and hermeneutics. Not everyone will agree with the particular construction of a theological hermeneutic which I have put forward here. Nevertheless it should illustrate the way in which a hermeneutical approach is constructed from basic theological decisions, and serve as a starting point for a critical interaction and discussion.

I have hinted at the relation between hermeneutics and methodology (as the theory of method) and the methods the theologian applies. It is of utmost importance for the intellectual integrity of the theologian that his or her theology, hermeneutics, methodology and methods are coherent. This applies for the interpretation of texts, reflection on theological issues and theological writing or speaking as well as for moral action. And a theologian must speak and act with integrity. One does not only owe this to oneself, but also to the community to which one is responsible.

Further reading

Anselm of Canterbury, 1974, *Basic Writings*, edited by S. N. Deane, 2nd edn, La Salle, Ill.: Open Court.

Austin, J. L., 1962, *How to do Things with Words*, Oxford: Clarendon Press.

Bonhoeffer, Dietrich, 1966, *Christology*, London: Collins.

Bonhoeffer, Dietrich, 1978, *Christ the Center*, San Francisco: Harper & Row.

Bonhoeffer, Dietrich, 1996, *Dietrich Bonhoeffer Works*, edited by Gerhard Ludwig Müller, Albrecht Schönherr et al., Minneapolis: Fortress Press.

Borg, Marcus J., 1994, *Meeting Jesus again for the First Time: The Historical Jesus & the Heart of Contemporary Faith*, San Francisco: HarperSanFrancisco.

Borg, Marcus J. and N. T. Wright, 1999, *The Meaning of Jesus: Two Visions*, San Francisco: HarperSanFrancisco

Crossan, John Dominic and N. T. Wright, 2006, *The Resurrection of Jesus: John Dominic Crossan and N.T. Wright in Dialogue*, edited by Robert B. Stewart, Minneapolis: Fortress Press.

Giannaras, Christos, 1991, *Elements of Faith: An Introduction to Orthodox Theology*, Edinburgh: T & T Clark.

Jensen, Alexander S., 2002, 'Martin Luther's "sin boldly" Revisited: A Fresh Look at a Controversial Concept in the Light of Modern Pastoral Psychology', *Contact: The Interdisciplinary Journal of Pastoral Studies* 137, pp. 2–13.

Jensen, Alexander S., 2004, *John's Gospel as Witness: The Development of the early Christian Language of Faith*, Ashgate New Critical Thinking in Religion, Theology, and Biblical Studies, Aldershot: Ashgate.

Jüngel, Eberhard, 1983, *God as the Mystery of the World: On the Foundation of the Theology of the Crucified One in the Dispute between Theism and Atheism*, Edinburgh: T & T Clark.

Lutheran World Federation and The Catholic Church, 1999, 'Joint Declaration on the Doctrine of Justification' (website, cited 7.11 2006). Available from http://www.vatican.va/roman_curia/pontifical_councils/chrstuni/documents/rc_pc_chrstuni_doc_31101999_cath-luth-joint-declaration_en.html1.

Philp, H. L., 1975, *Freud and Religious Belief*, Westport: Greenwood Press.

Theissen, Gerd and Dagmar Winter, 2002, *The Quest for the Plausible Jesus: The Question of Criteria*, Louisville; London: Westminster John Knox Press.

Wittgenstein, Ludwig, 1967, *Philosophical Investigations*, Oxford: B. Blackwell.

Wright, N. T., 1992, *The New Testament and the People of God*, Minneapolis: Fortress Press.

Wright, N. T., 1996, *Jesus and the Victory of God*, Minneapolis: Fortress Press.

Wright, N. T., 2003, *The Resurrection of the Son of God*, London: SPCK.

Zizioulas, Jean, 1985, *Being as Communion: Studies in Personhood and the Church*, London: Darton, Longman and Todd.

Notes

1 Borg published his views in accessible form in Marcus J. Borg, 1994, *Meeting Jesus again for the First Time: The Historical Jesus & the Heart of Contemporary Faith*, San Francisco: HarperSanFrancisco.

2 Marcus J. Borg and N. T. Wright, 1999, *The Meaning of Jesus: Two Visions*, San Francisco: HarperSanFrancisco; John Dominic Crossan and N. T. Wright, 2006, *The Resurrection of Jesus: John Dominic Crossan and N. T. Wright in Dialogue*, edited by Robert B. Stewart, Minneapolis: Fortress Press; N. T. Wright, 1992, *The New Testament and the People of God*, Minneapolis: Fortress Press; N. T. Wright, 1996, *Jesus and the Victory of God*, Minneapolis: Fortress Press; N. T. Wright, 2003, *The Resurrection of the Son of God*, London: SPCK.

3 Friedrich Schleiermacher, *On Religion: Speeches to its Cultured Despisers*, edited by Richard Crouter, Cambridge: Cambridge University Press, p. 52.

4 Dietrich Bonhoeffer, 1966, *Christology*, London: Collins (English edition); Dietrich Bonhoeffer, 1978, *Christ the Center*, San Francisco: Harper & Row (American edition), pp. 43–5 in both editions. These lectures are also forthcoming in volume 12 of Dietrich Bonhoeffer, 1996, *Dietrich Bonhoeffer Works*, edited by Gerhard Ludwig Müller, Albrecht Schönherr et al., Minneapolis: Fortress Press.

5 A more detailed account of this dynamic and its implication for biblical interpretation can be found in Alexander Jensen, 2004, *John's Gospel as Witness*, Aldershot: Ashgate.

6 Anselm of Canterbury, 1974, *Basic Writings*, edited by S. N. Deane, 2nd edn, La Salle, Ill.: Open Court, pp. 171–288.

7 Alexander S. Jensen, 'Martin Luther's "sin boldly" Revisited: A Fresh Look at a Controversial Concept in the Light of Modern Pastoral Psychology', *Contact: The Interdisciplinary Journal of Pastoral Studies* 137 (2002), 2–13.

8 H. L. Philp, 1975, *Freud and Religious Belief*, Westport: Greenwood Press, pp. 21–37.

9 Eberhard Jüngel, 1983, *God as the Mystery of the World: On the Foundation of the Theology of the Crucified One in the Dispute between Theism and Atheism*, Edinburgh: T & T Clark. Jüngel is an interesting example here, as his hermeneutical approach is influenced by Heidegger's philosophy.

10 Jean Zizioulas, 1985, *Being as Communion: Studies in Personhood and the Church*, London: Darton, Longman and Todd, pp. 36–9.

11 J. L. Austin, 1962, *How to do Things with Words*, Oxford: Clarendon Press.

Conclusion

The inner word

In the previous chapter, we explored the implications of a consistently hermeneutical approach, that is, an approach which takes seriously that the problem of understanding lies beneath all theological questions, and developed one possible approach to such a theology.

In this final conclusion, we will return to the recurrent theme of this study: the inner word. As we have seen, throughout antiquity it was generally assumed that a text is meaningful, that it contains *logos*. The *logos* of the text was understood to be the thought of the author, which was seen as the product of the silent inner conversation of the soul with itself.

When texts became problematic, for instance when an ancient and authoritative text such as the *Iliad* was found to contain unacceptable depictions of gods, then the meaning was to be recovered by critical operations, most commonly by allegorical interpretation. Hermeneutics, in this context, referred simply to the removal of obstacles to understanding. The recovery of the inner word, the meaning of the text, was still seen as unproblematic.

It was Augustine of Hippo who identified the fundamental problem of understanding, the obstacle that cannot be removed. This is that the thought, the inner word, cannot be translated into external words without loss. The earlier simple identification of the *verbum interius* with the *verbum externum* was not sustainable any more. Augustine recognized that thoughts are essentially unspoken, pre-verbal and non-conceptual. When the thought enters speech, even the silent speech of thinking, then something is inevitably lost.

From this follow a number of important insights, but also some questions that need to be resolved. First of all, hermeneutical theories from antiquity onwards emphasized that utterances do not refer to simple facts in the world, but to the speaker's or writer's thoughts. These thoughts may well be a perception and interpretation of occurrences and events, but they are not the occurrences or events themselves. We saw that a naïve realism which assumes that we have direct access to the things themselves, either directly or indirectly, that is, when they are reported, only developed during the Scottish Enlightenment and brings more problems with it than it solves (see pp. 83–4).

Second, if understanding is always flawed because of the loss that occurs when the internal word enters the external word, then everything that involves interpretation, be it the interpretation of speech, of the world around us, of God and of the self, is essentially problematic. The obstacle to understanding is universal, and therefore hermeneutics, which is dedicated to the analysis and removal of obstacles to understanding, needs to form the basis of all human sciences.

Third, interpretation always involves interpretation of the self. Every utterance contains the speaker's or writer's interpretation of his or her existence. For hearers or readers to understand the utterance, they will reinterpret their understanding of existence in the light of the interpretation of human existence offered in the utterance. Although this insight was only made explicit early in the twentieth century by Martin Heidegger, it is not only consonant with the earlier hermeneutic tradition from Augustine to Dilthey, but it builds on it and complements it.

Finally, because thoughts are never expressed without distortion, interpretation must be critical. We saw above that language carries with it a surplus of meaning, which refers to the author and his or her situation, state of mind, prejudices, social circumstances and psychological issues (see pp. 145–6). If interpretation is meant to recover the inner word, then it must be critical in order to account for those influences that may distort the expression of the inner word. Although this critical approach to hermeneutics was only formulated by Jürgen Habermas and Paul Ricoeur in the second half of the twentieth century, it solves some problems that arose within the hermeneutic tradition when a new critical approach to language developed and the possibility of systemically distorted discourse became an issue.

From these insights a number of questions arise. To begin with, if the internal word is contained in the external word, then it is still open to debate how this embodiment is to be understood. We have seen that different traditions of thought approach this issue differently. This question is particularly burning for theology, because it carries with it the question as to how the word of God relates to the human word. The way in which one answers this question will doubtlessly determine one's methodology for the recovery of the inner word from the utterance.

An even more fundamental question, which lies at the heart of the debates surrounding postmodernism, concerns the very existence of the inner word. As we saw in our discussion of post-structuralism and deconstruction, these approaches are based on the assumption that the external word, the utterance, does not contain anything like an internal word. According to them, language is essentially meaningless, and all meaning is imposed on it from the outside by the reader or hearer.

Although at first glance it may appear extremely dissatisfying, I do not believe that it is possible to solve these two questions, namely, if there is such a thing as the inner word, and if texts and other utterances have any meaning apart from that which the reader or hearer imposes. One's attitude towards them is most likely to be pre-rational and largely influenced by unconscious factors. Consequently, it is not always open to rational argument.

Nevertheless, dialogue between the positions is necessary and useful, as it will exercise some critique and force proponents of both opinions to be intellectually accountable. A good example is Paul Ricoeur's theory of symbol and metaphor, which takes seriously the post-structuralist notion that signs refer to a potentially unlimited number of other signs, which, in turn, refer to even more signs (see pp. 146–7). Ricoeur accepts this notion and uses it when he speaks of the 'universe of *logos*'. At the same time, however, he modifies it and roots the endless play of metaphors in the life-world using his concept of the 'symbol', which builds a bridge between the realm of *logos* and *bios*. Thus Ricoeur makes the attitude that language contains meaning intellectually accountable in the dialogue with post-structuralism.

The same applies to the intermediate positions between these extremes. We saw in the discussion between Lutherans and Calvinists that their respective hermeneutical approaches were deeply related to their respective sacramental theologies and Christologies (see pp. 70–4). Consequently, the way in which one relates the inner word to the external word is intimately connected to one's explicit or implicit religious beliefs.

Again, this does not imply that dialogue between these positions is not desirable or not possible. On the contrary, it is the very task of theology to give account for deeply held beliefs, and expose them to dialogue and critique. Thus, in theological hermeneutics the theologian must take seriously the connection between fundamental theological decisions and the resulting hermeneutics. In this respect, the hermeneutical debate can never issue in a consensus as long as there are different theological approaches. Consequently, keeping the hermeneutical debate open and conceding that we do not have all the final answers is an admission of human finitude and limitation.

The significance of hermeneutics

From all that was said above, it is clear that hermeneutics is significant for theology in a variety of ways. On the most basic level, hermeneutics is involved whenever we interpret an utterance. Theology is a text-based field of study, in which the interpretation of texts and the proclamation based on these texts is the focus of the intellectual endeavour. Consequently, hermeneutics as the theory of understanding cannot be avoided.

This insight applies to all text-based disciplines, to law, philosophy, the study of literature and history. In theology, however, hermeneutics holds a particular significance. Christianity is not a religion of the book in so far as its heart is not the revelation of the divine nature or God's will in a book of divine origin. Christianity is essentially about God's transforming action in the person of Jesus Christ. The Holy Scriptures of the Christian Church are the authoritative witness to the transformation brought about by the encounter with the risen Christ (see p. 213). Consequently, the subject matter of the New Testament is the transformation of the world, of the totality of meaningful relationships of being. Thus at the very heart of the Christian proclamation lies an act of interpretation, which is the interpretation of the new life, the new creation made possible in the cross and resurrection of Jesus Christ.

A second act of interpretation is to proclaim the saving transformation to which the biblical writings and all subsequent Christian literature bear witness. The texts, the biblical texts as well as liturgical, doctrinal and devotional texts that refer back to it, mediate the saving presence of Christ in the Christian community.

Thus there are two fundamental acts of interpretation involved in the Christian religion. One is the interpretation of the new life in Christ through language, the other the interpretation and proclamation of these texts, which, in turn, mediate the transforming presence of Christ. All obstacles to understanding which we have discussed in this study, from the simple ones such as lack of knowledge of the ancient languages to the identification of systemically distorted discourse, need to be removed in the interpretation of biblical and other Christian texts.

The main obstacle to understanding remains, however, the recognition that when the *verbum interius* enters the *verbum externum*, there is always a loss; we do not have direct access to another person's inmost, pre-verbal thoughts. This means that the interpretation of texts is always open to challenge, and that there will never be one undisputed authoritative interpretation of biblical texts and of Christian faith. As long as we live in this world, we have to live with this uncertainty and with the conflict of interpretations. From a Christian point of view, however, the uncertainty has certain limits – for 'by grace alone, in faith in Christ's saving work and not because of any merit on our part, we are accepted by God and receive the Holy Spirit'.[1] Any merit on our part also includes having the 'right' theology. Thus, taking seriously salvation by grace, theologians are released from the pressure of getting it 'right'. So they can engage in the theological debate, of which we are part as long as we live in this transitory life. Thus we are free to acknowledge what Hans-Georg Gadamer once called the soul of hermeneutics; the possibility that the other person may be right.[2]

We recall that Augustine of Hippo recognized this and located the overcoming of this ultimate obstacle to understanding in the heavenly Jerusalem (see p. 48). Only in the beatific vision, which he describes in the final chapter of the *City of God*, will understanding be without impediment, and our thoughts shall be fully transparent to one another. In this world, we live with imperfect communication and distorted discourse, and we will not be able to escape the hermeneutical question.

Notes

1   Lutheran World Federation and The Catholic Church, 'Joint Declaration on the Doctrine of Justification'. Available from http://www.vatican.va/roman_curia/pontifical_councils/chrstuni/documents/rc_pc_chrstuni_doc_31101999_cath-luth-joint-declaration_en.html (accessed 7 November 2006).

2   Gadamer at the Heidelberg Colloquium, 9 July 1989. Quoted in: Jean Grondin, 1994, *Introduction to Philosophical Hermeneutics*, New Haven: Yale University Press, p. 124.

Index of Subjects

Index of Names